Logic of the Digital

Also available from Bloomsbury

The Bloomsbury Companion to Philosophical Logic,
edited by Leon Horsten and Richard Pettigrew
The Bloomsbury Companion to the Philosophy of Science,
edited by Steven French and Juha Saatsi
Critical Theory and the Digital, David M. Berry
Software Takes Command, Lev Manovich

Logic of the Digital

Aden Evens

Bloomsbury Academic
An imprint of Bloomsbury Publishing Plc

B L O O M S B U R Y
LONDON • OXFORD • NEW YORK • NEW DELHI • SYDNEY

Bloomsbury Academic
An imprint of Bloomsbury Publishing Plc

50 Bedford Square
London
WC1B 3DP
UK

1385 Broadway
New York
NY 10018
USA

www.bloomsbury.com

BLOOMSBURY and the Diana logo are trademarks of Bloomsbury Publishing Plc

First published 2015
Paperback edition first published 2017

British Library Cataloguing-in-Publication Data
A catalogue record for this book is available from the British Library.

ISBN: HB: 978-1-4725-6673-7
PB: 978-1-3500-2747-3
ePDF: 978-1-4725-6674-4
ePub: 978-1-4725-6675-1

Library of Congress Cataloging-in-Publication Data
Evens, Aden.
Logic of the digital / Aden Evens.
pages cm
Includes bibliographical references and index.
ISBN 978-1-4725-6673-7 (hb) – ISBN 978-1-4725-6674-4 (epdf) –
ISBN 978-1-4725-6675-1 (epub) 1. Human-computer interaction–Philosophy.
2. Digital media–Philosophy. 3. Ontology. 4. Logic. I. Title.
QA76.9.H85E957 2015
004.01'9–dc23
2015010429

Typeset by Deanta Global Publishing Services, Chennai, India

For my elder son, Felix …
Which means I have to write at least one more book.

Contents

"It is therefore true that God makes the world by calculating, but his calculations never work out exactly, and this inexactitude or injustice in the result, this irreducible inequality, forms the condition of the world. The world 'happens' while God calculates; if the calculation were exact, there would be no world." (Deleuze 1994, p. 222)

Introduction

All digital technologies share one thing: they operate on the basis of a discrete code. Usually this code is binary, constructed from sequences of binary digits or *bits*, each of which can be in one of two states, named 0 and 1. The most basic contention of this book is that the binary code, which defines and enables digital technology, is consequential; the 0s and 1s that allow a machine to operate digitally lend to that machine something of their character or way of being. *Logic of the Digital* articulates this ontology, describing how the binary code reveals itself throughout the digital and so also in the thought and action of those who live with and within digital technologies.

The interface of a computer does not appear obviously to be made of 1s and 0s. The binary code encodes the images and actions that take place in the interface, but where is that code, and how does it make possible the computer's expansive possibilities? By tracing the path from the media that read, write, and store individual microscopic bits to the icons and menus of the graphical user interface and to the people who use digital devices and constitute digital culture, *Logic of the Digital* exposes the logics of the digital and its engagements with the human. A code such as the binary code is not a neutral surface of inscription but lends its character to the objects and actions it encodes. Given the breadth of the digital domain, the great swaths of life that now pass through or in digital media, the character of the bit should be widespread, if diffuse. Examining further the nature of the code, *Logic of the Digital* pursues its influence across the grand scale of the digital, looking at the shape it gives to cognition and behavior.

This is not a technological determinism; the digital does not impose a way of being on its users. On the contrary, the digital is embraced precisely because of its way of being, for it reproduces already dominant values. The digital makes an excellent companion to rationalist epistemology, instrumental reason, positivist notions of truth, and so colludes with ways of thinking on the rise for a number of centuries. Our culture chooses the digital because *it works so well*—it does what it is programmed to do—extremely quick and very efficient, predictable, transportable, ubiquitous. And the digital works so well largely due to the binary code.

Digital specifies neither binarity nor encoding; rather, it signals discreteness. Like the ten digits we use to represent decimal numbers and the ten digits we use to type, the digital code is discrete. In fact, it is doubly discrete: each bit is distinct from each other bit and each of the two bit values is distinct from the other. This double distinction defines the bit and gives it its possibilities; digital technologies cannot function should these distinctions falter. This sort of distinction, an absolute and immaculate distinction between values or between bits, is an abstraction, a generalization or idealization. The remarkable ability of the digital is to make concrete the abstraction of the bit, to materialize an idea, and this is a formula for the power of computers. The digital allows its users to engage with an abstract world, semimaterialized but still made of ideas. Realizing perfect distinction in the actual world, the digital gains its extraordinary efficiency, its seeming weightlessness, its rapidity, its general lack of material resistance. But abstraction, the basis of the digital's power, also establishes its limits; the abstract bit substitutes formality for actuality throughout its operation, semantics collapsed into syntax, free expression replaced by constrained choice, material trace overwritten by formal sign, and generative difference supplanted by static identity. This is another central theme of this book: abstraction is the digital's glorious motor, but also its tragic deficit.

This also points to the chief motive for this research: the intuition that something important may be lost in the headlong rush to *go digital*, the easy embrace of abstraction. The spread of digital technologies is unprecedented, reaching into countless areas of human endeavor and inventing plenty of new ones. Commerce and communication, work and leisure, archiving and organizing, reading and writing, design, production, dissemination, and presentation—the digital is the medium that does it all. It therefore becomes urgent to understand how the digital works, to get a clearer sense of what kinds of thinking and acting it admits, and what cognition and what behavior it encourages. What are the limits of the binary code and how do those limits show themselves in the uses of digital technologies? These questions impel much of the analysis of *Logic of the Digital*, which is haunted by a cynicism that it cannot always justify. The book does not finally answer the question of what is lost; it does not ultimately discover a precise limit of digital encoding, but the pursuit of those limits drives the inquiry herein.

Skepticism about the digital does not begin with this book, as criticism and fear of the digital have accompanied it from the beginnings of the computer era. Digital culture includes the nagging worries that its associated technologies are rotting our brains, narrowing our thinking, and separating us from ourselves and from each other. *Logic of the Digital* is thus unusual, not because it expresses insufficient reverence for the digital, but because it advances its analysis and critique on the basis of the techno-logical principles of digital operation, primarily the binary code. Criticism of the discrete has only recently begun to attract attention, so this book was written largely in intellectual isolation and outside of the currents of digital studies. Many people provided much-needed encouragement and collegiality as I completed the rather long arc of writing, and I am especially appreciative in this regard of my colleagues in the Department of English at Dartmouth College. Professors Sean Kelly and John Cayley kindly read an early manuscript and offered several hours of critique and advice, as did Amy Allen, Tom Luxon, and Alex Halasz. I am indebted to a number of readers for various presses, who affirmed the value of the project, and to one anonymous reader whose bracing critique inspired a wholesale recalibration of the book's argument. The first two chapters have benefited from the sensitive attention of Josh Hudelson. Anna Guenther provided some desperately needed research assistance. Humphrey Morris has probably made all the difference. My primary reader has been Dr. Sally Ackerman, who is my partner in more and more ways. And it is reassuring to know that Sandy Baldwin is writing too, as he always says it better than I can.

Following the trajectory of the book's claim—the ontology of the bit as an influence on the digital's way of being—the chapters move roughly from the inside out. Starting with an exposition of the bit and its operation in Chapter 1, the subsequent three chapters *zoom out*, to focus on programming and software, the user interface, and the World Wide Web. The fifth and final chapter marks a shift in tone, as I attempt to draw together themes common to the first four chapters, offering a rough account of the general characteristics of the digital and a more speculative analysis of digital dynamics, which concludes that the digital consistently encounters its limits, but also consistently displaces them, expanding its reach indefinitely.

1

From Bits to the Object

Begin with the bit. Bits are a de facto universal language of the digital. Whatever happens *in* the computer, all the input and all the output and whatever transpires in between, all of it is encoded as bits, lists of 0s and 1s. In computing, a bit, contracted from *binary digit*, is a device something like a switch obtaining one of two states. The two states of a switch often distinguish *on* and *off*; in a bit these values or states are usually called 0 and 1, but a bit can equally be thought of as *true* or *false*, *yes* or *no*, + or −, or any two distinct, exclusive values. The meaning of a bit, and thus the meanings of its two states, depend on how the bit is employed, what it gets used for. For the bit and its two states have no intrinsic meaning, or at least none aside from an assertion of one state and not the other. In particular, though bits are often used as numerals to represent numeric values, there is nothing inherently numeric about the meaning of a bit's value, and its two states do not inherit the rich histories of the numerals that label those states.

In the right context, a given bit could designate that a particular pixel on the monitor manifest one shade of orange rather than a slightly darker shade. In another context, it could store a datum corresponding to a user's gender as masculine or feminine. (More bits would be necessary to store a fuller range of genders.) Elsewhere a bit could tell the computer to skip the next instruction if the result of the previous calculation was a positive number rather than telling the computer to skip the next instruction if the result of the previous calculation was a negative number. This does not begin to hint at the enormous flexibility and ubiquity of the bit. All information in the computer, both data and instructions, is materially instantiated and logically encoded in bits. The bit is the basic building block of digital operation.

As a material entity, a bit is a structure in some substrate with a property that can exhibit either of two detectable, distinct, defined states. This structure typically occupies a small area in or on the surface of the hardware substrate. The state of the property can be altered (*written*) once or many times depending on the nature of the substrate; to write a bit is to set the selected property to one of the two designated states within that small area such that it represents the state understood to mean 0 or the state understood to mean 1. This state can then be measured (*read*) to yield its value, 0 or 1, and so can play a role in a system that produces different results depending on which of the two states obtains. In a nutshell, that is how the digital works: if such-and-such a bit is 0, do *this*; if 1, do *that*.

Just as the bit can be turned to many purposes or meanings, so does it find accommodation in a variety of materials. Though there is no digital technology or experience that is not irredeemably dependent on its material, the digital can be stored, transmitted, and manipulated in disparate materials, and notwithstanding significant differences in efficiency, size, etc., the digital results are the same, as though the digital demonstrates a degree of indifference to its material. To accommodate digital data, a material must have some property that allows orderable, localizable, persistent distinctions between two states; common examples of such properties include electrical resistance such as on a computer chip, magnetic field strength on a hard disc surface, and optical reflectivity on a compact disc. In fact, any medium that admits such a configurable distinction between two states can store bits, and any medium that allows a *re*configurable discrete distinction can host digital calculation.[1]

The physical property used in a digital machine to represent the two states of a bit need not of itself present discrete states, but might range over a continuum of values. (For comparison, a light switch is usually spring-loaded as to allow one of two discrete states, on or off, whereas a volume knob on a stereo console allows a continuous range of values between silent and very loud.) With a continuously variable property, two particular values within the range of possible values of that property are chosen by convention to represent the two distinct states. For example, electrical potential relative to a reference voltage can vary, measuring from 0 volts (equal to the reference voltage) to large positive or negative values, including noninteger values. When electrical potential is used on a computer chip to actualize bits, two values, such as +2 volts and +5 volts, are chosen to represent 0 and 1, and that chip is engineered to operate according to that standard. As material flows of electricity, the conventional values chosen are idealizations; the circuits that act on bits are designed to treat as homogeneous a range of values around the conventionally chosen values. A reading of *approximately* +2 volts is taken as *exactly* 0 and a reading of *approximately* +5 volts is taken as *exactly* 1.

Taking a range of different voltages and treating that difference as a self-identical sameness, this digital bow to the inscrutability of the material presents a preliminary and basic example of the founding principle of the digital, namely, abstraction. The digital assigns an ideal, self-same value to a material difference in order to constitute the bit. In its material construction, the bit is defined through a materialized ideal, an abstraction that replaces (a range of) difference with a homogeneous value.

Functioning as a switch, an individual bit can mean *yes*-or-*no* or *true*-or-*false*, and there are contexts in which a single bit takes on such a specific meaning, definable independently of other bits. More typically, though, bits are not treated in isolation, but in lists or sequences; eight bits in linear sequence, which constitutes a *byte* in many computing systems, has been a historically popular sequencing convention.[2] Whereas a single bit can obtain one of two states, a sequence of bits, like a row of switches, can obtain many states; two bits allow four possible states (viz., 00, 01, 10, 11), three bits express eight distinct states (000, 001, 010, 011, 100, 101, 110, 111), and in general, n bits taken together can obtain 2^n distinct states.

There is a natural correspondence between sequences of bits, as in the examples just given in parentheses, and the whole numbers, starting with 0. Just as our decimal numbering system, with ten different digits, uses m digits in sequence to represent any number from 0 to $10^m - 1$, a sequence of n bits, with only two different digits, can represent any number from 0 to $2^n - 1$, and any unique sequence of bits can be read as a binary representation of a unique integer. Picture a three-digit number in the familiar decimal system. Grade school students learn that the rightmost digit is the 1s place, the middle digit is the 10s place, and the leftmost digit is the 100s place; if there were a fourth digit (on the left) it would represent the next power of 10, the 1000s place. So the decimal number 206 means six 1s, plus zero 10s, plus two 100s. The binary number system represents the same numbers as the decimal system, but it uses only two symbols, 0 and 1, instead of the ten symbols of the decimal system, 0, 1, 2, 3, 4, 5, 6, 7, 8, 9. With two symbols, the binary system counts the *places* according to powers of two rather than powers of ten: instead of the 1s, 10s, 100s, 1000s places from right to left, the binary system counts the 1s, 2s, 4s, 8s, 16s, etc., places. For example, the binary number 01110110 represents the number written 118 in the decimal system, which can be verified by adding up the *places*: from right to left, zero 1s, plus one 2, plus one 4, plus zero 8s, plus one 16, plus one 32, plus one 64, plus zero 128s. The leftmost 0 could be left off, just as one can leave off leading 0s in decimal numbers, but leading 0s are often included by convention in binary representation, perhaps because binary numbers are often taken as lists of independent bits rather than exclusively numeric values. Because a list of bits can represent not just 0 or 1, but any numeric value (limited only by the number of bits used), it provides a very adaptable encoding system.

Note that this method of encoding numbers as bits is by no means the only possible encoding nor is it the only one in common use. Systems are distinguished as *big endian* or *little endian* according to whether the bit values of higher significance (larger powers of 2) are taken to be to the left or to the right in the sequence of bits. Further, an adequate integer encoding scheme requires that a method be designated to indicate the sign, positive or negative, of the number represented by the bits. For reasons of engineering efficiency, negative values are often encoded using a *twos-complement* scheme, which allows many arithmetic operations to be carried out as though the numbers had no signs, as in the simple scheme of the previous paragraph where no bit was set aside to represent the sign of the represented integer. The variety of codes attests to the bit's lack of inherent value or meaning, and so can be employed by hardware and software engineers as they will. Representation of *anything* representable by bits is always a matter of convention, though some conventions, such as those of simple binary logic, are so widely respected as to have become practical principles.

The openness of the bit, its indifference to its employment, its complete availability, evinces the digital's central technique and principle of operation. The bit is drained of all inherent value by the *abstraction* that is its primary action and the result of this action; the bit is "not just tiny but abstract" and "insubstantial," as James Gleick puts it (2011, p. 10). It is as *abstraction*, divorced from its concrete material meaning, drained of substance, that the bit undergirds most of the digital's extraordinary contributions, its powers of efficiency, speed, and size, its powers of reproduction, alteration, communication, and so on. All these possibilities of the digital depend essentially on the abstraction made possible by bits and realized through bits.

Though the discussion thus far treats the bit in its aspect as foundation of the digital, another perspective places the bit and its code in a mediate role, interposed between, rather than at the bottom of, (digital) things. In between what the user puts into the machine and what she gets out of it, in between programmer and user, in between idea and its digital realization, in between either end of every digital communication, transaction, calculation, etc., lie streams of 0s and 1s.

This would place the binary code not at an edge but at a strait or *wasp waist* of the digital medium. The computer (or digital device) admits input in different modes (mouse gestures, keyboard clicks, voice commands, Ethernet messages, etc.) and generates output likewise (images, text, tables, windows, light pulses, rumbling noises, . . .), but whatever passes through and whatever goes on in between takes the form of a code of 0s and 1s, and its transformations in the machine are governed by a code of 0s and 1s running on hardware whose intricate design was created using 0s and 1s. Input and output sandwich the binary code, which serves as a medium of construction for digital objects and actions. What can it capture using its seemingly simple tools of 0 and 1? For the straits of the binary code must inform whatever transpires using a digital machine.

If the bit is a universal of digital technologies, that is because it plays a unique and crucial role as the tool of abstraction, the digital's chief technique. Abstraction achieves in the bit an apotheosis. This maximal abstraction drains the bit of a native sense of its own, which lack opens it to any purpose. With no meaning of its own, the bit readily adapts to any information need, offers itself to any articulable meaning. A common maxim of computer programming holds that one should "be conservative in what you produce; be liberal in what you accept"; the bit practically makes a definition of this, as it confines itself to the homogeneity of two values, which allows the heterogeneous accommodation of any information. It is the largest breadth of application using the fewest possible symbols.

Each bit, a maximal abstraction, is both the greatest and the least difference. The least, for it represents a minimum of information. No amount of information may be transmitted in less than one single bit. The mathematics of information theory measures amounts of information in bits. In cases where the information includes some redundancy, or where all messages are not equiprobable, the *amount* of information transmitted in a particular case may be fractional. It takes one bit to transmit a yes-or-no response; if you are 99 percent certain that you will receive the message "yes," and then you do receive the message "yes," you did not really find out anything that you did not already pretty much know. Information-theoretically speaking, you received less than one bit of information, although it still took one bit to send the message. In that sense we might speak of an amount of information less than one bit, but the bit remains the least meaningful amount of information.

The bit is also the greatest difference in that its whole principle is discrete difference. The bit is occupied by its assertion of 1-and-not-0 or 0-and-not-1, the simple but absolute difference that allows the representation of any discrete difference. For a bit, the meaning of 0 is that it is absolutely not 1, and vice versa. It makes difference its genesis and being, such that the bit is the greatest difference that is nothing but the posit of difference as perfect distinction.

This formula must be further elucidated. The abstractness of a bit is maximal not only because it represents the smallest measure of information but also because it denies any grounding in the concrete. The bit includes an indispensable materiality, but as abstraction it divorces its meaning from the material conditions in which it is realized. The actual material of bits not only instantiates them but also carries out their meanings, making sense of their processual logic by exhibiting flows and inhabiting states of electrical, magnetic, and other properties. The working logic underlying the creation in hardware and software of bits depends for its *existence* on that remarkably refined materiality, but its sense is both constructed out of and authored through its logical meaning, realized in, but semantically divorced from, its materiality. The bit should not be confused with any token, with any meaningful or sensible stand-in, with any symbolic reminder of its function. A bit is not a 0 or a 1, not the glyphs, 0 and 1, we use to represent these digits, not the sonic tokens, "zero" and "one," that name them, and not the numbers, 0 and 1, that might end a countdown. On its own, the bit does not mean *on* and *off*, or *up* and *down*, or *true* and *false*. These figures, sounds, and concepts are all laden with meaning, inseparably bound to their histories, and embedded in materialities of embodiment and sensation that define their ways of being and determine their signifying contexts. Perhaps the numbers 0 and 1 come close to the ontology of the bit, for they also show a considerable degree of abstraction in their way of being, as well as an unusual relationship to instantiation and existence. Still, numbers and their relationships and histories offer an insistence or intractability, sometimes taken as a claim to truth (such as the purported truth of simple arithmetic statements), which gives them singular meanings, in contrast to the indifference and semantic void of the bit. The bit's sense has been abstracted away to a minimum, a formality: a bit means only *that it is not its other*.

But are not bits themselves symbols? We have noted already that they function in (linear) sequences to encode meanings, which ascription applies as well to the letters of the alphabet, and those are surely symbols. C. S. Peirce's most well-known typology of signs characterizes a symbol as a sign that relates to its intention by convention, taking on a particular meaning "because [it] will be so interpreted," and this would seem to hold for bits, too (1958, p. 368). However, as will be said below of icons, bits may not belong to the realm of signs at all. Unlike the bit, figure and phoneme are irreducibly tied to their materialities: a letter or written symbol has a shape (or a family of related shapes) by virtue of which it both is what it is and does what it does (which is to present the figure that it is). A letter can escape its figure only by entering another symbolic order: one can invoke the letter in speech, for instance, where it still cleaves to a materiality now aural rather than textual. What about encoding the letter using bits? Undoubtedly, the bits that store or process the encoded letter retain a specific materiality, but no longer does that materiality bear any inherent or sensible relation to the letter it encodes. Common figures such as letters are usually stored as numeric values referring to standard look-up tables indicating which figure is associated with a given value according to the standard in use. The ASCII standard, for example, associates the values 0 through 127 with the lower and upper case letters of the English alphabet, the decimal numerals, a space character, punctuation marks, and some control codes intended to offer instructions to a printer or other output device, such as *backspace* or *line feed*.[3] The bits associated with the letter *c* stored in ASCII encoding represent the (decimal) number 99, or as a row of bits, 1100011. Neither the numeric value nor the pattern of bits bears any inherent relation to the letter *c*, but that only affirms that the relation between the bits and the letter is a matter of convention.

Complicating the question of semiosis, bits do not, except in unusual cases, offer themselves to human sensation and so do not operate by sensible representation. Even magnified, the hard drive platter or logic surface of a computer chip would not reveal its value-state to the eye; those states are realized as invisible magnetic and electrical properties, producing meaning by generating a detectable magnetic field or by allowing a particular amount of electrical current to pass through. The semiotic relation, with its human component, emerges only after a decoding process that once again produces the letter in one of its singular material incarnations (as figure or sound). The relation between the bits and the figure or sound they might indicate is conventional, but that convention, being entirely automated and unavailable to perception, does not depend, as signs usually do, on the subject or enunciative group that would typically maintain a standard by respecting, or enforcing, or disseminating it. Which is to say, if bits symbolize, their interpreters are not people but machines, as Friedrich Kittler despairs.[4] Encoded in hardware and software, the standard does not stand above or apart from that which it conventionally governs; they are of a piece. The digital representation in bits must first be read by the machine, an automated reincarnation of the *symbol* to be presented. Whereas material symbols appeal to their sensible materiality, tying themselves necessarily to a place and time, the bit pushes its materiality aside by a kind of indirection, a shift of registers from the symbolic into a still more abstract domain.

This challenging semiosis of the bit we might call its *bare materiality*, borrowing loosely from the notion of *bare life* articulated by Giorgio Agamben and others. Bits are not immaterial, but they are engineered and employed in a manner that selects certain material properties related to data storage and isolates them from other physical or materially variable properties such as temperature, noise, and vibration.[5] Bits neutralize and stabilize material resistance to subordinate the material to the bit's logic. The material of the bit remains to some degree intractable, for the bit occupies space, imposes temporal duration, demands energy, and occasionally fails to operate properly due to poor design, deterioration, or improper operating conditions such as dust or unstable power sources. Given the statistical infrequency of such errors and the wide range of temperature and other environmental conditions under which digital technologies can operate, the bit's materiality becomes uniquely disconnected from its content.[6] Thus, a bit operates the same way: it blindly follows nothing but its deterministic role in a simple logic, enabled and bounded by its materials but functioning in a different register from them. Below the thresholds of perception, bits are decoupled from the human world and minimally materialized as to reduce as much as possible the resistance of materiality; bits are designed to go as fast as possible using the least energy in the smallest space. Aside from its posit of 1 or 0, the bit is only the simple fact of a material instance, its content and container mutually indifferent. If the bit is a symbol, it is a strange symbol that operates only at a distance and in no sensible relationship to its materiality.

The separation or gap between a bit's materiality and the logic that gives it meaning in practice offers more than just an efficiency. This gap chiefly characterizes the ontology of the bit, which is riven by a divide that founds the digital's distinctive and extraordinary powers. Separating the bit's meaning from its material conditions sets bits in a realm apart, a domain where they can operate nearly perfectly, without interference from the contingencies and inconsistencies that riddle almost any materiality. For example, this ontologically significant gap determines the unusual relationship between the digital and error. A breakdown in the materiality of the bit, as when operating conditions exceed the limits of material tolerance, generally produces catastrophic failure; the machine simply stops working or crashes. Whereas technologies more closely tied to their materialities might bend rather than break as they surpass their operational parameters, the digital either works or breaks, with only rare in-betweens. Quoting Claude Shannon, Wolfgang Hagen puts it succinctly: "A single error in the components, wiring, or programming will typically lead to complete gibberish in the output" (2006, p. 166).

Jim Campbell's digital-analog artworks make visible (a representation of) the normally implicit function of the bit as well as the process of its transformation into a legible symbol. In his *Portrait of a Portrait of Harry Nyquist* (2000), Campbell uses a twelve-by-sixteen rectangular matrix of 192 white LED lights to render a low-resolution image of Harry Nyquist, who formulated a basic principle of digital information capture that governs relationships among the range of information captured, the sampling frequency, and the distortion called *aliasing*.[7] Campbell's LEDs allow variable brightnesses and so exceed the binarity of the bit (which would be more precisely instantiated by a light that could be only on or off), but viewers nevertheless encounter the bit's enigma in the contrast between the simple stupidity of these individual white LEDs and the remarkable, eerie image of a blurry face that comes to exist only by virtue of the aggregative act of seeing on the part of the spectator. The face presents its precarity, its almost not being there, its tendency to dissolve into its component pixels, and so explores the related limits of digital information capture and perceptual reconstruction. Campbell mitigates this precarity by placing a translucent scrim in front of the LED matrix, hiding the individual pixels and diffusing their light to emphasize the ghostly appearance of a just-recognizable face and to illustrate by direct demonstration a digital-to-analog conversion process that takes place in sensation, rather than prior to it.[8]

Cadence Kinsey works to rematerialize the binary code, recognizing and protesting the abstraction that conceives the "binary as a zero-sum game, an all-or-nothing form of representation" (2014, p. 897). Her analysis advances on two fronts, one phenomenological and the other ontological. First, she reads Nell Tenhaaf's sculpture *Push/Pull*, to show how a differently materialized interface can leverage algorithmic behavior to introduce *contingency* into the user's experience of the digital, defying the digital's typically deterministic, "all-or-nothing" style of interaction. Second, she locates the bit's history in the punch cards used to control Jacquard looms in the early nineteenth century, distancing bits from the abstraction of the numbers 0 and 1 that many theorists conflate with the values of digital bits. Punch cards have spaces that are either punched or not, and they can thereby store and instruct a pattern of binary states, raising or lowering threads attached to hooks on a loom according to whether a given space is punched or intact, but many other factors contribute to the produced textile, such that the resultant visual meaning of the punched holes is determined only in context and bound to an intractable materiality.

Though I share Kinsey's critical relation to the history of the (conceptualization of the) bit as formal and rigid, her optimism regarding a shift away from that rigidity is unfounded. Kinsey's analysis of *Push/Pull*, for instance, attributes a contingency to the autonomous digital agents constituted through software as patterns of LEDs, as programmed by Tenhaaf or programmers working under her direction. Emphasizing the destabilizing experience of the interactive sculpture, Kinsey includes "the hardware and software that process and display the information" as "sites of possible interference" in the subjective encounter (between observer and sculpture) and, thus, as loci of contingency (2014, p. 903). But, in fact, any contingency involved in the user's experience of the sculpture—and it is at the level of experience that Kinsey locates an alternative to the formal rigidity of the binary code—is introduced by the user and to a lesser extent by the nondigital materiality of the sculpture and its installation. The complexity of the algorithms that determine how the LED lights turn on and off may foil an attempt by the user to exercise a strict, intentional control over the sculpture's (interactive) behavior, and this complexity is redoubled by the sculpture's responsiveness, which uses sensors that react to the user's position in space. Along with the unfamiliar interface and its organic contours, this complexity of the artwork disrupts the traditional relation of dominance by the user over the digital machine. But nothing in this analysis (or in the sculpture itself) overturns the strictly deterministic and "all-or-nothing" character of the underlying binary code, the absolutism of which may be softened by other aspects of the work but which retains its rigid process throughout. The sculpture may feel unpredictable and even haunted by a subject (or a group of subjects), but this feeling is generated through complex, yet finally deterministic, digital processes that do not introduce a contingency at the level of the bit.

Her analysis of the phenomenology of the artwork, focused on the dimension of experience, does not speak to the ontology of the binary code, but Kinsey also examines that code directly, considering its origins in the punch cards used to control the thread hooks of a Jacquard loom as well as the gendered reading of the binary as analyzed by Sadie Plant. Acknowledging the authority of Plant's feminist critique of the binary, which maps the binary 1 and 0 onto (respectively) penis/male/presence and vagina/female/absence, Kinsey rightly insists that this mapping mistakes the digital binary code for the numbers that share names with the bit's values. As has been discussed above, 0 and 1 are convenient names for the values of a bit, and are not the same as the whole numbers that bear those same names and glyphs; as Kinsey puts it, "what is important in binary is not the digits themselves but the places where they occur" (2014, p. 920). The bit value 0 does not designate an absence, as Plant proposes, but takes its meaning from its context, where it might well indicate a presence, as in the loom where a hole in the punch card causes the warp thread to rise above the woof thread, hiding the woof and showing (*present*ing) the warp in the finished textile. In digital graphics, a 0 bit value often means a black pixel, which acts as a positivity when deployed against, for example, a white background. (The letters on many a printed page or displayed in my word processor as I write this are black against white, such that black or 0 is much more presence than absence.)

Divorcing the values of a bit from the numbers that would make those values abstract, Kinsey aims to bind bits to the materiality exemplified in the holes and intact spaces of punch cards. She concludes that bits cling to a spatial and temporal specificity rather than an abstract numeric value. But this appealing conclusion overlooks the degree of abstraction of the bit as employed (not in looms but) in digital technologies, where even place in a sequence is largely abstracted from the material restrictions of space and time. Adam Nash offers the countervailing perspective:

> It is important to note that a digital file does not usually contain instructions on how to decode it in order to reconstruct a copy of its semantic source. Rather, digital files simply note which protocols are required to do so, in order that the system can employ the appropriate software to attempt a decoding. Such software is itself subject to the same process and so on. The point is that digital data is *essentially* formless and plastic. It requires an intentionality external to itself in order to be reconstituted as a copy of its semantic source. (2012, p. 12)

On a punch card, the values of the "bits" operate according to an explicitly material regime in which the meaning of a punched or intact spot arises through a mechanism that engages concretely with the physical hole or continuous surface. But in a digital machine, these values are abstracted, not as the numbers "zero" and "one," but as the "*essentially* formless" values named 0 and 1 that can be turned toward any meaning whatsoever. As Nash points out, nothing about a bit lends it to any particular purpose, and it awaits its determination from without. It is not the abstraction of numbers but an even more severe and deliberate abstraction, the evacuation of all inherent meaning, that allows the bit to be turned toward whatever purpose, offering no resistance of its own. Thus does Wendy Chun refer to software as "fundamentally ephemeral" (2011, p. 3).

* * *

We started with the bit but continually refer to the digital. Taking a cue from its etymology, we define *digital* as *marked by discrete distinction.* This is a concise if baggy definition, with the advantage that it underlines the foundational abstraction of the bit: the discrete distinction between 0 and 1 and the discrete distinction between each bit and each other, by means of which the bit works. The binary code makes discrete distinction the first principle of its being, but other things from fingers to numerals to technologies are digital because they too feature or rely on discreteness. The word *digital* derives from *deixis,* the act of pointing out, pulling something out of its immediacy to set it against and before its background. Digital technologies, then, are digital foremost because they rely on a discrete code; by convention it is a binary code, but it would be logically equivalent to a code with three, or ten, or sixteen digits instead of just two.[9] What is essential is that there are discrete values, identifiable as absolutely other than each other. Note that being digital, according to this definition, does not rule out also being analog: a computer chip is digital because its operation relies on a discrete code, but it instantiates those operations using analog circuitry that admits a continuous—not discrete—flow of electricity. The chip is also, therefore, an analog device.

Even if the etymological connection between *deixis* and *digital* refers more directly to the finger as both pointer and digit than to the more abstract notion of discreteness, the finger serves as pointer precisely on the basis of its discreteness. It is not just a matter of orienting one's body in the direction indicated by the pointing finger; for the finger also in*dic*ates that there is some*thing* to see or encounter. A closed fist but for one extended finger makes a symmetry by analogy with the thing being pointed out against its background of what is not being pointed out (or only as background). One points with one's in*dex* finger, which becomes an index into the world. One of the contentions of this book is that what is digital about the finger is in the main also what is digital about the digital, namely, operation by indirect, encoded action. The digital works only by pointing, not by touching, even in the case of so-called touchscreens, which still separate the user from what she touches, turning the touch into a pointing.

How does the discrete distinction of the bit, based in abstraction, found the operation of the digital? Another definition is overdue: *abstraction* substitutes an idea for something tangible or a general idea for a more specific one. In the case of *digital* abstraction, formal distinction substitutes for generative difference. The digital represents everything, objects and operations, as sequences of precise, distinct values. Instead of a singular quality like color or texture, the digital substitutes an integer or a sequence of them. Rather than a sensory manifold of overlapping experience extended in time and space, the digital deals with a tidy list of binary digits, constructing its world from separate parts, each with a set of qualities precisely defined by numbers. What could be more abstract? Digital processes are not events whose borders blur into the indefinite ramifications of expanding consequence and receding precedent, but sequences of exact, repeatable steps, each defined by a particular value determining a logical configuration of electrical flow.[10] In each case, and, in fact, in every case, the digital discounts variegated complexity and irreducible singularity in favor of the simple abstraction of a precise number. (As has been emphasized, the digital code need not be understood to represent numbers, though it is expedient to do so.)

Abstraction is not only the result but also the mechanism of the digital. Looking again at etymology, *abs-tract* means *to draw away*. At the basis of the digital, the principle of discrete distinction abstracts from or draws away the plenitude of material, semantic, and perceptual difference, to leave only the formal differences between 0 and 1 and between one bit and another. Constructed as lists of bits, a digital object is thus an abstraction that results from a process of abstraction. Though every technology relies to some degree on abstraction, the digital uniquely makes abstraction its chief technique. A screwdriver ignores many differences among screws, treating its objects as essentially the same even when they are of different sizes, different materials, different ages, textures, and colors. The Philips head figure at the tip of the screwdriver requires only a general conformity to this shape and size, so that most screws that have a + inscribed in their heads will work with most Philips head screwdrivers.[11] The screwdriver handle accommodates many hands, as different sizes and shapes will still find a grip that can take advantage of the simple machine to transform a force of rotation in a plane into a force of linear motion along a perpendicular axis. This bracketing of difference, characteristic of any technology, is abstraction, privileging or selecting something general out of a field of specific difference.

Relative to other technologies, digital technologies promote abstraction to a central position, not just one maneuver among others but the founding and sustaining principle of digital operation. The digital abstracts *all* difference; whatever it does not simply ignore, it treats as a number or as a numerical relationship among numbers. Constructing its entities and actions out of abstract numbers instead of plastic, metal, or paper, the digital avoids the fragility, irregularity, cost, and resistance to change of those materials. And as easily as they can be digitally instantiated, objects can be altered through logical or numerical transformations, again without contending with the resistance and unpredictability of the material. In the digital there is no question of a tolerable difference between the screwdriver and the inscribed furrows in the head of the screw; represented digitally as precise integer values, a digital object is exactly defined and will necessarily submit to any algorithm whose formal parameters it satisfies. Every number, a sequence of bits, is equivalent to its own formality, and difference amounts to a subtraction problem, itself amenable to digital capture. *The power of the digital lies in its confinement as much as possible to this rarefied, ideal realm of pure form, for there it might operate unfettered by the most severe constraints of materiality.* Numerical representation offers more than convenience; it also displaces the action to a domain that avoids the messy materiality of the actual world.

This most basic operation of the digital, an abstraction that discards difference to distinguish *and connect* two domains or two dimensions, establishes a simple structure that will arise many times through the subsequent analysis of the digital. As we will see, digital abstraction takes place not only in the encoding process that generates bits or numbers but also in the organization of the code itself and in the organization of objects and their parts that it produces. Arising deterministically from that code, the objects of the interface and the operations available there also convey the abstraction at the heart of digital operation. We will see too that an interface made of partial abstractions is not without an influence on the one who would engage with it. Throughout this digital space, from bits to icons to users to digital cultures, abstraction draws away difference to establish or codify distinct domains, both separating and conjoining. And in each case, digital abstraction shows a double edge, as it both opens and forecloses possibilities of action.

By removing or neutralizing the generative difference, the contingency and accident, the excess and play that inhere in material, semantic, and phenomenal things, bits approach their own ideality, for the difference that remains in the bit is almost entirely formal. The history of computing participates in this progressive idealization, chipping away at the materialities of time, space, and energy that stand between the actual computer and its idealization in a perfect logic. Moore's law codifies the trend, forecasting exponential improvements in the size and speed of digital technology and exemplifying the rhetorical stance surrounding high technology more generally.[12] Representative of the powerful futurist strain in digital culture, Moore's law embraces material abstraction as an engine of digital advance. For thirty years, microprocessor manufacturers played leapfrog, each offering frequent incremental improvements in processor clock speeds.[13] This particular shouting match over operations-per-second has diminished in the last few years, as abstraction targets other chip measurements, such as the number of processing cores and dye size, which are related to clock speed, but are not the same thing.

Improvements in energy efficiency, size, and speed have also made possible an ongoing shift from wired to wireless technologies, freeing the user to move without leaving her machine behind. The popular slogan of *ubiquitous computing* evinces the fantasy that would take this particular trend to its ideal conclusion, computing anywhere and anytime. Constructed and imagined environments for ubiquitous computing often use screens along with gesture and speech for passing information between user and computer. The parallel fantasy of *immediacy* also imagines the computer everywhere, not by virtue of ubiquity but rather by its disappearance; the machine no longer signals its presence, but answers to our intuitions and desires seemingly unbidden. Like ubiquity, immediacy exerts a significant influence in the use and development of digital technologies, though there is also a countervailing tendency toward "hypermediacy," as Jay Bolter and Richard Grusin thematize in *Remediation* (1999). (Chapter 4 discusses these fantasies in greater detail.)

The bit, a shadow flitting across a plane of logic, encodes the processes and products of the digital. Treating the two values of the bit as digits 0 and 1 and identifying distinct bits in linear sequence produces a straightforward encoding of whole numbers, the binary or base-2 number system, as explained above. How do bits, or the numbers they encode, also encode the objects and operations that inhabit digital devices, all the many things—programs, databases, messages, images, mouse clicks, copy-and-paste, etc.—that make up *computing*? If writing or the alphabet offers one model of how to encode meaning using symbols, this encoding depends essentially on the way in which its materiality makes it perceptible, and so does not provide a model adequate to the bit, which is generally imperceptible. That is not to say that the model of writing can provide no assistance in understanding how the digital works, but only that it does not account for the general case. So what do bits do and how do they do it?

Consider the reach of number as a code. Anything measurable, anything categorizable, any distinctly identifiable property of a thing, real, imaginary, or in between, whatever can be information can be captured by a code of numbers and thus ultimately by a code of 0s and 1s. The long history of the ascent of numbers and statistics in sciences, medicine, economics, and the many systems of control and administration means that a lot of the world is already enumerated, ready for digital processing. Moving and still images and recorded sound become digital through the innovation of sampling, but are thereby also rendered as lists of numbers. Note that even in cases where the information to be captured has no inherent numerical or logical order, an encoding by a local or widely adopted convention can be employed: 0 for girl and 1 for boy, or 0 for Africa, 1 for Antarctica, 2 for Asia, 3 for Australia, etc. The assignment of a number to a particular quality can be motivated (the continents could be numbered from east to west, or alphabetically, or by size of landmass, or by population, etc.) or arbitrary, as long as the chosen scheme is consistently employed. That is, both the encoding process that generates the data and the decoding process that re-presents or manipulates those data must respect the same coding convention.

In these latter examples, the bits in question could correspond to qualities of an object in the interface and thus be, in a sense, directly readable in the interface: a database where each record stores information pertaining to a person might include a data field for *Sex* and another for *Country*, where a single bit stores the response to the question, *Male* or *Female*, while eight bits yielding 256 distinct possible values would be sufficient to designate one of the (arguably) 196 countries of the world (with leftover values for future expansion, perhaps). A user who knows the codes, that is, whether the program employs the convention that 0 = *male* and 1 = *female* or vice versa, could know the value of the bit stored in the database corresponding to *Sex* for a given record appearing in the interface. On a computer, bits on the hard disc or loaded into random access memory (RAM) can correspond directly to data legible in the interface; but most bits that course through a digital device are less immediately intelligible to the user. Much of the data that bits encode characterize objects that do not simply present themselves on the thick surface of the interface but work behind the scenes, in layers of organized code whose most immediate effects do not yet appear as objects in the interface. Programming is largely a matter of authoring and administering such objects, where the user interface, if even there is one for a given piece of software, is only one component among many dozens or hundreds to be managed. Thus bits also encode the dynamic logic that governs the storage, transmission, recall, and alteration of the objects in the interface and elsewhere; both data and instruction, the object and the operation on it, are made of bits and the numbers they encode in the computer.

A closer look at the basic method of digitizing images reveals some general characteristics of *sampling*. A static image to be digitized, such as a photograph, is divided into a grid of small boxes, rectangular or otherwise. Each small region is a *sample* of the whole image, hence the term *sampling*. To create a digital representation of the image, each box is replaced with a numeric value (or a set of values) that assigns a uniform quality to that small region of the whole image. For a gray scale (monochrome) image, the value represents the luminance of the box, how bright it is, ranging in discrete steps from totally black (a value of 0) to totally white (the maximum possible value, which would depend on how many bits are associated with each individual box). To capture in the digital code the dominant or average color of a box (and not just its brightness) requires additional values to be assigned for each box. One popular encoding system breaks down the color space into three channels, red, green, and blue, and represents each color (that it can represent) using three numbers to quantify the *amount* of each channel's contribution in a given box. Something like mixing paints on an artist's palette, different mixtures of red, green, and blue can produce a wide and useful range of colors; many display devices assign for each on-screen pixel three sub-pixels, red, green, and blue, mixing their individual contributions to reproduce a wide and dense range of discrete colors. A low *green* value with relatively high *red* and *blue* values would represent a shade of purple, for example. In this *RGB* (for *red*, *green*, and *blue*) system, each pixel is associated with a sequence of three numbers, one for each of the three colors being mixed.[14] The more bits available for each number, the more values that can be distinguished within each channel, and so the more gradations or differentiated shades of color available to be assigned to a pixel. Gray scale or color, the basic principle is the same: each small region in the original image corresponds to a set of values in the digital data that represents a single color (chrominance and/or luminance) associated with that region. As a digital object, an image is a list of bits with particular values.[15]

The encoded image demonstrates a hierarchy in its structure. To regard a list of binary values as an RGB-encoded image, the list of values is taken as a sequence of groups of bits, where each group is a number in the binary system. These groups are further grouped into triplets (a number each for red, green, and blue), such that each triplet represents the color of a pixel. The triplets are themselves sequenced, so that successive triplets represent adjacent pixels in the image. Further, higher-order grouping operations take a sequential set of pixels as a row of the image, according to the pixel width of the image.

Numerous abstractions mark this conceptually simple maneuver. First, the division into small regions treats a visual field as relatively (or momentarily) static and composed (or composable) from elementary parts, an assumption common to every digital representation.[16] Second, the assignment of a single value (or a single set of values) to a region treats that region as uniform or homogeneous over its surface while also rendering it comparable to others. That is, not only can its value be compared to the values of other pixels, but third, its *properties to be valued* have also been fixed, made uniform. *Digital sampling not only defines the values of an image but also defines what counts as an image*, namely, a sequence of triplets of, say, sixteen-bit numbers. The possibility of digitization already assumes that the object to be digitized is one of an abstract type, amenable to capture by a technique that makes substantive assumptions about the nature of the object and, in this case, also about the nature of seeing. On a small scale, the result is an imposed homogenization in the digital world. Two rectangular patches of an image might look somewhat different before digitization, but if they have the same average color over their surfaces, they will be assigned the same values and will thereafter be digitally equivalent.

Writing about artificial intelligence, but with applications to digital devices generally, Jean Baudrillard recognizes the limitations of predigested models as the possible categories of computer objects:

> So-called intelligent machines deploy artifice only in the feeblest sense of the word, breaking linguistic, sexual or cognitive acts down into their simplest elements and digitizing them so that they can be resynthesized according to models. They can generate all the possibilities of a program or of a potential object. But artifice is in no way concerned with what *generates*, merely with what *alters*, reality. Artifice is the power of illusion. These machines have the artlessness of pure calculation, and the games they offer are based solely on commutations and combinations. (1993, n.p.)

Baudrillard condemns computers as “celibate machines” because their dependence on rigid models denies them a more open creativity; they can reorganize what is already given in the model, "commutations and combinations," but they cannot produce something more novel. Jaron Lanier extends this analysis, noting that social media and communications technologies increasingly attempt to simulate aspects of human being in the computer and consequently reduce human being to abstract qualities. "I fear that we are beginning to design ourselves to suit digital models of us, and I worry about a leaching of empathy and humanity in that process" (2011, loc. 707–8).

In the process of sampling, the thing to be captured is divided into small pieces, each of which is assigned values associated with its qualities as compared to other pieces. Apprehending its object as a set of parts with properties, the sampling process enforces as a metaphysical rule that things, at least the things it is interested in, are constituted of qualified parts. Sampling of sound treats sound as variation in air pressure over time (at some point in space).[17] Typically, sound to be recorded digitally is initially captured by a microphone, which transduces the variation in air pressure over time into an analogous wave of varying electrical potential over time. Passing from the microphone to the recording device, at the analog-to-digital converter, this varying stream of electricity is measured at regular, rapid intervals: the machine includes a sample-and-hold unit that, when triggered, reaches into the electrical flow and generates a static bundle of electricity with a voltage matching the voltage in the flow at that moment, a sample of the varying voltage of the flow of electricity. This static bundle of electricity is assigned a numeric value, for instance, by running a timer that measures how long it takes for that static bundle of electricity to drain out of a capacitor. And that number is then designated as the value of that particular sample. By a series of analogies, the resulting list of numbers thus describes the rising and falling of the air pressure that constituted the original sound to be recorded. A suitable mechanism can reverse the process, using the list of numbers to generate a variable electrical current that feeds a loudspeaker to create a variation in air pressure whose rapid ups and downs are thus determined by the original list of numbers, reproducing (something close to) the original sound from its digital code. Sound is encoded not by parceling up space (such as the flat space of an image) but by dividing sound into parts spread out over time. Each part has a specific value, which constitutes that qualified part.

This structure, division into parts made of qualities defined by (assigned) values, applies not only to digital images, but to digital things of all kinds, and it serves as a template for understanding what I call the digital *object*. Take textual encoding as another example. Textual symbols (alphabetic or otherwise) must be encoded according to a convention that regards the symbols as discrete entities and then associates each with a *character*, a generic abstraction of the original material and perceivable symbol. That character is given by its numeric value, which allows the computer to look up (and produce as image in the interface) the image-data that describe the visible form of that symbol. ASCII is one such convention that matches characters with numbers, but there are many available conventions for textual encoding, for different languages, extended symbol sets, diacritical inflection, technical and specialized symbols, and more. As in the cases of image and sound sampling, the text as digital becomes a list of numbers, but it must first become a list of abstract symbols in a determinate sequence. Word processors, seeking to offer text-processing flexibility beyond that of a sequence of characters, populate the sequence with additional numeric codes that, for example, specify orthographic characteristics such as italics or colored text, or that update the displayed characters according to the time or some other criterion. The practice of *markup* establishes conventions (markup languages and extensions and implementations of those languages) for including in the sequence of characters *tokens* that make reference *to* or *about* the text rather than being strictly *of* it, adding a logical dimension to the flat stream of characters and so multiplying possibilities of textual display, analysis, and manipulation.[18]

The digital object is characterized by a structure of parts constituting the whole, but it ramifies this structure, each part itself decomposing into parts, and so on until one arrives at the level of bits. The above examples of image and sound sampling demonstrate the tiered hierarchy of digital objects. Even when it is a question of describing or capturing not data but processes, the hierarchical pattern persists. Programming offers numerous examples of digital objects, structures made of parts that iterate hierarchically. Coding languages are distinguished as *higher-level* or *lower-level* according to how abstract or conceptually distant from the machine the language in question is. A relatively high-level language might include in its vocabulary terms that correspond to complex processes requiring thousands of machine operations to complete; for example, a language could include a *compare* command that compares two objects, such as documents, and reports their differences. To write down the code to execute this command could be a matter of a few words and symbols in the high-level language: something like, `compare "Document A" to "Document B"`. Through software tools that encode the logic of the language as described by an official standard, the high-level code undergoes a sequence of translations into (abstruse) lower-level codes that are typically not intended for human readers, until it arrives at a rendering in the machine language of the machine on which it will execute. A low-level language, including the machine language for a given machine, addresses the computer directly as a mechanical-logical device, with individual instructions on the order of moving data around from one memory location to another or multiplying two integer values. Thinking beyond even the machine language, which is based on the logical architecture of the central processing unit (CPU), the engineers who design that architecture might employ an even lower-level language of a first-order binary logic, which would correspond to directing the flow of electricity through gates on the CPU chip, the flow of individual bits.

High-level languages often are *compiled* languages; a compiler is the main piece of software used to translate high-level code, which can be read but not executed, through a series of steps into (binary) machine code, which executes but is so granular (that is, low level) as to make human reading a challenge. Though *compilation* is used casually to refer to the whole process of translating program code (also called source code) into machine code, there are often many steps involved, including linking, assembling, precompiling, and parsing, and, sometimes, refactoring. The programmer writing the high-level code works in *compile-time*, the time of the code-text. But once that code-text has been compiled into a binary executable, it runs on the computer according to the machine time, *run-time*. These two times or divergent temporalities are mostly exclusive: for example, the running program (such as a word- or image-processing program) cannot generally be altered while it runs, while the high-level code is inert prior to being compiled.[19] Precompiled software does not run, whereas once it has been compiled, just type the name of the application (or double-click it) and off it goes.[20]

The difference between compile-time and run-time spans the gap rent by the grand abstraction of software and the complementary abstraction of code. The concept of software divorces instruction from machine, erects an abstract domain of standardized logic: "Every programming language defines a virtual machine, for which it is the machine language" (David Eck quoted in Chun, 2004, p. 38). A virtual machine here means one that exists as an idea, but it is an idea that can be realized in an actual machine. Designing digital objects and logical relationships among them, the programmer crafts or constructs a space in which the user might interact, fixing certain possibilities or structures and leaving others indeterminate until run-time when they can be assigned and altered. One distribution of possibilities manifests in the coding distinction between *variables* and *literals*: a variable can change at run-time while a literal cannot.[21] As a sequence of characters, code-text includes tokens such as the commands and symbols that are recognized early in the compilation process as elements in the vocabulary of that code language. Other tokens stand for variables, which work something like the variables *x* or *y* familiar from high school algebra: they can be manipulated by the code without specifying their particular values, so that their values (can) remain indeterminate until run-time. Many languages give variables a *type*, and the compiler ensures that the program code respects this type, generating an error if, for instance, the code includes an instruction to divide a variable of numeric type by one of character-string type. The compiler recognizes this error on the basis of the mismatch between data types without assigning the variables determinate values. Coding with variables offers immense power, for not only are the variables abstracted from their particular values but they are also abstracted from any value, their "insides" isolated from the code that treats them from without. Variables offer a basic example of the powerful coding mechanism of *abstraction*, both data abstraction and procedural abstraction. "Data abstraction is a methodology that enables us to isolate how a compound data object is used from the details of how it is constructed from more primitive data objects."[22] As in the case of the bit, abstraction divides and relates two worlds, isolating inside from outside, and offering an interface, in this case the name of the variable, to connect the two worlds.

`xyc` could be the name of a variable, but `"xyc"` (with quotation marks) would be a literal in many programming languages, a string of characters that signifies not an associated process or abstract value but that stands for just those very characters *xyc* written into the program code. Literals are used for various reasons, including the simple reason that unlike a variable, which hides its insides behind its name, a literal presents its value as its name, and so can be easily read in the source code and directly manipulated. In fact, it can only be directly manipulated, as it lacks the abstraction of a variable and must be handled *in situ*. Whereas programmers read and write literals because they reveal their meanings on their surfaces, compilers treat literals as opaque, leaving them relatively unchanged as the code around them is translated into machine commands. Thus, literals can often be discovered intact in the otherwise arcane executable code. By contrast, a variable at run-time is a value in a memory location, a value that does not necessarily exist until the program actually starts running and allocates memory for that variable, and which may change while the program executes.[23]

Compile-time and run-time are distinct domains of experience: the programmer works in compile-time, while the program runs (and the user works) in run-time. More fundamentally, these two temporalities have different structures or moments, which characterize their operation. Compile-time is structured as *modular*, while run-time is *linear*.[24] Modularity refers to an abstract or logical characteristic of computer code, that it is divided into chunks, each of which is relatively independent of the others. Linearity refers to the executing process of the machine, where each moment is a fixed state, defined by the values of the bits in the whole system at that state, and pointing according to logical rules toward a next state. Modular structure characterizes the organization of high-level program code: distinct processes and even distinct files that group together all of the code relating to a particular module. Modules have boundaries, and we can thus regard an entire program as a module, divisible at compile-time into smaller modules. Linear structure is not so much a logical organization, but a feature of hardware, built into the design of the personal computer; the *program counter* points to the memory location that holds the currently executing machine command, and this program counter gets bumped to the next command at each iteration, each tick of the system's clock. Linearity is a constant forward march that is in itself almost dimensionless; it is a fixed state pointing in a direction, toward a next state, which does not even constitute the single dimension of a line.

The difference between these two structures or moments acts as an engine of the computer's operation. The computer progresses by converting the modular into the linear, by feeding a static sequence of commands into a focusing lens, a point of realization, that makes of each command a fixed state. When the computer operates, it proceeds from one fixed state to another, reading the modular code one "frame" at a time, moving its lens (the program counter) through successive memory locations that contain the modular program arrayed logically in sequence. Only because modularity and linearity are already mutually imbricated can the computer perform its transformation from one into the other. The modular structure of the program breaks down into submodules and eventually into linear sequences of commands, while at run-time, the program counter often retraces its steps through the commands to be executed, performing the same algorithm, the same set of actions, over and again.

Different programming paradigms offer different ways of organizing code and of characterizing the parts (modules) of that organization. (Some programming languages are associated with a particular paradigm, but many languages admit more than one approach.[25]) Procedural programming structures code into procedures, subroutines organized around different operations or functions. To conceptualize a procedural program is to list the various functions that need to be performed while the program executes, such as *Save the file* or *Calculate whether or not the projectile has hit the target* or *Scroll down one page*. Each function to be performed corresponds to a procedure, and procedures are constructed of smaller procedures, eventually reaching the lower level of lists of sequenced individual commands. Scrolling down by one page might involve many other actions such as getting data from a buffer, updating the location of the scroll bar indicator, redrawing the screen, etc., and each of these more detailed tasks would warrant its own procedure in the source code. (Procedures are also called *methods, algorithms, processes*, and *routines*. Programmers speak of *routines* and *subroutines* in a program, but the distinction is not strict and any routine could be a subroutine of some other routine.)

Procedures are distinguished from each other by formal textual conventions, each bearing a different label in the code-text. The lines of code—code-text is typically divided into lines that are logically significant, dividing one command and its associated objects from the next, as well as visible in the orthography of the text—the lines that constitute a given procedure are grouped together in the code-text, generally in the sequence in which they will be executed. This sequence of the text is not faithfully preserved at run-time, however; codes frequently instruct the processor to branch to a new subroutine or to bypass the next group of commands, which conditional branching is crucial to the operation of automated, interactive software. Nominal, typographical, and physical conventions help to keep procedures separate from each other in the source code. But the main principle that *encapsulates* a procedure, distinguishing its inside from its outside, is *scoping*.

The *scope* of a variable (or procedure name), as enforced during the compilation process, ensures that a name (of a variable or procedure) is associated with a particular value in a given context, while outside of that context it may have a different value or no meaning at all. In many high-level languages, variable names must be declared before the variables can be used as values in the program code. To declare a variable is to give it a name and, in many languages, also to specify its type, such as text or integer or list or array (the latter of which is a special kind of list). Variable declarations sometimes also include the assignment of an initial value to the variable. A variable declared within a procedure is "known" only to that procedure, and an attempt to reference that variable in another procedure will produce an error during the compilation process. Hiding its insides, a procedure does not allow other procedures to "see" its internal variables, and one procedure cannot directly alter the variables of another. In order to communicate with each other, procedures provide a public *interface*, keeping their insides private. The interface in procedural programming environments is generally the name of the procedure along with a set of values that can be passed to the procedure when it is called (triggered).[26] For instance, a procedure to find the average of a list of integers would be passed a reference to that list: `FindAverage(varList)`, where `FindAverage` is the name of the procedure and `varList` is a variable whose value indicates the address in memory where the list of data to average is stored. The name `varList` would refer to that list of data only within the code-text for the procedure `FindAverage`. Outside of the scope of `FindAverage`, `varList` might be undefined or otherwise defined. Like the computer itself, and like the programs that run on the computer, procedures are opaque machines that accept input and produce output, offering no access to what goes on in between.[27]

Scoping helps to enforce modular design: a procedure that keeps its variables to itself can be (more) easily transported and used elsewhere. Distinguishing its inside from its external interface, such a procedure does not depend on circumstances outside of its purview, and so can be used in other code-texts, other programs, with few, if any, changes.[28] Scoping helps to ensure that a procedure is relatively self-contained, more modular. Not only is it therefore transportable, but it is also easier to maintain and debug: errors in the program can be isolated because the functions and variables of procedures are isolated.

Scoping maintains the interiority of a procedure; the procedure presents its name (and list of variable parameters) to its outside. Some languages allow one procedure to be defined within another, the outer procedure defining the scope of the name (and availability for execution) of the inner one, which mirrors again the hierarchical structure of the digital object. Organizing code into procedures, this objective order dividing inside from outside places more emphasis on structure and so relieves the code of some emphasis on detail. That is, the construction of an organizational dimension, the program module, allows the programmer to capture some of the intended algorithmic behavior in the structure of the code, which leaves less behavior to be coded in individual commands. Through procedures, the programmer is distanced from the relentless sequentialism of the machine, establishing an intermediate layer of organization between the aim of the program and the sequence of commands necessary to institute it. In addition to reducing the amount of code the programmer needs to write, scoping and encapsulation provide the programmer with a way to think about her task, a template for structuring her code.

The programmer hence aims at discrete abstractions, parceling the computational task to be performed, sometimes described in a design specification or *spec*, into modular procedures and their subprocedures, representing the goal as an abstract aggregation of these distinct code-texts with insides and outsides. Division into parts each with its character or quality as determined by its (sub-)parts, both programming and sampling demonstrate the abstract idea of an object, whose outline can be found throughout the digital domain. By virtue of this object, a structure of inside and outside, of showing and hiding, the digital divides worlds from each other but at the same time joins them together to offer the advantages of a dematerialized abstract world to the corporeal and perceptive user. A further wrinkle and another paradigm will provide a more formal conception of the digital object, allowing its examination in the interface and in its broader implications.

2

From Objects to the Interface

The paradigm of *object-oriented programming* (OOP), which substantially informs this book's conception of a digital object, multiplies the organizational abstraction of procedural programming, encouraging a tighter modularity and allowing the programmer structural possibilities for organizing code that capture still more of the operation of the program in its architecture rather than in its sequential commands.[1] Procedural code—while dividing the program (and its code-text) into separate modules, each of which is designed to perform a particular function—does not organize these modules into categories, nor does it organize the most general data that the program must operate on. Local variables, those scoped within a particular procedure, "belong" to that procedure, but other data structures may be global data that every procedure can access. These *global* variables muddy the distinction between the insides and outsides of procedures that access those global data structures, making the code harder to transport and harder to debug, which is to say, less modular. To tighten the inside/outside distinction would mean drawing the data themselves into the inside, while at the same time organizing the procedures through an even more general abstraction. This is the foundation of OOP.

Instead of organizing the program primarily by dividing it into tasks to be performed, the OOP programmer organizes the program by dividing it into entities that operate within it, such as windows, files, icons, filters, datasets, functions, shapes, etc. The programmer specifies the procedures and data structure for each of these different *categories* or *classes* of object. At run-time, these class descriptions are used to instantiate individual objects (particular windows, files, etc.), each of which adheres to the data structure associated with its class, but populates that structure with particular data. The class in the source code describes the general characteristics of its members; a `Menu` class might include a variable, `Number_of_Items`, used to store the length of the menu. The instanced object at run-time fills in those general characteristics with specific values; an instance of the class `Menu` might assign the value 6 to the variable

`Number_of_Items`, to indicate that this particular menu is six items long. Thus, OOP code-text includes an abstract description of a category of object; the programmer writes code representing object categories, providing a template or structure for the data associated with the object but not yet specifying particular objects. At run-time, the computer creates instances of these categories, that is, objects, with particular values filled in to its categorical structure.

Here is an imaginary sample object class, described in a pseudocode corresponding to no real programming language. "Data" and "Procedures" define the object class, while the "Instance" is an example of the values of the data structures for a particular instance of that category of object. In this invented example, the object category is `Menu`, which would describe the class of objects that are menus. Each menu, which is to say each instance of the `Menu` category, has associated data including a name, a count of the number of items in the menu, the memory address of the list of items in that menu, a yes-or-no datum indicating whether the menu is currently visible in the interface or only stored in memory but not on the screen, and more. The category also includes a number of procedures (*methods*) that operate on individual menu objects, such as a procedure for responding when the user clicks the mouse on the menu name and a procedure for adding an item to the list of items associated with an instance of a menu object. Note that some procedures are related to user actions (such as responding to a click) while others involve internal administrative tasks (such as a building of the menu by adding items before displaying it in the interface). Though this example is simplified relative to the syntax of most object-oriented programming languages, the basic structure and concepts correspond to actual object-oriented programming languages.

```
Category: Menu (Child of: Category: List)
Data:
    Menu_Name
    Number_of_Items
    Items_List_Address
    Is_Visible?
    Is_Active?
    Menu_Type
    Location

Procedures:
    Name_Click
    Add_Item
```

```
    Remove_Item
    Item_Click
    Pull_Down
    Pull_Up
    Deactivate
    New_Menu
    Destroy_Menu

Instance:
    Menu_Name: "File"
    Number_of_Items: 12
    Items_Address_List: $3A0F
    Is_Visible: Yes
    Is_Active: Yes
    Menu_Type: Pulldown
    Location: MenuBarPosition3
```

Going beyond procedural organization, OOP folds more structure into its inside, heightening the *encapsulation* that was already part of procedural programming and variable names. The data for a given object category can be accessed only by procedures belonging to that object or through the public interface that allows data to pass between inside and out. The interface to an object category consists of a number of *public* procedures within that category, allowing other objects to request information about an object or to request that an object alter its data. In the above example, the procedure for `Item_Click` would send a message to the appropriate `Menu_Item` object telling it to do whatever it does in response to being clicked. Notably, the `Menu` object would have no direct access to the action triggered by clicking on one of the entries in the menu. Rather, the menu item instance itself would be responsible for responding appropriately; if the clicked menu item were "Save As . . .," for example, the menu item object would send a message in turn to the (active) document object, passing along the "Save As" instruction to the thing (instanced object) to be saved-as. Another example: a graphics program might have a graphical operator object that sends a request to a circle object to multiply its radius by three. The circle object would modify its data, but only if it accepted this command. It might reject the command because the object is "locked" by the user, or because the resulting circle would exceed the boundaries of the drawing area, or for any number of other reasons. As with the relationship between the `Menu` object and the items listed in that menu, the graphical operator object need know nothing about the object to which it sends its commands. The user has selected some graphical object and then has chosen the command "multiply by three." The object responsible for this command blindly forwards the command to the selected graphical object without distinguishing that object as square, circle, polygon, or something else. An object is a black box, a structured part as enforced from without, but a set of values and possible interactions with those values from within.

Alan Kay describes some of these features in relation to Smalltalk, the first object-oriented programming language and one that he helped to invent. Kay emphasizes that object categories begin to allow a language to model itself, offering a reflexivity associated with certain kinds of intelligence.

> Smalltalk's design—and existence—is due to the insight that everything we can describe can be represented by the recursive composition of a single kind of behavioral building block that hides its combination of state and process inside itself and can be dealt with only through the exchange of messages. Philosophically, Smalltalk's objects have much in common with the monads of Leibniz and the notions of 20th century physics and biology. Its way of making objects is quite Platonic in that some of them act as idealisations of concepts—*Ideas*—from which *manifestations* can be created. That the Ideas are themselves manifestations (of the Idea-Idea) and that the Idea-Idea is *a-kind-of* Manifestation-Idea—which is a-kind-of itself, so that the system is completely self-describing—would have been appreciated by Plato as an extremely practical joke. . . . In computer terms, Smalltalk is a recursion on the notion of computer itself. Instead of dividing "computer stuff" into things each less strong than the whole—like data structures, procedures, and functions which are the usual paraphernalia of programming languages—each Smalltalk object is a recursion of the entire possibilities of the computer. Thus its semantics are a bit like having thousands and thousands of computers all hooked together by a very fast network. Questions of concrete representation can thus be postponed almost indefinitely because we are mainly concerned that the computers behave appropriately, and are interested in particular strategies only if the results are off or come back too slowly. (1993, p. 70)

Insisting more forcefully on the integrity of the inside, this new encapsulation, a further abstraction of abstraction, makes it possible to treat objects as integral, as entities, allowing their manipulation as individuals. For the code no longer consists of a flat list of procedures, loosely tied together by mutual references. The code now exhibits a ramified structure, organized into objects (or rather, object categories) that are further organized, in one of the most powerful innovations of OOP: *inheritance*. A category is generally derived from another category, the child category inheriting all of the characteristics (procedures and data structure) of the parent. The programmer need only specify those aspects of the child category that differ from the parent as well as any new parts or procedures that apply specifically to the child, and the remaining details are filled in automatically with the parent's data and procedures. In the example above, the category `Menu` is a child of the category `List`, and would inherit from `List` some of its features. For example, the `Number_of_Items` datum would probably already be one of the data structures belonging to the category `List`, and would not need to be included again in the description of the `Menu` category.

A `shape` category might include among its associated data a variable for `center`, as many shapes would be defined in part by their centers. A child category of `shape` named `square` would already have a `center` inherited from `shape` and would add variables for `side_length` and a `rotation_angle` to make a basic but complete definition. The `circle` category, also a child of `shape`, would inherit `circle.center` from `shape` (where it is named `shape.center`) and would also add to it a `circle.radius` datum, defining a circle. `polygon` could be another child of `shape`, augmenting the data in the `shape` category to include not only a radius but also `polygon.num_sides` and `polygon.orientation`, specifying, respectively, the number of sides in the polygon and the angle at which the polygon is rotated. (Syntactical conventions often specify a period between an object name or class name and a data structure associated with that object or class.) These four categories (`shape`, `square`, `circle`, `polygon`) are written in the source code (code-text) at compile-time. At run-time, the user might choose the *circle* tool or the *polygon* tool from a *palette* containing a host of such tools. A mouse click would trigger the instantiater (or creator) method of the appropriate class to instantiate a `circle` or `polygon` object, with a particular center, radius, number of sides, etc. Central to the operation of the program would be the instantiation at run-time of these various shapes, children of the `shape` category, but while circles, polygons, rectangles, triangles, and more could all be instantiated, there would likely be no way to instantiate a pure `shape` object. (What would such a thing be?) The `shape` category functions as an organizational abstraction, containing data structures and procedures common to all shapes, thus saving the programmer from having to include these data and procedures in each of the child categories. (In the coding language C++ for example, a category like `shape`, which is used organizationally but is not intended for instantiation, is called a *pure virtual* class. See Figure 2.1.).

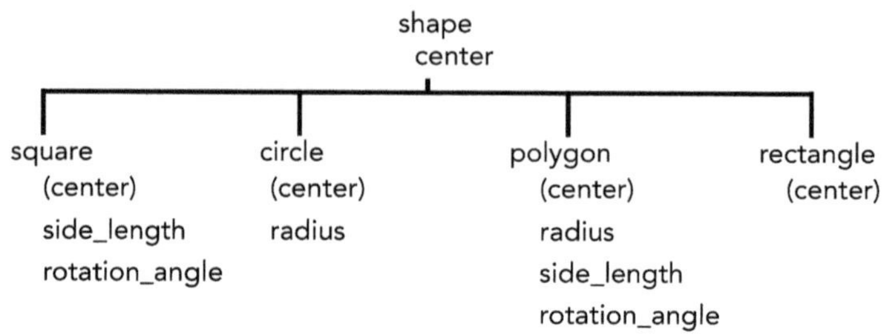

Figure 2.1 The child classes inherit the variable `center`, from the parent class, `shape`.

"If you view the right data structure you will have most of the result computed almost automatically as part of its inherent structure" (Kay 1986, 1:10:00). Certainly, inheritance saves a great deal of labor, but its advantages go beyond programming efficiency. For it directs the activity of programming toward an even greater focus on structure, such that the programmer's cognitive field shifts from an attention to the details of a binary logic to an attention to structural relationships among semiautonomous objects divided into characteristic categories. The inside of the object takes on a greater integrity, as the object is itself more articulated and complex, while the outside is no longer merely a horizon, but becomes a manipulable element of the program. OOP, given its direct operation on structure, effects most profoundly what Chun (2004, p. 30) characterizes as a shift from "numerically oriented" to "problem-oriented" programming. We might also say that the programmer has shifted her focus from coding tasks to design tasks. Working on the structures of objects and the relationships among those structures—in other words, working with human problems rather than machine language—the programmer inscribes her desire more directly, more immediately on the surface of the machine. Kay states the advantage bluntly: "The move to object-oriented design represents a real change in point of view—a change of paradigm—that brings with it an enormous increase in expressive power" (1999, p. 56).

Numerous commentators recognize the link between the increased abstraction of OOP and a shift in the cognitive approach of the programmer. "Object-orientation . . . does take programming one step further away from the idiosyncrasies of individual machines and closer to the ways in which people normally look at the world. In the example above, it allows us to think of a box, a carton, and a cube as things that are similar but not quite identical" (Kohanski 1998, p. 155). David Berry emphasizes not only the essential function of the object, independently of the particular programming paradigm, but also the move toward a more human and less machinic style of programming cognition.

> The further the programmer is positioned from the atomic level of 0s and 1s by the programming language, the further from the "metal"—the electrical operation of the silicon. Therefore the programmer is not required to think in a purely mechanical/electrical fashion and is able to be more conceptual. At the humanised level of abstraction of third generation languages, *delegated code* can become extremely expressive and further abstraction is made easier. Away from thinking in terms of *digital data structures* or *digital streams*, the programmer begins to think in terms of everyday objects that are represented within the language structure, so rather than deal with 0s and 1s, instead she might manipulate another ideal-type which I will call *code objects*—such as "cars" or "airplanes" which have related properties such as "gas tank" or "wing span" and functions (i.e. methods) such as "accelerate" or "open undercarriage." There is a growing use of the relatively new concept of the discrete "object" within computing. It is used as a monad containing a protected internal state, methods and interfaces to its external environment. (Berry 2008)

Frederick Brooks suggests that the increased abstraction avoids an unnecessary complexity, in some sense pushing programming toward its fundaments.

> What does a high-level language accomplish? It frees a program from much of its accidental complexity. An abstract program consists of conceptual constructs: operations, data types, sequences, and communication. The concrete machine program is concerned with bits, registers, conditions, branches, channels, disks, and such. To the extent that the high-level language embodies the constructs one wants in the abstract program and avoids all lower ones, it eliminates a whole level of complexity that was never inherent in the program at all. (1986)

The digital object that presents the digital in different ways and across a variety of digital contexts takes its structure from OOP. The notion of an object in OOP adds a new dimension, organizing the code into a hierarchy that includes the procedures and data that lie relatively flat in procedural programming.[2] In fact, there is more than one additional dimension: procedures and data are gathered into objects, while objects are themselves gathered into a hierarchy of categories through inheritance.[3] The subtlety and complexity of this many-layered encapsulation is experienced by the programmer as an emphasis on design over code production, but is evinced most powerfully in the curious `this` referent.[4]

As in procedural programming, OOP uses scoping to enforce encapsulation, ensuring that references to an object's (private) data and procedures are meaningful only within the code associated with that object category. In OOP the integrity of the inside has sufficient force to create a context, an inside that has a meaning beyond just the formal or nominal conventions that hold procedures together. `this` is a keyword in many object-oriented languages that points to this context, referring as in English to the here-and-now, the object of the moment. In most cases, `this` serves as a simple shorthand for the name of the current object, the object that "owns" the procedure in which the token `this` occurs. Such usage is unremarkable albeit useful, as it can make the code easier to write and read. (In practice, many languages and many compilers assume that a variable that is not otherwise specified is associated with the current object, thus making it unnecessary for the programmer to include the `this` keyword explicitly in most code.)

Whereas `this` might suggest via its English-language cousin ("this") a kind of self-reference in the code, its resolution purely in terms of local syntax is in a sense disappointing; if the referent of `this` can be determined simply by looking at where the word appears in the program code-text, then it fails to escape the literalness that closes the circuit of meaning production in programming. That is, if `this` were like any other variable, then while its value (the specific instanced object that it refers to) would be determined at run-time, its meaning (as a reference to some object of a specified class) would be already available at compile-time. But what happens when the meaning of `this` is not strictly determinable from syntax? For instance, suppose the object referred to by `this` is an instance of the category `circle`, and the source code tells it to draw itself using the command `this.drawme`. But `circles` are also `shapes`, and it might be the case that the `shape` category also has a `drawme` procedure. As the object is effectively both a `circle` and (thus) also a `shape`, it is not clear which procedure should get executed.[5]

In at least some cases, the ambiguous *polymorphism* of the reference `this` is not resolved by the compiler. Instead, determination of just which object `this` is is deferred until run-time. John Kopp uses slightly different terminology to make this same point: "Said another way, in our code a base class pointer or reference is used to access an object of some subclass, possibly unknown at compile-time and *known only during execution time* when the program is running" (2008, "Lesson 30: Polymorphism," my emphasis). The deictic quality of `this`, its reference to a dynamically changing context, carries over from the source code into the machine code, resolving to a specific object only when the program executes. The appearance of the word `this` in the high-level code is, at compile-time, ambiguous, in that it cannot be decided based purely on syntactic context which (category of) object it will refer to at run-time. As in its English usage, `this` functions in OOP as a floating or deictic signifier. Thus the program, and with it the programmer, cross the gap between compile-time and run-time, enmeshing one in the other.

To defer until run-time the calculation of the object referred to by `this` requires a set of tools collectively called Real-Time Type Identification (RTTI). The most straightforward uses of RTTI tools allow polymorphic ambiguities of object reference to add significant productive power to software. Innovations, in the form of augmentations to C++ (and other object-oriented languages), push RTTI further, to the point that key decisions about the nature of the software do not take place until run-time. Not only does the user enter anticipated input into the software, but it is also becoming increasingly possible for the user to shape the very software she is using while she uses it, as RTTI and related tools allow for the code itself, or at least its behavior, to be restructured at run-time.

This change breaks the strict mechanism that pulls code toward the literal. Using RTTI, an OOP programmer can write code whose results she cannot anticipate. Say a programmer writes code using the `this` pointer. That code gets compiled into an executable, ready to run on a user's machine. Running the program, the user can take advantage of RTTI techniques effectively to create new categories of object, categories whose properties were not known to the original programmer. At run-time, the original code's reference to `this` can point to objects in categories that only came to exist after the user created them. That is, the programmer writes code whose capabilities she does not fully anticipate, run-time code that defies her compile-time expectations.

Furthermore, since RTTI allows object types (categories) to be determined at run-time, the object hierarchy or structure is made available for manipulation by the user. The object is not just a programmer's tool, a means of organizing code, but becomes part of the interface to the running software. Relationships among object categories are offered to the user's manipulation in the running program, which ties very closely the structure of the code to the structure of the world. OOP thereby invites a more direct inscription of desire onto the surface of the code, but only by defying the literal character of code production. Deferring decisions about the code and its values until run-time, a technique more generally known as *late-binding*, will be further discussed at the end of the next chapter.

`this` reaches across the gap between compile-time and run-time, folding them into each other. The deictic is placed by the programmer at compile-time in order to resolve its reference only (unknowingly) by the user who runs the program, oblivious to most of the details of its objects and their structure. `this` coordinates the here of the modular with the now of the linear, generating a context in the running software. This logic, this organization of ideas that become possibilities for the user, this structure of 0s and 1s connects programmer to user, extends the possibilities of the programmer across the straits of the digital into the run-time environment of the user. At the limits of this logic, as in RTTI, the software appears haunted by its autonomous awareness of a context and a deictic operator, while the object manifests an ever more convincing coherence. The object has gained a limited autonomy, an ability not only to name itself but also to distinguish itself dynamically (and not just syntactically or formally) from the objects around it; `this` indicates an inside that recognizes itself as such.

The reflective autonomy of the object folds code-text into executable, compile-time into run-time, and programmer into user, deferring the "now" of the former into the "now" of the latter. The deferred reference of `this` invites a contingency into the running software, a contingency formerly absent from the literal mechanism of the machine. Autonomous objects that incorporate a relationship to their context allow for (at least an opening onto) the unexpected. The programmer does not know what the context will be at run-time; the running program reacts to events that are not available or not yet determined at compile-time.

* * *

With these logical structures in the background, what does this make of a digital object? It is a collection of parts, data structures, along with methods for acting on the object by acting on its parts. The parts may also be objects (and in some programming languages such as Smalltalk every *thing* referenced in the language has to be an object, including an object's parts). An abstraction, or a number of abstractions, encapsulate objects, distinguishing an inside and an outside and encouraging a relative autonomy of tiered, hierarchical modules.

The parts of an object both constitute it and qualify it, as is most evident in the case of sampling; an object's parts are the data structures that store its properties or values, which can be manipulated and otherwise processed by the methods that are also parts of the object, written in the code-text of the associated object class. The difference between a part and a quality is a matter of perspective; an object is a part when regarded from without while it expresses a quality when understood with regard to its inside. Instantiated in the same bits, parts and their qualities are, nevertheless, independent determinations. The mechanisms that take a sequence of bits as an object (or, equivalently, a part-quality), differ from the mechanisms by which bits are assigned particular values and made part of some object instantiated in a digital device. While the distinction is not strict, structure comes from a different perspective than does value, the former more the programmer's domain while the latter more the user's.

As a set of autonomous parts each with a value independent of the others, the object presents no essential coherence or integrity; no principle generates an object in an organic unity such that the value of a part comes to be alongside the part itself, but its parts and hence its values are determined in separate gestures. The digital always carves out a place before filling it with a quality or determination. In natural evolution, a wing develops in and through its qualities, such that it becomes a wing in immanent relation to its weight, size, shape, and matter, and also in relation to the rest of the body and, crucially, the animal's milieu. In the digital, the wing determines its quality as its inside, which need bear no relationship to the (outside) body to which it is appended; the wing can be appended as a module, its qualities determined independently of any characteristics of the host body. It is as though a bird were to develop a wing-shaped anatomical structure independently of its size or the particulars of the wing's weight, internal articulation, materials, etc. Recent research suggests that many birds are good at counting; perhaps they can choose their wings from a menu, too.

Actual objects are not equal to themselves but are dynamic, generative, and relational, while digital objects have static states and prescribed possibilities. The same pulsive or generative power through which each actual object produces itself within its milieu also constitutes an objective integrity for that object. Of course this integrity is not inviolable; actual objects can be sundered or combined, dissolving their integrities and creating new coherence (or no coherence). But the unity of an actual object is more than the coincidence of its parts. A person's unity, his consistent recognizability, is more than the contingent mutual proximity of his limbs and organs. The digital lacks this essential surplus that holds objects together in the actual. A digital object is nothing but the sum of its parts, a fact easily verifiable by examining its associated code. Any unity, any endurance, any sense in a digital object must be placed there from outside, a conclusion we will approach again below.[6]

Software design practice may recommend simulating the missing integrity of objects. Though modular methods (procedures) hide their insides, the methods associated with an object share in common the data structures of that object and may enforce relationships among the qualities conveyed by those data. (For instance, a `mass` value could be maintained in a proper arithmetic relation to `volume` and `density` values.) The attempt to establish this absent coherence responds to the design objective of creating a structure that makes sense, a set of object classes that not only respects the modularity of object-oriented design but also expresses the logical autonomy of each class and so suggests that the invented division into object classes finds a purchase on the structure of the program as a logical task/text. The programmer may therefore attempt to establish the absent coherence of an object, to rescue it from its syncretism. In good code, the structure of the code-text mirrors an underlying ontology of the program, a way of dividing the program into a group of objects that offers the desired set of possibilities but at the same time makes sense of the task(s) to be performed.

Even the bit demonstrates the original structure dividing part from quality, each bit twice articulated. Digital encoding relies on the division of the bit into its definitive two possible values, but this single articulation of the bit is not adequate to empower digital encoding. Encoding requires a second articulation, one that distinguishes each bit according to its place in a sequence. Digital code needs both articulations, one of value from the inside, and one of order from without. Even the most basic cases manifest this double articulation. Each bit is assigned a value, 0 or 1, an implicit, internal distinction. And each bit takes its place within the sequence, an explicit distinction, independent of the internal one and determined from without. In numeric representation, a bit's place in the sequence determines not its value but the magnitude of its value, its *power* or how much of a contribution its place ("ones" place, "twos" place, "fours" place, etc.) makes to the number overall; people who work with bits refer to the *least* or *most significant bit* (lsb or msb), meaning the bit assigned to the ones place (lsb) or the bit assigned to the opposite end of the binary representation, the 2^{n-1}s place (msb), where n is the number of bits—eight or sixteen, etc.—the system uses to store numbers.

The two articulations are logically separate but the bit makes its sense by relating them to each other. A value can be understood only with the correct index indicating where the value is located in the sequence of bits, which determines its power. Groups of bits are themselves grouped, and so on, each grouping treating internally determinate subgroups according to an externally imposed structure. Digital objects and whatever is built from bits demonstrate this same onto-logic. A part of an object takes on an internal value associated with its property, while its structure arrives from its outside, discrete distinctions imposed from beyond. Objects and their parts exhibit this basic double articulation, an abstraction in two dimensions: an internal set of values that are determined when the program is run and an external structure determined by the programmer who designs the architecture of the program.

The object understood as a hierarchical arrangement of formally distinct structures, themselves objects, could be called a *dividual*. An *in*dividual asserts its coherence according to a sense evolved and evolving in relation to its self and its world, an inherent and incipient sense. Individuals do not generally admit separation into parts, and to break an individual apart is to destroy it along with its sense. Digital objects, by contrast, offer no resistance to their dissolution, for their parts, which may be very well matched to each other, nevertheless assert no belonging, no particular allegiance to other parts or to the whole. An image, being a collection of pixels (at some resolution), can be easily parceled into bits and pieces as small as pixels and even smaller (such as one color channel of a pixel, or only the most significant bit in each channel). Digital objects such as digital images are dividuals, collections of dividuated part-qualities that are also dividuals. Under these circumstances, where divisibility constitutes a basic potential of the object, a combinatorics illuminates the haze of possibilities surrounding each finite discrete state of the computing machine. It is not just the combinatorics of bits, where the ready switchability (equivocation) built into each bit suggests that any combination might proceed. Dividuals invite a combinatoric approach by virtue of their modular and divisible structures expressed in a common language of a binary code.

The term *dividual* is due to Gilles Deleuze, who offers a related conception in his "Postscript on the Societies of Control" (1992). In that short text, the dividual names the structure of (something like) personhood in the society of control, which Deleuze introduces in a section called "Logic": "The numerical language of control is made of codes that mark access to information, or reject it. We no longer find ourselves dealing with the mass/individual pair. Individuals have become 'dividuals,' and masses [have become] samples, data, markets, or 'banks'" (p. 5). It is a shift from integral individuals to flows of bits and samples in their recombinant possibilities. The *in*dividual is the person of *disciplinary societies*, passed from one modular domain to another, hospital, to barracks, to factory, to echo Deleuze's examples by way of Michel Foucault. The structure of control societies breaks modules down into granules to maximize recombinant efficiency and speed. Constituted of granules, domains cease to enforce strict boundaries and instead fade diffusely into each other; the person who traverses those domains is constructed in partially continuous aspects, modules that can be divided and reorganized to accommodate the sliding of the domains against each other. This is also the era of the password, says Deleuze, that grants access to the coded logic of society and its diffusion of bits and pieces. Deleuze proposes money as the abstract universal to express this slippery logic, but over the past two decades, bits have become the more obvious choice as the logical element of our time.

Friedrich Kittler offers an example of one powerful political consequence of dividual organization, as it allows homogeneous indexing and piecemeal manipulation.

> Now, for the first time in the history of optical media, it is possible to address a single pixel in the 849th row and 720th column directly without having to run through everything before and after it. The computer image is thus prone to falsification to a degree that already gives television producers and ethics watchdogs the shivers; indeed, it is forgery incarnate. It deceives the eye, which is meant to be unable to differentiate between individual pixels, with the illusion or image of an image, while in truth the mass of pixels, because of its thorough addressability, proves to be structured more like a text composed entirely of individual letters. (2001, p. 32)

Alexander Galloway reads Deleuze's concept of the dividual also with an emphasis on its technological and specifically computational context, and he locates the dividual in motion across the gap between user and machine. "The dividual therefore does not so much carry pleats in its soul, as Deleuze says of the baroque subject, but a tessellated, recombinant soul, if soul is still the proper word, forming and reforming across the metastable skein of the bioinformatic ecosystem" (2012, p. 524). Though Galloway's account of a soul "forming and reforming" expresses a vitalism that may not survive translation into the formal logic underlying digital objects, he characterizes (Deleuze on) the digital in the same basic terms as does this book; for Galloway reading Deleuze, the digital is a process of synthesis "in which a universe grounded in the univocity of an identity of the same becomes a universe grounded in discrete distinctions between elements, elements that, although divided, are brought together and held in relation, suspended opposite each other like cliffs over the banks of a great river" (2012, p. 519).[7] Elements divided but related, determined by discrete distinction, and maintained in their separate identities according to an extrinsic principle, this description of the digital dividual is complete but for the idea of hierarchy. But, in fact, what I have called *hierarchy*—the recursive combination of parts to make a new part alongside others—arrives in the culmination of Galloway's essay in his speculations about Deleuze's elliptical concept of the *superfold*, which Galloway reads as an ontological structure of recursive folding: "First the fold, then the double fold, the triple, on up to the multiplicative folds of the superfold" (p. 525).[8] The superfold names the topology of control societies, where everything is made of folds, each articulating side from side, establishing a gap and relating across it. Within the superfold, the human and the digital machine are themselves enfolded and so can be folded into each other. Galloway offers the superfold as one answer to the question of how the digital and the human encounter each other, but the general ontological structure of the fold, the passage across the "metastable skein" that laces digital and actual together, must be described with attention to the details of *digital* ontology. If the bit, by virtue of its two values and also its double articulation, satisfies the ontological condition of the fold, and if the digital object constructed from bits is also made of folds, then we have still to understand how the user enfolds herself into this pleated machine.

* * *

It is a computer game. You are running down a long, dank corridor, urged ahead by thick-looking stone walls decorated as is customary with sconces holding flickering wooden torches. You tend to run wherever you go, but you have an added incentive at the moment: you are being chased by a giant worm, whose throaty growls and gnashing teeth indicate a less-than-friendly intent. In fact, you know full well that the worm will eat you should it catch you, as you have been consumed on your last six tries. An idea occurs to you: you stop directly in front of a sconce, jump up toward the torch, and, with the flame inches from your face, press the *grab* key on your keyboard. Landing, you turn toward the worm, hoping to intimidate it or possibly injure it with the open fire of the torch. But, as experienced gamers will anticipate, you discover that you are empty-handed; the torch remains in its sconce and you are soon again engulfed in the gaping maw of this neogothic cliché.

Why can't you grab the torch off the wall? Many objects in a computer game are just for show and serve no function in the game beyond appearing as part of the two- or three-dimensional space of the game (as rendered on a two-dimensional screen). Mountains in the distance cannot be approached, do not block the sun's light, influence local weather conditions, or signal the proximity of a fault line or volcanic activity. A doorknob cannot be turned; in fact, it cannot even be grasped, and it does not catch on your clothing or deflect the blade of your passing sword. The doorknob is effectively painted onto the door, just as the mountains might as well be painted onto the horizon, and games sometimes reinforce the superficiality of some game objects by rendering them in two dimensions: a tapestry that does not flutter and has no backside, for it is rendered directly on the wall's surface. Walk right through a dead body; it appears on the screen as a three-dimensional object but offers no dimensions of simulated material resistance; it might as well not even be there as far as the logic of the game is concerned. Many digital graphics systems formalize the superficiality of appearance in the digital by formally distinguishing an object's *texture* from its other physical properties such as shape and location; the texture is effectively painted onto the object's surface when rendered.

Perhaps the torch on the wall is more than just a painted surface. Though it cannot be grabbed or otherwise manipulated, it does appear in proper perspective, sticking out from the wall and changing its visual relationship to the wall as you circumnavigate it. Moreover, its flickering flame is not only something to look *at*; for it shares its data with algorithms that determine how far down the corridor you can see, as well as algorithms that draw shadows when objects or creatures pass by. But no matter where you jump or how determinedly you press the *grab* key, the torch refuses to become a full-fledged thing, and you cannot relate to it within the simulated materiality of the game except as something to be seen. Your face can pass through the flame when you jump, but you feel no heat and suffer no ill effects of this proximity to fire. You cannot soften the metal of a coin by holding it in this fire, and you cannot even ignite the wick of a candle placed near this torch. Looks like you have to use your sword, yet again.

It is not just the happenstance of video game conventions that torches cannot be removed from their sconces and wielded. According to a *principle of simplicity*, what happens in the digital is what has been designed to happen. If an object behaves in a particular way, it does so because that behavior has been *put there* by designers and programmers. The nature of computer programming dictates that nothing comes for free; every digital object, every part-quality, and every possible alteration thereof must be explicitly programmed, vested in the code.[9] "From this perspective, there is no future in computer games. To play a computer games [sic] represents a loss of time, since nothing happens, *except what was programmed*" (Mackenzie 2002, p. 267).

One result of this principle of simplicity is that the appearance of an object is effectively independent of its behavior. The code that governs how an object appears on the screen has almost nothing to do with the code that governs what a player can do in relation to that object. Appearances are generated by a graphics engine, a set of subroutines that accept standard data describing a three-dimensional space and a perspective in that space, and then render that space from that perspective in two dimensions on a monitor. Objects in this space have a set of properties: location, orientation, size, shape, texture, color, opacity, reflectivity, etc. The methods that govern the *behavior* or possibilities of that object are, at the discretion of the programmer, connected to the variables used by the graphics engine. If it has been coded to do so, an object can behave somewhat in accord with the way it appears. But this connection is inevitably deliberate; any relationship has been explicitly assigned. Only behaviors that have been coded to do so will alter the appearance of an object, and there is no inherent connection between appearance and behavior. A virtual wall has a texture that determines how it appears under different lighting conditions or from different angles. But this texture does not give the wall any solidity or resistance, and an avatar will pass right through the wall unless additional collision detection programming intervenes to disallow such passage. (Of course, most virtual environments do include collision detection algorithms to ensure that users cannot pass through walls.)

At least in computer gaming, the disconnect between appearance and behavior often establishes the problem of the game, to discover what possibilities the game offers and how best to deploy them according to the changing conditions of game logic. Play is guided and motivated by a Cartesian anxiety, the threat of a tenuous and ultimately arbitrary relationship between the world as it appears and the world as it actually operates. One key to successful play is to discover where these worlds align and where they do not, exploiting that knowledge to solve the puzzles or overcome the obstacles that the game places before the player. Learning to play means finding out how objects work, exploring the possibilities and limits of one's avatar and its world, and while this process of discovery is guided by representations, there is no guarantee that an object that looks as though it can be used in a particular way actually can be used that way.

Its recombinant ontology distinguishes the digital object from worldly ones. In the material world, objects *must* behave something like the way they appear, and while this rule has to stretch to cover some liminal cases (such as optical illusions, clever hoaxes, sci-fi holograms, hallucinations, etc.), its normative force underpins the possibility of making sense of the world (as one that generally conforms to expectations). A tangerine is throwable because it has a particular mass, which also determines (in part) its appearance as a certain size, shape, etc., and these properties enmesh with many others to constitute the tangerine according to a grand sense that implicates the whole tangerine, its openness to its possibilities, and ultimately also implicates the rest of the universe. A tangerine, like almost any worldly object, does not equal the sum of its parts or properties, but has an integrity that testifies to the sense in which it comes to be where and how it is, a sense that also regulates and qualifies its parts.

Digital objects bear a different sort of relationship to themselves and their possibilities. A digital object is an instance of a particular category, a type or token that defines its inside only by making it a generality, a set of parts-qualities in a structure shared with other members of the category. Constructing an object class, the programmer decides everything about the structure and possibilities of the object, its parts, its qualities, and its methods. An icon for a disk volume can be dragged into a folder to effect a change in the file indexes that coordinate the physical location of the files stored on a magnetic disc with the logical structure of files and folders constructed by the user and the operating system; the possibility of dragging the icon into a folder is in no way ensured by the appearance of the icon, but depends on a set of encoded instructions entirely independent of the way the icon appears or the fact that it appears at all. This aggregative rather than integrative being could be thought of as an absent depth, a missing center; the digital is all façade and no thickness. The tiered layers of a digital object, stacked in the space between the digital and the actual, do not amount to a depth, but only to a set of deterministically related planar surfaces, images of the same object at different levels of detail.

"Rather than converting structures into events, the realtime animated computer game seems to assimilate events to pre-existing structures, to select amongst the possible events only those that can be processed in terms of translations of polygons around the screen. Rather than realtime play triggering events, the very systems on which it relies seem to contain events within a strictly controlled permutation of marks" (Mackenzie 2002, pp. 266–7). The separation of behavior from appearance as a dimension of play is well known to the gamer. The programmer creates objects, which orient the player in a world made of granulated time, space, and logic. Thus fixated by the objects of the interface, the player recognizes appearances as indicators of possibility, indexes of the options available in the interface—build a fortress or activate a power-up or purchase more ammo. Appearances cease to represent a world outside the game and intend only the data and behaviors of the digital objects of which they are part.[10] Cut off from the world outside the game, the circuit of affection and logic that passes from computer to user and back closes onto itself. The player of a game takes all her cues from the game, devoting herself to this world of play. As Charles Bernstein observes of the computer game's "fixed system of control, *all the adapting is ours*" (1991, §53, emphasis in original). Given this short circuit of affective logic, the player ultimately plays herself. Her aim is to use the computer as a biofeedback mechanism to instruct her body to react in a manner governed by objects of the game and according to a strategy developed also in terms of those objects.

At least in regards to digital gaming, this phenomenon of logical adaptation is widely recognized, sometimes celebrated, and occasionally contested. In Chapter 4 of *Gaming*, Galloway acknowledges the representational ideologies that games present, but then notes that these meanings are effectively trumped by an *informatic* signification, wherein the game inculcates its logical and algorithmic foundation (rather than its representational significance) as its instruction (2006, p. 99ff.). McKenzie Wark (2009, card 67), defending the claim that gaming characterizes the logic of the digital in general, uses different terms to describe the same structure as Galloway: "[Games] are not just an allegory but a double form, an allegory and an allegorithm. Appearances within the game double an algorithm which in turn simulates an unknown algorithm which produces appearances outside the game." Appearance becomes logic, which becomes lower-level logic, which the player comes to experience and express. This is Wark's formula for the "topology" of a digital encounter. Ted Friedman counters the cynicism of Galloway and Wark, suggesting that the adaptation of gamer to game logic produces the pleasure of the game:

> The way computer games teach structures of thought—the way they reorganize perception—is by getting you to internalize the logic of the program. To win, you can't just do whatever you want. You have to figure out what will work within the rules of the game. You must learn to predict the consequences of each move, and anticipate the computer's response. (1999, p. 136)

And in the same essay he writes, "The style in which you learn to think doesn't correspond to the way any person usually makes sense of the world. Rather, the pleasures of a simulation game come from inhabiting an unfamiliar, alien mental state: from learning to think like a computer" (p. 135). The player programs herself according to the logic of the game. Does the user program himself according to a digital logic?

Games and gaming are object-oriented. Programmers write objects and players pursue them. Data and algorithms—*objects*—define a logic by which the programmer determines the nature of the game. Creating objects, the programmer fixes the possibilities that the player can choose, the paths of play, the objects of the game. The player defines her goals in terms of the properties and behaviors of game objects; not only her overall strategy but every individual move is oriented toward the available objects provided by the programmer, the algorithmic possibilities for affecting the behavior of game elements. Will Wright, inventor of *The Sims* games, describes the phenomenon as "reverse engineering":

> The more accurately you can model that simulation in your head, the better your strategies are going to be going forward. So what we're trying to [do] as designers is build up these mental models in the player. The computer is just an incremental step, an intermediate model to the model in the player's head. The player has to be able to bootstrap themselves into understanding that model. (Pearce 2002, n.p.)

If she wishes to succeed according to the objects of the game, the player avails herself of precisely those objects, those dimensions of play that effect success. She disciplines herself, training body and mind in response to the underlying logics of the code. "Eventually, your decisions become intuitive, as smooth and rapid-fire as the computer's own machinations" (Friedman 1999, p. 136). As the player focuses on selecting object behaviors in a manner that promotes progress toward in-game goals, all the parts of the game, including the appearances of objects, take their meanings primarily from those same goals. Appearances turn inward toward the game and away from the rest of the world; with no reference outside of the game, they serve as *icons* for behaviors, indicators of an underlying algorithmic logic.

In a digital game, the player must learn the conventional language of the game, likely an extension of familiar conventions from other games. This conventional language is a set of associations between visual (and sometimes extravisual) cues and events/objects in the game. An alien body twitching in a particular direction foretells an imminent missile salvo. A pulsing green glow and high-pitched hum mark the location of the next power-up module to collect. An arched eyebrow and tilted head reveal that the enemy queen is skeptical and likely to be easily angered by lowball deal proposals. The player learns to recognize these signs (icons) and makes them hinge points in her tactics for play. The signs tend to isolate themselves experientially from their surrounding contexts (or to turn their contexts into symbolic backgrounds). For the entrained player, the angle of the queen's head and the twitch of the alien's body ceases to refer, except incidentally, to their representeds—a (fictional but) actual person's head, an actual missile-toting humanoid—and become embodied triggers of habituated action. The player reacts not to the impression of a twitchy body but to the conventional signal of the start of an action sequence, action as icon. Diane Carr's analysis of the simulation game *Civilization* concludes that

> for these experienced users there is little or no link between the various in-game variables (be it barbarians, nuclear weapons, character ethnicity or despotism) and the real-world instances of these phenomena. . . . Objects and actions—their value, status and meaning—are read solely in terms of their role and strategic value within the closed world of the game. (2007, p. 227)

The player orients her habits of thought and motion according to this algorithmic logic. To play a game is to engage immediately with abstractions, which are defined by the logic of algorithms. "The similarity between the actions expected from the player and computer algorithms is too uncanny to be dismissed" (Manovich 2001, p. 222). Appearances of game objects cease to represent anything outside of the game; instead, they produce meanings wholly internal to the circuits of affective logic that flow in a closed loop from player to computer and back. Representation is digitized, as computer objects stand for abstractions that could never be presented. Representation relaxes its grip over sense, and the player enters a digital world, at play between actual and digital. It is in part this divorce from external reference and simultaneous hermeticism of the player-computer circuit of affect that leads gamers to describe their playing experience as *immersive*.

Matthew Fuller recognizes the shift from representational to functional significance in the interface. He notes that the metaphors prevalent in computing (desktop, icon, hand pointer, etc.) rapidly lose their value and become impediments to efficient computing. "With every interface metaphor, there is a point at which its explanatory or structure-providing advantages collapse in the face of the capacity for mutation in the universal machine, the computer, and what it connects to" (2003, p. 102). Presenting this mutability as interactive possibility, the icon's representational dimension becomes increasingly extraneous. "Software will need to be seen to do what it does, not to do what something else does" (p. 100).

Chun recapitulates Brenda Laurel who makes a similar point.

> Laurel's emphasis on action underscores the crucial difference between the representation of tools and the tools themselves: she argues that people realize when they double click on a folder that it is not really a folder, and making a folder more 'life-like' is not helpful. What is helpful, Laurel contends, is clear causality: events must happen in such a way that the user can accept them as probable and thus narrow probability into certainty. Causality, she claims, ensures universality, ensures that the users will willingly suspend their disbelief. (2004, p. 41)

Not only does Laurel thus assert the internal logic of digital objects as the basis of their meaning, as opposed to their representational referents, but she also emphasizes the rigidity of that logic, which conveys its meaning when it enforces a sense of necessity.

Appearances peel away from behaviors, to become superficies, their capacity for representation now incidental, hardly relevant. The brief glint in the eye of the invader from Jupiter no longer signals malice, but only the familiar and experiential pattern of an imminent feint and attack. The blue glow at the end of the hallway is not the luster of a magical gem, but only the ego-syntonic aura of another marker of progress soon to be obtained. The putrescent corpse of a long-dead soldier evokes no sympathy or disgust, but serves as a waypoint in the search for more loot. To play is to transform the principle of simplicity that divides appearance from behavior into a practice of simplicity, wherein one ignores the appearance except inasmuch as it continues to indicate the affordances of an object. Commenting on the disturbing reduction in games of race and gender to a simplistic visual iconography, Jill Rettberg notes the divorce between appearance and behavior: "Plato's theory of the Ideal forms that have faint copies on earth seems to suit this world well. The Ideal is the code, and the Actual is the way it looks on different characters. The properties or game mechanics of the item remain the same no matter how it is expressed visually on different genders and races" (2008, p. 180).

No doubt some contexts outside of gaming and the digital also encourage a collapse of appearances into iconic pointers. Human soldiers must repress the knowledge that they are shooting at human beings and experience the battlefield as a field of signs of opportunity, markers that enable the translation of learned strategy into immediate tactic. But would it not mark the best soldiers so that they remain open to the possibility that appearances will exceed their reduced meanings as symptoms of behavior? Smoke surely means something, but not always fire.

To follow Wark's suggestion, extend the analysis of the logic of gaming into the digital in general. If appearances in games lose their representational significance (Wark says "allegorical" meaning) to become iconic indicators of a set of possible behaviors ("allegorithmic" meaning), then we might look more closely at the *icon* as the object's representative in the interface. The icon, itself an iconic fixture of the *graphical user interface* (GUI), designates a kind of sign according to C. S. Peirce's definition. Peirce calls *icon* a sign that refers to its object in respect of a similarity between them, a similarity of quality, of structure, or of a relation among structures. The icons of the GUI represent digital objects; if they bear a resemblance to their referents, it is not first of all a qualitative resemblance. The computer icon resembles its referent by virtue of a structural analogy, which obtains in relation to the icon's context or type. A menu, a character, a file, a window, a scroll bar, a button—each of these icons represents information, but in each case by a different structure, indicating different possibilities for that information, different relations. The icon resembles its referent inasmuch as it indicates states of its referent (properties of the underlying digital object) and possible states of its referent (available alterations of the digital object). Parts of the icon (color, number, relation, size) reveal the structure of the associated digital object, its composition, its data, and the organization of those data. In their relations to each other, icons also exhibit an interactively explorable structure analogous to the logical structure of their represented objects. As Peirce's icon sign operates by similarity, it makes no appeal to a direct connection between icon and object, and "would possess the character which renders it significant, even though its object had no existence" (Peirce 1955, p. 104). But this last criterion disqualifies the icon of the interface as a Peircean icon; whereas Peirce's icon relates to its object only by similarity, in the GUI, icons both stand for and directly affect their objects: throw an icon in the trash and the associated file is (logically) marked for deletion.

If its reliance to a degree on similarity nevertheless commends the GUI icon to Peirce's category of that name, his conception of the *index* promises a still better match to the function of GUI icons. An index is

> a sign, or representation, which refers to its object not so much because of any similarity or analogy with it, nor because it is associated with general characters which that object happens to possess, as because it is in dynamical (including spatial) connection both with the individual object, on the one hand, and with

> the senses or memory of the person for whom it serves as a sign, on the other hand. (1955, p. 107)

Certainly, the file icon demonstrates a dynamical connection with its (dividual) object and also with the visual and sensorimotor senses of the user. The index operates not by convention, "association by resemblance," or "intellectual operations"; rather, indexes "direct the attention to their objects by blind compulsion" (p. 108). It is an inescapable compulsion wrought in the material or metaphysical circumstance of the indexical sign. To understand and work with GUI icons as Peircean indexes is to grasp their direct connection to the objects they indicate, to recognize at least in practice the operation of the digital as mechanistic and deterministic.

But does the user connect icon to object through a blind compulsion or through force of habit? Peirce calls a *symbol* that sign that relates to its object through a law or convention of human behavior.

> The Icon has no dynamical connection with the object it represents; it simply happens that its qualities resemble those of that object, and excite analogous sensations in the mind for which it is a likeness. But it really stands unconnected with them. The index is physically connected with its object; they make an organic pair, but the interpreting mind has nothing to do with this connection, except remarking it, after it is established. The symbol is connected with its object by virtue of the idea of the symbol-using mind, without which no such connection would exist. (p. 114)

Is the user's grasp of the relationship between an icon and its object an "intellectual operation," and so, more symbolic than indexical? Do we know the small pictogram on the desktop to represent an available compact disc, ready for playing, based on its resemblance to an actual compact disc or as a result of previous experience? The possibilities offered in the interface are those of digital objects, possibilities for the presentation, analysis, and modification of parts and qualities. The GUI icon shows the status of something digital, evincing not so much the existence of a file or process but its availability. Existence alone is not a sufficient condition to produce an icon; the interface shows information but at the same time hides much information, placing some possibilities within more immediate reach and others farther away. A file icon signals the availability of certain possible manipulations of that file, for instance. The interface icon most generally indicates that something can be clicked, operated upon, gotten a hold of. It also serves as the handle by which the user gets a grip on the file or process it stands for.[11] It asserts that there is "in" the computer an encoded object, a data structure or algorithm, but this *there is* is not a passive or static being. The stood-for data are significant because the icon might be clicked, because it might be altered, because it might be other. The interface icon is part of the object, a face of it, offering a certain grip on that object and so opening a particular set of possibilities. The user hesitates between two signs; on the one hand, she recognizes and relies upon the immediate, logicomaterial *indexical* connection between icon and object without which she could not use the icon effectively; on the other hand, she also recognizes the break between icon and object that characterizes the ontology of dividual digital objects and so places the GUI icon in Peirce's third category of sign, the *symbol*. The connection of icon to object is fragile, subject to the combinatorics of the digital; it is a weaker logical connection rather than a deeper metaphysical one, requiring that the user provide the missing coherence according to a rule or convention.

That the computer icon should borrow characteristics from each of Peirce's categories of sign violates no Peircean interdiction; though he offers numerous negative or exclusive definitions in his discussion of the categories of sign, he generally allows that a sign might fall into different categories depending on how it is understood or contextualized. Stepping back to his description of the general notion of a sign reveals an important dimension of the computer icon. A sign for Peirce is "something which stands to somebody for something in some respect" (1955, p. 99). The first *something* is the sign itself. The second *something* is its object, what it stands for. And the *somebody* is the person (though Peirce acknowledges that other things besides persons might count as somebodies) who recognizes the standing-for relation between something and something else. Peirce articulates the notion of standing-for as the mental production of an idea (in "respect" of which the standing-for happens), "understood in a sort of Platonic sense," that idea being called the *interpretant* of the sign. The idea or *ground*, which is the content of the sign (though not necessarily its object), is abstract not only because it happens in the mind but also because even in its definition, it involves a generalization; the sign stands for its object not in all the object's particulars (for then it would simply *be* its object), but only in respect of the object's self-same ground or idea. Peirce underlines the essential abstraction of this "sort of Platonic" idea through the definitional criterion of self-identity: the ground of a sign cannot be an immediate sensation but must be an enduring idea, a generalization over time "insofar as a thought continues to agree with itself during that time" (ibid.). What constitutes the ground is what remains the same in the idea when it is recalled at a later time or when it is "caught" by another person.

The ground mediates the relation between sign and object via a process of abstraction. Though the effective reality of this abstraction is evident in the fact that the sign successfully signifies, the abstraction itself, which makes the sign a sign, requires more than sign and object. Abstraction requires a "somebody," an interpretant, as Peirce says. The sign is tied to its object but only because there is an "Interpretant" determined by the sign to "assume the same triadic relation to its Object in which it stands itself to the same Object" (1955, p. 100). The interpretant arrives at this relation partly on the basis of a prior familiarity with the object; that is, the object must already be known, for the sign can only "represent the Object and tell about it" but, due to the gap between material sign and abstract ground, the sign cannot offer a direct knowledge of an object that is not already known. The sign points to its object but does not present it.

The GUI icon points to its digital object, and the user must conceive an idea of that object as a set of available possibilities to grasp the meaning of the icon. In the interface, the connection between icon and object—the icon as a set of possibilities for an object—arises at first in the symbol-using mind of the programmer as an idea of the object. The icon then induces this idea in the mind of the user who understands the set of possibilities it indicates and symbolizes. The important point was already evident in Galloway's account of the dividual recombinant soul, which passes *across* the "bioinformatic ecosystem." Crossing goes both ways: it is not only that the icon and its object are indexically connected to each other; in order for the icon to operate as the sign that it is, *the user must offer an essential contribution*: she must intend an *idea* of the digital object, an idea of the object indicated by the icon.

This invested idea answers to the missing coherence of the object, constructing that coherence as a syncresis of the object's possibilities. In *New Philosophy For New Media*, Hansen emphasizes the user's essential contribution to the experience of the digital, but he theorizes a contribution not as idea, but as embodied action. As the digital always threatens to decohere into its data, its bits and pieces, it can only make sense, become sensible, when the body offers it a *frame*. "In this way, the act of enframing information can be said to 'give body' to digital data—to transform something that is unframed, disembodied, and formless into concrete embodied information intrinsically imbued with (human) meaning" (2004, p. 13). For Hansen, enframing is always fundamental to sensation but the digital provides an acute example because its recombinant ontology underlines the need for a frame imposed from without. "This means that with the flexibility brought by digitization, *there occurs a displacement of the framing function of medial interfaces back onto the body from which they themselves originally sprang*" (p. 22). Despite the modularity of the code that makes an icon appear on the screen, despite the scope rules enforced by the compiler to determine the inside of the object and the homogeneity of the interior of the icon, despite the existence of precise boundaries between each pixel on the screen and the next such that the icon has a perfect definition, it is, nevertheless, only the user who makes the icon function, makes it mean, gives it a sensible relationship to an object by providing its frame. This follows from the nature of the dividual object, that it does not finally hold itself together except in the idea that the user intends (often) through its icon. The purely formal structure of the digital object, its layered hierarchical organization, arises out of no coherence and so always threatens to dissolve into its granular flow, the minimal module of the bit.

Hansen locates his account of the digital initially through a contrast to Deleuze's reading of Henri Bergson's discussion of sensation. The upshot of Hansen's critique is that by extending the formal filmic technique of the cut to describe the enframing of sensation in general, Deleuze locates the frame within the medium, rather than recognizing, as does Bergson according to Hansen, that enframing is a selection made from an embodied "center of indetermination" and not through a formal determination. Characterizing the digital as "formless" in itself, Hansen does not discover a digital object that would be a structured aggregation of bits produced by code, but, instead, proposes the concept of a "digital image," a process that includes the transformations and recombinations associated with images on computers, but at the same time includes embodied enframing, without which, Hansen says, there could be no meaning at all, nothing to recognize of the digital. By treating the digital as formless, opaque, a black box, Hansen underlines the body's role in giving sense to the digital and demonstrates, moreover, that not only clicking but also already seeing and hearing in the interface must be interactive, for the user could neither see nor hear without the frame that she contributes to sensation. But black boxing the digital, Hansen sets aside *the digital's contribution to making sense*, treating the digital as unassimilable and alien, with a strange remainder manifest in the problematic aesthetics, disturbing and uncanny, of the digital artworks he describes.[12] He, thus, does not acknowledge the tiered formal hierarchy of the digital object.

That the user contributes first of all an idea to the digital object, without which it would not be that object, offers a new perspective on the ontology of the digital, for the idea, unlike all of the other structures constituting the object from bits to parts and qualities, does not reduce to sequences of 0s and 1s. The nature and function of the idea must be analyzed, but the icon first needs a few further comments. The visual interface follows the logic of the icon throughout. Not just the small images that stand for files and folders, not just the pictograms that populate palettes and toolbars, but most elements of the visual interface, from menu items to scroll bars to characters of text, all demonstrate an iconic logic. Each object in the interface stands as representative of some set of relatively close possibilities, represented by an abstract image that relates to those possibilities according to deterministically encoded, but also learned, conventions. A word or a paragraph in a word processor takes on the character of an icon, inasmuch as those units can be formally recognized and treated according to the combinatorics discovered throughout the digital domain.

Other interface elements fit even more comfortably into the logic of the icon. Menus and their elements trigger digital processes, occupy clearly defined spaces, and indicate a `mouseover` event by lighting up. The desktop itself acts as an empty icon that stands only for itself, accepting clicks indifferently over its whole surface, and playing host to an image without any particular computational significance. The great variety of fonts attests to the iconicity of individual text characters. Each character stands for the idea of itself across many different standard forms and inflections, fonts, styles, and sizes. A given character is significant primarily by virtue of the ideal for which it stands, the immaterial form of the letter that takes on a particular material instantiation in a given font at a given size. In a digital text, everything is encoded, encode-able, nothing escapes; the digital letter too bears an oddly arbitrary relationship to its presentation, as even its material appearance no longer grounds its meaning. Instead, it is the digital code "behind" the letter that undergirds its significance in the machine, and this is the hallmark of the icon, an essential relationship between an ultimately superficial appearance and an immaterial ideal of code "inside" the machine, the user's ideal contribution.

Let us return to computer gaming to consider the breadth of the icon in the interface. Computer games frequently simulate three-dimensional spaces, and their on-screen presentations are dynamic and supple, which would seem to contrast with iconic logic. But gamers recognize and respond to a more rigid underlying logic, which dictates that active items in games appear in a certain way that signifies a status and available possibilities. The player reads the possibilities from the iconic images and adjusts her algorithm accordingly. Not just the images but also the habits, the twitches, the tics, the slogans, the patterns. In the game persona of a hard-boiled but good-hearted rogue hero, you are crossing the street, on your way to execute an evil terrorist boss. Suddenly a siren sounds, then a voiceover cop follows the squeal of police-band radio, "We've got him, boys. Close in." Next come shots fired, a *ricochet*, maybe the incidental music changes pace. The first time you experience this sequence, you are so busy figuring out what to do, which buttons to push, how to escape, that you do not really notice what is going on. But after two or three sequences, identical in their generalities, if not in all particulars, you come to recognize the signs, the elements of this icon as it unfolds predictably. Soon you develop a strategy for evading the cordon of police (perhaps taking to the rooftops?), thence employing it at need, with the siren triggering your response so rapidly that you have fled the scene before the gunshots ring out. (Perhaps you still hear the shots if the icon is especially stubborn.) "The exclusion of the unforeseen, that is, what Virilio names the accident is made evident by the First Person Shooter game in the very achievement of that winning performance where each enemy attack is dealt with *exactly* as if it is seen before it arrives" (Crogan 2004, n.p.). In its generality, the icon incorporates both past and future possibilities, circumscribing its instances according to a formula that entails a substantive definition of what counts—what counts as a file, what counts as a trap, what counts as a lie, what counts as a moral good. Even the unfortunate and persistent stereotyping around racial representation in games evinces the logic of the icon. Citing studies showing that as many as 90 percent of protagonists in games are white, André Brock notes that "while Black and Brown bodies are increasingly represented in current-gen videogaming, they are depicted using stereotypes of criminality, athleticism, or terroristic threat. These characters rarely achieve high levels of narrative involvement or character complexity" (2011, p. 432). Henry Jenkins generalizes this prevalence of iconic representation to the whole computer game: "Everything is streamlined: the plots and characters are reduced to genre archetypes, immediately familiar to the boy gamers, and defined more through their capacity for actions than anything else" (1998, p. 279). Meaning is about a consistent and predictable action, leaving appearance to mark this underlying consistency as stereotype.

The iconic character of the visual logic of the digital reveals both the user's engagement with the machine and the strange ontology of digital objects. Image sampling not only treats images as discrete and independent parts but it also determines in advance what counts as an image, what it means to be an image (in a digital context). And this is true for sound sampling as well, that it determines not only the piecemeal construction of sound in the digital code but also the nature of sound as something that can be thus sampled to encode an adequate representation of it. The point is that this same structure of symbolic representation carries over into digital interactions generally. It could not be otherwise, for any digital representation is constructed from elemental parts, requiring a principle of construction, a conceptualization of how to constitute, phenomenally and (onto)logically, the object in question. Digital objects are types before they are particulars, and constituted by structured numbers, they are never singular but always generic, reproducible, simulacral.

Any digital representation of an object—a word, an image, a video, a sound—presupposes a conceptualization of sensory experience as well as a conceptualization of the object to be experienced. There is always a model that determines what aspects of the world (and the objects in it) should be digitally encoded and how those objects or aspects correspond to the material capacities built into the prostheses that constitute most of the computer's physical mass, such as the monitor, speakers, keyboard, etc. Because those prosthetic abilities are almost always tied to widely observed protocols or norms so common as not to require a formal protocol, these capacities too reflect a conceptualization of sensory experience. Computer monitors present images of objects that persist over time, that have only so much detail, that can be visually represented using stacked lines made of dots, each of a particular shade and brightness. Another example: whereas vision typically takes in objects bathed in light from many sources and scattered off other objects, every object rendered on a computer monitor emits light, as emissive light is the only kind of lighting possible using the technology typical of a monitor. Which is to say that the presentation of visual information on a monitor presupposes a substantive theory of visuality, and in this case, it is a theory-in-practice that we know to be significantly incomplete as a description of how people actually see the world.

The icon introduces its generality as a capture of particular instances; it serves as both category and example of that category. There is a symbolic relationship between representation and represented, a conventional association that is learned rather than intuited. The object on screen is a symbol that the user associates with a particular digital object, but that interactive symbol is necessarily generic, iconic, separated from the actual by the boundary of a world, the boundary that divides the actual from the ideal. It does not matter whether the object resembles its referent as long as the user knows to connect the two. Thus, icons need not look like the documents or applications they stand for, and one can operate Illustrator (or Photoshop or Maya or Excel or MAX/MSP) without ever noting the match or mismatch between the programs' icons and the functions they perform.

3

On the Interface

We might think of the digital as having the shape of a *wasp waist*. The discrete code of 0s and 1s, the binary, marks a waypoint through which passes everything digital. Plenty of other aspects of computing are richer than this binary code, semiotically richer, materially weightier, historically more laden. Research tends rightly to focus on these areas of the history of computing where the stories to be told are more subtle and complex. But for all this thick penumbra of meanings around the digital, its being digital depends on the austere binary code that defines it as such. The binary code stands between input and output, between programmer and end user, between electrical impulses in silicon and the ideal logics that determine the computer's design and operation.

All that passes through the computer takes the form, at some point, of these 0s and 1s, the code that provides the digital's power of abstraction and serves as its chief technology. The central problem of computer design, then, is how best to make this power available to the user, how to effect passage back and forth between human being and binary code. This is the problem of the human-computer *interface*. The interface mediates between binary code and human world; it negotiates an accord between digital and actual and thus also between programmer and user, between input and output, between desire and its effective expression at the computer. The image of a dynamic interface that negotiates, mediates, and operates should discount the notion that the interface is a mere formality, a liminal surface defined by the insubstantial juncture of two genuinely real entities, digital and actual. Only an active and substantial interface could enable the rapprochement of digital and actual across their ontological disjunctions. The material world and the binary code do not operate according to the same logics, do not readily translate one into the other. The contention of this book is that there is no one solution to the problem of the encounter of these ontologies; rather, the digital meets the actual by traversing a series of singularities, running along an edge. Thus the only rule of the interface is definitional: the interface, as the locus of encounter between digital and actual, necessarily occupies both territories, keeps one foot in each camp. The interface inhabits both worlds at once, and its mission of mediation means that it tends to leverage the characteristics of each world in the other, isolating the digitality of the actual and the actuality of the digital.

Even if the problem of ontological compatibility is set aside, the interface resists easy definition as a surface of encounter. The interface is that part of the human-computer assemblage that necessarily includes both human and computer; but user and machine cannot easily be extricated, each interpenetrating the other, which means that the interface is thick rather than flat. In a sense, it is all interface, since each part of the machine functions in service of the user while the user orients herself, her behaviors, her intentions, toward the computer. A menu item is an element of the interface, which also includes the pixels that illuminate it on the screen, the magnetic charges that store its associated data on the hard drive, and the code that was compiled to enable its appearance at run-time. The spacebar on the keyboard is surely an interface element, but then so is the thumb that depresses it and even the cognitive habits of the user as her actions and thoughts find expression in discrete words and commands.

Though it has no distinct boundaries, the interface does have a mobile center. At its core lie those elements that structure and are structured by user actions at the computer, the sites where the human body touches the machine parts and the machine offers its data to human sensation. At this central meridian of the interface, human behavior most closely follows a digital logic, as user actions are atomistic, mechanical, linear, and processual, while the computer organizes and presents its data in forms most accessible to humanity—images and characters that signify in excess of the rarefied logic necessary for proper digital operation.

Beginning from this central surface of encounter, analysis of the interface proceeds from the inside out. Starting in the middle, we can ask whether and how the digital reaches out from the computer to encode even the user's body and thoughts. Exploring in the other direction, we can discover what about the images and characters on the monitor screen remains digital even as these artifacts become available to human sensation. This bidirectional analysis, from the center of the interface toward the two poles of user and machine, mirrors the two directions of data travel: input goes from user through the interface into the digital processor, output reverses this path. The rapidity of these traversals gives the appearance of an immediate receptivity of the machine, a direct connection between input and resulting output, but there are extensive territories of 0s and 1s, all of the complexity of the computer in between these two moments of user experience. The vast but concealed gulf between input and output produces in the computer a phenomenological split: hardware reflects the division between input and output, devoting separate components to each interface task, while the user applies distinct sensations and body parts to each direction of computer interaction. The mouse/keyboard involves the sense of touch in an input mechanism, while the monitor places the sense of vision in the service of digital output. These are the primary components of the interface—mouse, keyboard, monitor, touch, and vision—and this chapter examines these devices and their respective sensibilities, asking what they do, how they work, and where they connect.

Chapter 2 revealed at least two essential dimensions of the interface. First, it showed that the icon is the model of visuality in the interface, with a logic other than those of representation and presence. Second, it uncovered the crucial role of the user, who contributes an idea without which the object would not be an object. The interface is the site of this mediation, an alternative logic and an ideal investment. How do touch and vision enact this logic and mediate this investment?

Input

One expresses oneself at the computer almost exclusively through the mouse and keyboard. Vision is nearly indispensable and hearing plays a supporting role, but these senses are stereotypically passive at the computer, where the more active job of input gets consigned to the fingertips. At the computer, you express yourself, communicate your desires, by executing a gesture chosen from among a very few possibilities. You can click a key on the keyboard, move the mouse, or click the mouse. That's it. Specialized speech-based interface elements are available; there are eye-motion detectors and other alternative pointer-control techniques. The rise of mobile digital devices has made touchscreens widely popular. But computers continue to call first and foremost for the traditional mouse and keyboard, as a primary and even exclusive means of communicating to the machine. It is remarkable that so much desire gets expressed, such a breadth of different ideas passes through this restricted interface, fingertips against plastic. "We are increasingly naturalized to the idea that we should be ready to translate any sort of human notion or practice, into keystrokes" (Penny 2008, n.p.). The interface evidently assigns the sense of touch a particular prominence in the expression of desire. What kind of desire gets expressed via touch, and what kind of touch touches the interface?

The narrowness of the interface reveals itself as a sequence of elementary commands: the expression of desire breaks down into individual keypresses and mouse clicks. Atomized, self-identical, and absolute, each keypress or mouse click is an abstraction; the *k* key is not a particular *k* but only the command, *k*. In general, interface components transduce between the material and the abstract. This is an alternate definition of the interface: hardware and software that mediate between digital and actual or between abstract and material. The job of mouse and keyboard is to render materiality as abstraction, just as the monitor and speakers take the abstraction of the digital code and present it to material sensation. A single click, the paradigmatic action at the interface, might involve hundreds of muscles, a finely tuned machine of flesh and nerve, plastic and silicon. But in the end, the mouse button is either pressed or not at any given instant of mouse clock time; nothing else matters at the computer. The materiality of the press becomes the abstract binarity of 0 or 1.

The case of mouse *movement* is only slightly more complex: The mouse photographs images of the surface passing underneath it. A differential analysis of successive images yields the mouse's vector of motion. This differential mathematics is built into the mouse itself, housed on a chip designed specifically to perform these calculations. Motion (or stillness) of the mouse generates a pair of numbers, a horizontal velocity and a vertical velocity. Fifteen hundred times per second the mouse reports these numbers to the computer, passing them along through the USB bus (or over Bluetooth or whichever hardware standard is in use). The mouse cares not one bit about any other elements of touch. How hard you push, whether you are sweaty, touch type or hunt-and-peck, the interface does not so much ignore as exclude these facets of touch, rendering touch abstract even before the CPU gets a hold of the command.

Which is to say, even the materiality of the mouse is coded by the binary; it is as though the digital extends its effect by reaching out of the computer to determine the characteristics of its surroundings. The modern mouse takes photographs of the surface passing underneath it: an eighteen-by-eighteen grid, a snapshot taken so many times per second. Older optomechanical mice feature a mouse ball connected by gears to wheels inside the mouse, flat plates that turn along with the spinning of the mouse ball, one for forward-backward and one for left-right motion. The wheels have evenly spaced holes around their perimeters, admitting and interrupting a beam of light shining onto a sensor. The sensor reads a count per second of these interruptions to calculate the movement vector. (It must also include some mechanism for determining the direction of motion of each wheel, since the number of interruptions of the light beam indicates how rapidly, but not in which direction, the wheel is turning.)

An even earlier generation of mice used a purely mechanical mechanism, in which the wheels, connected by gears to the mouse ball, turned a counter like a turnstile. Mechanical to optomechanical to optical, the development of the mouse proceeds by replacing matter with light, abstraction as the motor of history. The mouse, whose principal operation is motion, operates better when it has fewer moving parts, when it is maximally dematerialized.

A key on the keyboard is just a specialized mouse button, a single click in 120 varieties. Keyboards are being progressively virtualized, mostly through the sometimes frustrating mechanism of the touchscreen. Though there remains an active fantasy of the dematerialized keyboard, realized in laser keyboards that project the keys onto any available flat surface and register interruptions in a beam of laser light that shines on that surface, this method is problematic, not least because typists desire tactile feedback. Modern keyboards tend to use a dome-switch, which employs a flexible rubber dome underneath each key that closes an electrical circuit when depressed. Many typists still prefer mechanical switches, which provide greater tactile and audible feedback to indicate a successful keypress. Whereas the mouse becomes increasingly dematerialized, we are unready to relinquish the tactility of typing, perhaps because of its intimate proximity to language. It is as though users are more prepared in the case of the mouse to accept the computer's ersatz materiality, the arrow moving on the screen. The arrow-cursor, whose closest associations are to the digital, does not invite a nostalgia nor provoke an anxiety over the lost materiality of the predigital world.[1]

We might focus on an ever smaller neighborhood at the junction of analog and digital, hoping to grasp the most basic move, the precise moment of transition between actual and digital. Binary devices such as a mouse button are relatively straightforward: the user's action physically closes an electric circuit, causing electricity to flow, signaling, for example, a one where before there was a zero. Scalar values are more complicated: given a variable voltage of electricity flowing through a wire, how does one convert that voltage to a specific value (or sequence of values) represented digitally, especially when that voltage is changing rapidly and must be frequently sampled to produce a stream of values? There are a number of methods to accomplish this task, relying on various physical properties of flowing electricity and on simple electrical circuit components. One common method is to allow the electrical flow to fill a capacitor, which acts as a reservoir, admitting an amount of electricity proportional to the voltage flowing in. Then shut off the influx of current and allow the capacitor to drain while running a clock. As soon as the capacitor drains fully, the clock is stopped and the resulting value, measuring the time it took for the electricity to drain out of the capacitor, is the value of the sample. The higher the initial voltage is, the more electrons are held in the capacitor and the longer it takes the capacitor to drain to 0.

In this simple example, there is a sense in which analog and digital never actually meet. The motive force of the electrical current, its voltage, is measured by a clock that does not interact directly with that current; analog and digital interoperate across a gap. Perhaps it is typical of analog-to-digital (A-D) conversion methods that they require a kind of break, where an analog flow cannot simply be directly converted but only measured from a distance, *inducing* a value that it never quite touches. Another method of analog-to-digital conversion, called *direct conversion*, compares a sampled voltage to a set of stable standard voltages, and when a match is found, the matched standard voltage yields an associated number that becomes the digital value of the sample. Again there is a break or gap in that the bank of standard values serves as an intermediary used in the actual measurement, while the conventionally associated number never makes any contact with the sampled analog signal. Another method, successive approximation, also introduces an intermediary flow of electricity, produced from stable references. In general, the digital and analog do not quite meet, do not touch each other, as the digits, the bits, must arise from within their own domain, from an already digital site. The nonencounter of actual and digital attests to the radical abstraction of the digital, which removes it to its own territory, free of the messy materiality and inexactitude of the analog. In Chapter 5, this gap that must be crossed in the transit between actual and digital will be analyzed as an *edge*, and it presents a characteristic ontology that can be discovered at every meeting of the actual and the digital.

Digitization and binarization do not stop at the plastic and glass parts of the interface. Crucially, the user's body, her habits of motion, her self-consciousness, these are also digitized even while the body remains irreducibly corporeal. The user orients her body toward the interface, adjusting her posture, down to the tips of her fingers, for the most efficient inputting of 0 and 1; even her body already effects the translation of desire into the binary. If the moving body invariably exceeds capture in a binary code, that excess is not only excluded by the computer but is also minimized by the user. We train our bodies to click, move, and type as efficiently as possible, keeping excess motion to a minimum. Angry or distraught clicking would only impede one's ability to input commands. Campbell spells out one implication, the instrumentalization of the interface: "Interfaces that involve discrete choices leave little room for intuition. Discrete choices generally cause the viewers to look for a logical reason to make the correct choice based on what they think the consequences might be. Unless it is a game, there is no correct choice" (2000, p. 135).

The interface poses the body of the user, as evinced by the variety and frequency of interface-related illness. Eyestrain and carpal tunnel problems are among the most specific, but computing also places demands on neck, shoulders, and back, not to mention the consequences of the rigidity, stillness, and consistent posture imposed by the circumstance of computing. Eyes are oriented by the flat plane of the monitor, the line of sight approximating a vector perpendicular to the plane of the monitor and near its center. But this desire for a vision that comprehends the whole screen (and pushes all else to the background of attention) also necessarily places the head, chin, neck, and back in a particular relationship to the screen. Efficient access to keyboard and mouse positions the fingertips (and thus also the wrists, arms, and shoulders) in relation to another plane, generally perpendicular to the plane of the monitor. Though the user is, in principle, free to move her body as long as she maintains the right relationships of eyes and fingers to monitor and keyboard/mouse, in practice these constraints are already almost entire, as very little large motion is possible with eyes and fingers held in place. Fixing only these terminal, superficial body parts, the interface ultimately controls the user's entire body, demanding the fealty of stillness and sameness. Note also that the division between eyes and hands is reinforced by this ergonomics, as they are intended to stay out of each other's way. Perhaps the body is itself divided (and conquered) by the split between input and output, each aspect of computing laying claim to different parts of the user's body. Ironically, the sensory division between vision and touch may contribute to the simulated wholeness of each, as their noninterference makes it easier to correlate their relationship: since eyes do not see hands, the user more readily believes that the hand manipulates the arrow on the screen rather than the plastic housing of a mouse. It is a strange contraption, isolating the senses in perpendicular planes so that they might work together, against their typical deployment. Touch never actually touches what it reaches for, and vision helps to sustain the illusion that masks this aborted tactility.

Consider Maurice Merleau-Ponty's famous analysis of the right hand touching the left hand while the left hand touches something else (1964, pp. 130ff.). His example draws attention to the reflexivity of touch, the way in which to touch is to be touched; but even more dramatically this example speaks to the way in which touching is tangible. The hand can only touch because the world is tangible, and in order to touch that world, the hand must be a part of it, itself touchable. Only what is tangible could participate in a world of touching. Likewise, vision is visible; the seeing eye can be seen and it can be seen to see. "It suffices for us for the moment to note that he who sees cannot possess the visible unless he is possessed by it, unless he *is of it*, unless, by principle, according to what is required by the articulation of the look with the things, he is one of the visibles, capable, by a singular reversal, of seeing them—he who is one of them" (pp. 134–5). Advancing this line of reasoning, Merleau-Ponty concludes that vision and touch must share the same world, for vision is tangible just as touch is visible. "Since the same body sees and touches, visible and tangible belong to the same world" (p. 134).

Giving a massage, playing the cello, kneading dough, writing with a pen, one feels the variable resistance of the material, and this essential resistance produces thought in the touch itself, a reflexivity that is the hallmark of thinking. This reflexivity constitutes not only the dynamics of touch but also, according to Merleau-Ponty, the tangible world (and also the visible world for vision). But precisely this haptic condition is disrupted in the digital. For one touches there what does not touch back; the keyboard and mouse do not offer anything variable to touch, they always feel the same no matter what command one gives, no matter what one is touching. The texture of the surface over which your avatar runs, the brightness of the filter you apply to an image, the amount of text to be pasted to a new location in the document, these factors do not alter the smoothness or bumpiness, the thickness or weight, the speed or precision of the input devices' operation.

This homogeneity of touch, though nearly universal, need not be essential in the digital interface. We can imagine a simulated reflexivity of touch built into the input components of the machine. In some cases, it would be helpful for the mouse to roll differently depending on the on-screen circumstances of the simulated world. A game might be more fun and intuitive if (virtual) running over ice felt smooth to the hand while jumping over rocks felt jerky and effortful. A drawing program might benefit from a mouse that could offer increased resistance to motion when working on fine detail, allowing greater precision, while larger movements could glide more easily to cover a lot of distance on the screen. But these are very specific contexts, in which a physical characteristic of the input device is associated by convention with a particular aspect of the simulated space. Though these examples add expressive possibilities to the input device, they only underline the simulated nature of touch in the digital, as the input features are turned on or off according to their value in a particular application and do not offer a general sense of variable tangibility or texture of the simulated world. It is not clear what simulated resistance is appropriate in the general case: how much should an icon weigh? Should a desktop picture be smooth or bumpy? Should the mouse vibrate when scrolling through a list? We could settle on conventional responses to these questions, but the virtuality of the world one reaches for at the computer, its ultimately immaterial nature, ensures that no simulated tactile resistance will ever finally close the reflexive circuit of touch. And much simulated resistance would likely feel fairly intrusive or contrived.

Working from Merleau-Ponty's understanding of touch as necessarily tangible, we might conclude that the interface includes no touch, since icons, windows, and menus do not touch back. Or that the world one touches at the computer is not the same as the material world at one's fingertips. It is another world, constituted by the digital code, a world generated by processes of abstraction, defined by an architecture of command and control. Given the gap between fingertips and the objects on the screen that they manipulate, the sense of touch is oddly curtailed. The objects one touches do not touch back, and the reciprocation constitutive of thought in touch is carried out not in touch, but in vision. One sees but does not feel one's touch in the interface, eyes offering an essential completion of touch that typically requires only fingers. (This was the founding principle of cybernetics: one steers the computer via a feedback loop, taking one's cues from mediated output rather than from the immediacy of the context of input. But this game of Marco Polo may have unforeseen effects when played directly in sensation without a necessary passage through cognition.)

Would we say the same thing about a hammer or a fishing pole, that it reaches for what it does not finally touch? Or rather that the user uses them to reach for what he does not touch? But the gap is different, for the circuit of touch remains complete, as the tug of the fish on the line is felt in the fingers and responded to there, as is the solid thwack or the buzzing resonance that indicates a direct or off-center contact with the nail. Touching is essential in using these tools whereas it is only a means to an end at the computer. Moreover, if one reaches for the fish or the nail, this reaching is for what is generic in these objects. Fingers (and the whole circuit of touch) are still necessary to accommodate a particular nail or a particular fish, and the gap only opens to the extent that one reaches for an abstraction, fish or nails in general.

This gap between touch and its object—the very distance that Merleau-Ponty debunks as metaphysically misguided[2]—allows for the interposition of the simulated world. (The computer thus realizes the fear that prompts a metaphysical distrust of vision: a distance, necessary to vision, that, nevertheless, threatens its authenticity, as though someone or something might interpose between object and eye, altering the seen before the eye actually sees it.) Cut off from the world that they touch, fingers finally reach a recreated materiality, a representation that uses the gap separating it from fingertips as an opportunity to downplay or hide its shortcomings, its unreality. What the computer offers to touch, what the fingers aim to grasp is a generic representation, not the variegated texture of a real object, but the algorithmic or perfectly reproduced pattern of a represented digital. Reaching for a generic object and curtailed to make room for an ersatz abstraction, touch in the interface becomes itself generic, a gesture with no distinction.

Merleau-Ponty's detailed analysis of touch in *Phenomenology of Perception* points to the strange poverty of digital touch. His concept of *optimum distance* implicates the body and the entirety of sensation in any attempt to reach for something in the world, as one's body discovers the best distance from which to apprehend an object, taking in its whole as well as its details. Touch happens against a negotiated backdrop that allows the touched to come forward and distinguish itself. Whereas actual, material touch thus always encounters an entire world, implying a place for one's whole body, digital touch reaches for and seizes upon a single, already distinct object, given independently of its background as determinate in itself. This narrowness of intentionality in digital touch is highlighted by the affective possibilities of the arrow-cursor: once grabbed, a digital object can be manipulated in a few different ways, which are derived almost exclusively from within itself. To grab a digital object is to approach the cusp of a few possible actions, whereas to grab an actual object is to open a world of potential.

The mouse click is a generality, the same click no matter what the intention, no matter what the context. One first designates an object and then specifies the particular action to be taken (usually by choosing from a menu). Typically, we act in the material world by reaching for objects with a grasp that anticipates the intent of the reaching. As Merleau-Ponty points out, visible and tangible are of the same world, such that the appearance of an object is not determined independently of its potential relations to the body and the rest of the world. In his reading of Merleau-Ponty, Hubert Dreyfus emphasizes that to reach for an object is to engage it in terms of one's embodied possibilities, an intentionality guided by the world and the place of one's body within it (2009, pp. 55–6). But on the computer, the particularity of the action is deferred until after its selection, such that objects are defined as (graspable) objects generically and independently of their possible uses.

Complementarily, the mouse reinforces the logic of abortive touch by restricting its gesture to the deictic. Separated from the object that it reaches for, a gesture performed with an input device is structured less like touch and more like pointing, action at a distance. Digital touch does not encounter its object in the flesh but indicates its object from a distance, the logic of the index. Lacking any distinction between center and periphery, occupied not by an attention but by a list of values, the computer does not distinguish between *this* and *that* as ontically distinct categories, but only distinguishes among values, a pixel and the adjacent pixel.

Even while it epitomizes the generic, the mouse click works against this digital reduction to abstraction. Though it asserts only the most general instructions—*this*, or *here*, or *now*—these deictic commands impose a human world on the sterile, indifferent domain of the digital. The computer, left to itself, has neither center nor periphery; it does not focus but only proceeds, each of billions of bits taking on a next value, 0 or 1, at each tick of the digital clock. The computer offers numerous possibilities as to what might happen next, but it prefers none of them, it leans in no direction, occupying itself with numbers whose values are all equally meaningful from the perspective of the operating machine. All the more significant, then, is the lowly mouse click, for the single click divides before from after according to a contingency that lies beyond the computer's reach. The click is the minimal human imposition, a punctuation in the otherwise untextured stream of bits that passes through the computer chip.

That the computer has no attention means that it has no about-ness, that it operates as though without context, that it makes meaning in a way that always threatens to collapse into mechanism. The indexical character of digital touch corresponds to and supplements this deficit of attention. Instead of a focused or pendant attention, the computer tarries in a state of indexed readiness, a random access potential that is only the fact of being ready to offer up any next data (given an index into the database). If it preserves a field or list of possibilities, a set of available next actions, this readiness derives from its indifference. It favors neither beginning nor end of the list, neither this one nor that one, which is part of its being generally (randomly) available. The deictic command is also an index that designates which path should next be pursued, a choice in the face of the computer's indifference.

The image of an intensive world of tactile sensation reduced to an indifferent flow of 0s and 1s might suggest that the key to a richer computing experience would be to disarticulate the interface, to find a way to restore the fullness of touch. No doubt, a simulated tactility could augment the computing experience, just as force-feedback in gaming controls plays a valued if limited role in popular console games, but more broadly, digital technologies do not deal well with the unarticulated. Thus, the science-fictional fantasy of a speech-based interface (like HAL from *2001* or the computer on the various starships Enterprise) does not respect the underlying nature of the digital. Speech is a (relatively) unarticulated continuum of sound and is thus often ill-suited to dealing with the digital. Fingers are digits, after all, and their suitability as interface components derives from their already digital character. (Of course, speech is very useful for some digital input activities, especially for people who do not or cannot type, but these applications remain specialized, as speech lacks the articulated finesse of fingers. Moreover, speech enlists powerful and resource-intensive parts of the brain, requiring energies less available, therefore, for other kinds of cognition.)

Even the touchscreen, increasingly common not only in advanced tabletop computing but also, and mostly, in handheld devices, enriches digital touch only ambivalently. Whereas the touchscreen may help to restore some sensuous intimacy to the realm of the digital, closing the gap that now tends to separate the deictic gesture from its object, it also reduces articulation. Fingertips on a screen are not as precise as a cursor, and keys make for faster and more exact text entry than does handwriting. Even on a touchscreen, the sensuous intimacy of tactile contact with the intended object is only simulated, as the objects under one's fingertips do not actually meet one's flesh. Not only does the surface of the screen stand between fingers and icon, a thick plate that refuses to disappear into the simulation, but so does a whole chain of code, which abstracts touch and then rematerializes images of the objects that one manipulates. As such, I suspect that pointing is here to stay as the primary input to the digital. (Touchscreens have not, for the most part, found their way onto desktop or even laptop personal computers, as the keyboard and mouse serve more readily most computing input tasks. Touchscreens are most frequently employed in contexts such as tablets, where the emphasis is on media presentation rather than production.) The power of the digital comes from its distinctness as another world, a world we can point to but not quite be a part of. We need to continue asking how the flesh manages to encounter this world of abstraction at all.

Mediation

The abortive structure of touch in the digital and, consequently, the indirect contact between the user and the digital object suggest a fairly banal conclusion: digital interaction is mediated. This will surprise no one, and it even calls into question the urgency of this analysis; after all, mediation does not arrive only with the computer and may even characterize human experience in general. Running throughout the history of Western philosophy, the problem of the connection between the subject and the object is the persistent preoccupation of metaphysics. Starting with the centrality of the subject, to follow Descartes' example, the philosopher is immediately confronted with the problem of how the subject relates to the objects that appear around her. Assuming objects are real, it would seem as though any contact with them is already mediated, if only by the subject's own body. A number of philosophers have challenged the primacy of the subject, and still others reject or revise the dualism that places the body as a mediator between mind and world. But the concern here is that digital objects, presenting themselves as mediated, may be raising only the oldest of problems and that the digital, thus, offers nothing particularly new to the philosophy of mediation.

However, this comparison between digital and actual worlds does not hold up under scrutiny. The problem of mediation necessarily takes a different form in the case of the digital. The problem of mediation in the actual world derives from the worry that we never manage to connect to the thing itself; separated from the real as it really is, we can never know reality, we can never determine reality, and we are therefore destined to live in an illusory world, trapped inside our own bodies, in thrall to the mere appearances that mock our inability to reach beyond or behind them. Having elevated self-knowledge, the cogito, to the highest degree of certainty and therefore the standard of truth, (dualist) philosophy achieves only a lesser knowledge of *things*, cut off from the world that surrounds and eventually comes to threaten the subject. We imagine that there is an unconditioned object, being for itself (just like the subject), that asserts its plenary reality, but we are forever separated from that object by our own bodies, an indirect contact mediated by sensation instead of an experience equal to the object itself.

In the case of the actual, the essential mediation, the mediation of the body, seems to be built into the conditions of being human, whereas in the case of the digital, the mediation is inherent to the nature of the (digital) thing. In the digital, there is no object that we might have a direct experience of. The object is not missing but neither does it have a necessary materiality. The digital object exists through material representations that are indispensable to its operations, but it does not equal those representations and maintains an *insistence* independent of them. Sensation cannot encounter the abstract ideal of a digital object, but unlike the thing in itself that supposedly lies behind the actual appearance, the digital object does not suggest even the possibility of an unmediated encounter. It comes from another world, a world of ideals, a world of perfection and pure possibility, and there is no question of an immediate relationship between human sensation and the digital object. We cannot imagine a direct contact with the object and, in fact, the object becomes more (not less) obscure as we approach its "essence" in the digital. To move from the appearance in the interface toward the underlying data is to leave the human world behind. Mediation is the essential condition of the encounter with the digital object, whereas an actual object presents itself as unconditioned.

We have arrived at the ontological bedrock. It is the unconditioned quality of the actual that most starkly marks its distinction from the digital. To assert that the actual object is unconditioned is not to deny its essential connectedness to history, to space, to other objects, or to human subjects. The unconditioned is not the autochthonous, the phallic posit that determines its own identity without reference, without relation. Rather, the unconditioned of the object is its contingency, its affect, its intensity, its potential, its propensity always to surprise, to offer something out of itself that manifests its creativity, or its participation in the creative principle of ontogenesis. An actual object always exceeds its appearance, not because it has more than meets the eye but because its appearance is the effect of a production.

But the digital object, insisting on its abstraction, does not generate an unpredictable resistance. It does not produce itself anew all the time but, on the contrary, provides an unequivocal standard of identity, a precise code of 0s and 1s that defines the object along with its possibilities.[3] This ideal is outside of the realm of experience not just in fact but also in principle. Any relationship to the digital must therefore be mediated due to the nature of the digital itself. It is made of logic, of structure, wrought by the power of abstraction, and, therefore, in a domain that does not present itself directly to sensation. (This basic but substantive claim lies at the heart of Johanna Drucker's [see 2001 or 2009] rejection of the digital as an ideal. She reasons that since experience can encounter the digital only as mediated, this mediated, individual experience of a particular artifact just *is* the digital object, and fantasies about an ideal that lies behind that object, an ideal made of code, are simply misguided.)

The deictic gesture that corresponds to touch at the digital interface is therefore mandatory. It is not a substitute for a more immediate contact to come, but is the essential structure of digital interaction. The interface functions as a surface of indication, a pointing mechanism, where what gets pointed at is necessarily something untouchable, not of this world. It is, therefore, not just that we never actually touch the representations on the monitor that we point to with the mouse. It is also that any encounter with the digital object is itself a pointing, to an ideal that is, in principle, materially unavailable; the digital is doubly mediated, which is its epistemological distinction. This is the structure that defines the interface: it is caught at the juncture of a double mediation, always passing the buck. But its role as surface of (double) mediation is part of its claim, which ironically gives it legitimacy, establishes its footing. Precisely because the interface does not claim to be the source of its own legitimacy, its claim is legitimate. It admits to its flatness and, embracing its inadequacy, it becomes adequate.

The analysis of touch in the digital focuses on the indirect or mediated connection between the user and the digital. The user points to but does not contact the objects for which she reaches. But an additional obscurity surrounds this deictic gesture, for it is not clear what the user reaches for. Does she aim for an image on the screen? Does she intend to alter data? Perhaps she desires to manipulate magnetic fields on the surface of a hard drive or flashes of light passing through glass cables crisscrossing the globe. If the user reaches for a digital object, what sort of object is this and where might it be found?

Output

In his recent monograph on the underappreciated role of software in new media culture, Lev Manovich notes the decisive influence of the *graphical user interface*:

> In short, while many HCI experts and designers continue to believe that the ideal human-computer interface should be invisible and get out of the way to let users do their work, looking at the theories of Kay and Goldberg that were behind

> GUI design gives a very different way of understanding an interface's identity. Kay and his colleagues at PARC have conceived GUI as a *medium* designed in its every detail to facilitate learning, discovery, and creativity. (2013, p. 100)

Introducing the computer for the rest of us, the GUI marked a decisive step in the history of the digital. During the 1970s, the computer was an administrative and research tool but was expanding its applications, increasingly adopted by hobbyists, by the upwardly mobile, and in classrooms. In 1984 the Macintosh brought the GUI, under development for more than fifteen years, into the mainstream. No more lists of commands to memorize, no more arcane codes and rigid syntax. Much of what the computer had to offer to the user was illuminated right on the surface by the shifting pixels of the monitor, outlining objects on which to act and suggesting possible actions for those objects.

Windows, Icons, Menus, and a Pointing device, the GUI is sometimes called a WIMP interface. Using these elements, the file system and its standard operations (copy, delete, move, list, rename, etc.) are laid out in virtual overlapping planes, loosely governed by the metaphor of the monitor screen as a desktop. This metaphor, stretched to incredulity from the start, is further taxed by the many applications hosted within the GUI, from three-dimensional projections in a gaming window to the hyperlinked space of a browser to the infinite, indexed cells of a spreadsheet. These are not easily recognizable as artifacts from atop someone's mahogany desk, but then we do not tend to decorate our cubicles with document icons, either. The desktop metaphor was only ever a thin contrivance for directing the intuition, to give a hint of the familiar to an esoteric technology. Young people, too naïve to be intimidated by computers and unburdened by the rigorous adult demand for metaphorical consistency, were possibly the perfect audience for the desktop and the GUI built on top of it. The GUI rendered the computer easier to use without expertise, but at the cost of some power and efficiency, a technology of a lower common denominator.[4]

Of his own considerable contribution to the invention of the GUI, computer scientist and interface guru Alan Kay dedicates much to the young people who were his test subjects and the "primary motivation" for much of the research he conducted in partnership with Adele Goldberg at Xerox PARC (1993, p. 79). Kay held that the computer offers extraordinary creative possibility, but he lamented that that possibility is out of reach for those lacking extensive technical expertise. Hoping to lower this barrier, Kay's team designed an interface simple enough for a child to operate, with a screen full of pictograms, symbols that resemble (at least somewhat) what they represent, and an intuitive pointing device for input that relies on an embodied sense of space acquired in early childhood. To generalize and popularize this interface, Kay helped to invent the programming language Smalltalk, including a visual environment wherein programming involves arranging icons within a window. Even children can use such a system to tap into the computer's potent possibility: Kay provides examples from toddlers through high school students (1986). Manifest in the immediacy of recognizable, iconic images, the computer's inner logic is revealed to anyone with eyes to see and so becomes wholly available to a general audience.

Under the guidance of reputed visionary Steve Jobs, Apple recognized (and capitalized on) the underlying principle of the GUI: it puts a human face on computing. The award-winning box art for the original Macintosh featured primary colors and iconic line drawings, penned so as to recall the crude and playful simplifications of a child's hand. A couple of system updates down the road, the Macintosh startup screen put the sign in the window (as it were), showcasing the "happy Mac," a drawing of an early Macintosh all-in-one computer with a smiley face on its screen. (See Figure 3.1.) The happy Mac eventually insisted even more literally on the amalgam of computer and human, becoming a rectangular figure of a monitor broken by a squiggly vertical line to suggest eyes, nose, and mouth.

Figure 3.1 Two versions of the "happy" Mac and the Picasso-style art from the original 128k Macintosh packing box.

What would be more iconic than a smiley face? The happy Mac is the epitome of the icon, the iconic icon. The smiling face—eyes, nose, and mouth—resonates deep within our brains, such that even the simplified line-drawing of a smiley refers immediately to an elemental experience, a neural structure basic to human being. But the happy Mac is not a face, only ever an icon of one. Its simplified features do not so much resemble as signify the face, as underlined by the generic figural language of the smiley, seen on t-shirts and bumper stickers. The happy Mac, an icon introduced in the late 1980s to indicate the successful startup of the Macintosh operating system, enacts a strange self-referential logic: shortly after powering up, the computer screen shows an iconic image of an early Macintosh "all-in-one" computer, on the tiny screen of which are the features of a generic smiley face. The on-screen representation of an iconic computer stages one of the central problems of the digital interface, namely, that the materials available to present on a computer are always already digital and hence iconic, generic, or reproducible. The interface can only present what is digital, offering to the user the computer "inside" the computer, revealing its essential mediation while sugarcoating and humanizing the message with a smile. The face on the iconic computer screen pushes back against this tail-swallowing digital trap; after all, the point of including a smiling face is to insist, against all evidence, on the underlying humanity of the computer. (An early print advertisement for the original 1984 128k Mac shows the computer with the word "hello" on its screen, drawn in a cursive script. This is a more subtle version of the same message: the human and the digital can indeed meet and can do so on human turf.[5]) Even at the time, these pseudo-human gestures flickering on the gray scale screen of the Macintosh felt awkward, foregrounding the clumsy mismatch of digital and human. With the distance of history, these miniature images—not just the small image of the computer, but also the smiling face on its little screen— have lost their humanity altogether, drawing attention not to any simulated emotion, but only to the pathetic fallacy of the digital.

Though Kay was not the creator of the happy Mac image, it might still be thought of as his signature on the Macintosh interface, for it underlines the core principles of his conception of how the interface should work. Kay inherits his pedagogy from American psychologist Jerome Bruner, who loosely adapts from Jean Piaget a developmentalism, modifying the relatively strict, preadult developmental stages of Piaget to allow for lifelong learning and change. Bruner identifies three stages of mentality, the enactive, the iconic, and the symbolic. The standard paraphrase holds that the enactive mentality, dominant in infancy, is about acting bodily on the world; the iconic, onset in early childhood, is about images and resemblance; and the symbolic, blossoming in adolescence, is about abstract connections.[6]

The driving force behind the GUI is the mediate position in this triad of the iconic, which leads learners from an infantile enactive mentality to a sophisticated symbolic one. By providing simple and legible icons that visually suggest their meanings, the interface is supposed to encourage users to pass from an understanding of the computer through embodied action (the mouse) to an understanding based on logic and symbolic reasoning (programming). Hence the rather trite title of Kay's well-known video lecture, "Doing with Images makes Symbols," in which Kay (1986) outlines some of the history of the GUI, tracing its principles to Bruner and its technical foundations (mouse and windows) to Douglas Engelbart.

The GUI does not merely substitute suggestive images (icons) where formerly there had been elliptical codes; it is not just a less intimidating means of accessing the same possibilities. Locating the icon between the material mouse and the symbolic binary, the GUI presents a different regime of possibility, a different structure of computing. How does the GUI convey the availability of the computer to the user? It encapsulates digital objects into icons, imbuing those objects with a visual and affective coherence. Arraying icons in space, the GUI establishes relationships (and potential relationships) among the represented objects. It provides an enduring visual presence to the objects "in" the computer, altering a fundamental tenet of computing: one need no longer already know what the computer can do in order to work with it. Its contents are laid bare by the GUI, such that the computer not only invites experimentation and use but also reveals its inner order to the eye, lowering its threat by voluntarily disclosing its innards.[7]

Prior to the icon, one would encounter a file only in the course of an operation on it. Now it (or its iconic proxy) sits in plain sight on the desktop ready to be clicked, indicating its existence and availability. The GUI renders some objects and some actions close at hand, promoting those objects and those actions, calling the user's attention to the set of possibilities surrounding those objects. Visuality rather than logic or memory comes to dominate the interaction with the computer, not only foregrounding certain choices, but also changing the kind of cognition associated with computer use.

Before the introduction of the GUI, the interface took its cues primarily from the computing hardware. The computer follows a linear process, accepting input, processing that input through a series of logical calculations, and then producing an output. Each tick of the clock yields the next state. The text-based, command line interface mirrors this linear process of computing. It spews out a stream of data, each character proceeding the previous one, each line following the last, and only the most recent information is current or active. The command line prompt represents the context of current operations, an edge between what has been established (above the prompt) and what is still to be calculated (below the prompt). The text already on the screen (or printed out on the printer) is inert, showing former states of the program that are not available except as a passive and static reference.

With a graphical interface, many items and many operations are simultaneously available, visible on the screen and ready to be clicked. Instead of entering codes according to an inflexible syntax, one need only point to a location on the monitor and click there. In Kay's view, this flat simplicity of the interface promoted creative possibilities: "The flitting-about nature of the iconic mentality suggested that having as many resources showing on the screen as possible would be a good way to encourage creativity and problem solving and prevent blockage" (2001, p. 129).[8] Filling the monitor screen with icons encourages the recognition of unforeseen connections, the choice of otherwise unfamiliar operations. In part, the novelty presented to the user derives from the flatness of the GUI: not only does the flat monitor surface allow only a limited representation of depth and a relative simplicity of structure, but this same interface also admits the juxtaposition of heterogeneous digital objects and operations. The icon for a volume of health-related data can sit on the desktop next to the icon of a text clipping containing a phone number. There is little in the interface to suggest the disparity of these two adjacent icons, and from the user's perspective they are, indeed, mostly equipotent. Each can be opened, copied, renamed, moved around, or removed from the desktop. The interface helps to hide the differences between these elements, and the consequent misrecognition may well spark some creative accidents. For example, a visual interface encourages unexpected connections by placing in the foreground icons that the user might otherwise never consider in a given context. A user will more likely try a different font when the possibility of switching fonts is immediately available right on the screen. An image filter represented as a button will be invoked more frequently and in more contexts than one buried in many layers of menus or only accessible by typing its name.

An immediate gain in creative possibilities is offset by a longer term loss. Unless the interface itself changes around over time (which would present its own problems), the available possibilities will become habitual instead of creative. The interface that promotes some possibilities encourages experimentation, but by burying other possibilities it also discourages certain creative maneuvers. It might seem as though the ideal would be an interface that becomes progressively more sophisticated as the user learns it, somehow demonstrating that one-click operations are actually instances of more complex, analogous operations that require additional clicks to execute.

Given that the possibilities of action are laid out on the monitor, a GUI—even a more moderate, less busy one—favors certain kinds of users, those who are *learning* to use the computer. With available options displayed on the screen, users can find what they are looking for without having to rely on memory or symbolic thinking. Offering options to the user through images that are self-consciously childish or caricature-ish, the GUI invites playfulness, and the very fact of an option being visibly available reassures as to the appropriateness or correctness of that option. The gentle GUI lowers the threat of the computer not only by offering immediate options but also by claiming implicitly (and not always correctly) that the available options are safe. By contrast, the codes of a text-based interface declare their esoteric status by being unreadable (to those lacking experience and expertise), and, as such, they always carry the threat of a tragic and consequential mistake. The warm and fuzzy GUI encourages experimentation, while comforting users and reducing the pervasive anxiety and intellectual effort of having to call forth an expertise. This is Kay's explicit goal, reflecting his philosophical commitments and his youthful audience of testers, but what about users who already know how to use the computer and now want to get their work done? For many years after Apple commercialized the GUI, expert users disparaged the Macintosh as an unsophisticated toy. The tired debate pitting Microsoft Windows against the Apple Mac remains a perpetuation of dueling philosophies: the computer as a learning environment versus the computer as a productivity machine. (Thus, it was never incidental nor merely a matter of marketing that Apple dominated in education while Microsoft ruled the business world.) "Hence we were thinking about learning as being one of the main effects we wanted to have happen. Early on, this led to a 90 degree rotation of the purpose of the user interface from 'access to functionality' to 'environment in which users learn by doing'" (Kay 1993, p. 84).

It may well be of benefit to an expert user to be able to call forth any file without having to navigate through layers of folders, without having to remove her hands from the keyboard, without having to engage in visual cognition at all. The command line may intimidate learners, but it provides a simple mechanism to invoke any process or any file with any modifying parameters, often using a single line of coded text. Moreover, the command line interface is consistent and efficient; input and output share a common form (text), and just about every character conveys essential information. By contrast, icons carry very little information relative to the amount of space they occupy and the amount of time they persist on screen. Unlike an icon, the textual interface does not tell the user (unbidden) what is available, but such information is at best superfluous to one who already knows what her machine can do. That Apple's interface (if not their operating system) ended up winning the desktop wars suggests that the manifest success of the personal computer required the warmth and fuzziness of the learning-oriented interface.

Designing an interface that functions in accord with the cognitive style of nonexpert human beings presented a new set of challenges. Experts could be counted on to follow a set of procedures, not just a precise syntax but an order of operations corresponding to the computer's own linear ordering of tasks. The two-dimensional visual layout of icons, menus, and windows invited a less linear interaction, with diverse possible actions on offer all at once and no strict constraints on the order in which actions may be triggered. To accommodate this loosened ordering of operations, the GUI emphasized *modelessness*; a modal interface, that is, an interface with modes, necessitates multiple steps to complete a given operation. Many operations require that the computer first be switched into the proper mode, and this involves exiting the mode in which the computer is currently operating. "This is what *modeless* came to mean for me—the user could always get to the next thing desired without any backing out" (Kay 2001, p. 129). In a modal interface, each application might institute its own mode, such that switching to another application means first terminating or suspending the current one.

We now take for granted that the operating system allows multiple programs to run simultaneously, and that we can switch easily among running programs and trigger a new one to run concurrently. When the Macintosh was introduced in 1984, its original operating system did not allow more than one running application at a time, such that a user would have to quit MacWrite in order to run MacPaint. Eventual operating system revisions introduced Multifinder in 1987, which allowed multiple simultaneous applications using cooperative multitasking. The maturation of this technology combined with multicore chips and multichip computers have now embedded this capability so firmly in our machines that we take it for granted. (Multifinder and other contemporary personal computing architectures did not yet perform true parallel processing, but simulated multiple simultaneous processes using a trick: one process would actively execute while the others waited their turn at the CPU, with rapid cycling among the various processes. Given the speed at which computers operate, this seemed to the user to be simultaneous processing. Personal computers contemporaneous with this writing perform true parallel processing, using multiple chips or multiple chip cores to execute multiple threads of operation concurrently.)

Given this description, modality might seem entirely undesirable, an unnecessary limitation on user choice that is at best clumsy and inefficient. However, on a computing system with limited processing and memory resources, modes allow greater efficiency, since programs can assume more control over the context in which they are run. In text-entry mode, a program need only interpret each input as either text to be entered or an instruction to exit the mode; no other inputs are possible, which limits what the user can (immediately) do, but makes the programmer's job a lot more cut and dried. Since the program only includes code to process limited, predetermined kinds of input, there is relatively less code necessary overall, less complexity in the code, and so a more efficient use of computer resources.

The gain of a modeless interface is a perceived efficiency for the user: no longer does she have to execute commands just to prepare for the next task. The administrative labor of computer use is reduced, with a savings primarily in terms of time. A mode functions as a temporal context; at a given moment, the computer is ready for one kind of task or for another, and switching modes takes some time. Instituting a kind of modelessness, the GUI trades space for time, laying out the options on a plane (or on a sheaf of overlaid planes).[9] Now instead of switching modes, the user clicks on an already visible icon or window and immediately begins working at her new task. She need not terminate her current operation before switching to another. In the GUI, (what were formerly) modalities are now represented by different icons or different planes or different windows, spatial arrays that reduce the amount of time spent switching modes.

Modelessness typifies progress in the history of the interface, as many interface innovations compress the temporal dimension of computing. Consider the historical shift in the interface from batch processing to interactive processing. For the first twenty years of commercial digital computing, computing resources were scarce and most computers were shared among many projects and many users. Rather than interacting with the machine directly, users would submit programs (e.g., on punch cards) to a queue, to be run in their turn. Fed into the computer, the program would run for the most part without human interaction: input program, output result. A bunch of programs to be run were a *batch*, so this style of allocating scarce resources over time with little interaction during program execution was called *batch processing*. Batch processing takes for granted the perspective of the computer, and does not work to accommodate the exigencies of human being. That is, a batch process assumes that the computer's state can be known in advance, that it will not generally get interrupted, that its task is intended to proceed from start to finish without extra-digital guidance. This structure understands the computer as task-oriented, designed to complete a series of tasks it has been assigned. It works on computer time, on clock time, as clock cycles are considered expensive or valuable and so must be used efficiently, getting the most computing done in the least amount of time and resources. A modal interface works well in this case, as the moments when the interface is available to the computer operator are relatively anomalous and separated from the actual calculations of the program.

Modelessness helps to accommodate the temporal incommensurability of the digital and human domains. The digital follows a linear progress, each tick of the crystal clock measuring a single-step advance; past and future narrow to a slice of present, the current value of the output, the command to be executed. For human beings, the world is confined neither to a linear progress nor to a narrow present; our world comprises a context of attention, a simultaneous manifold availability of a whole perceptual field, whose meaning derives from its relation to past and future. (Kay calls this the "flitting-about nature of the iconic mentality." [2001, p. 129].) The human world is wide. Modelessness expresses each world to the other, simulating in the digital the general availability of context by rapidly circulating among many options, one at a time, while the side facing the human retains its digital survey-ability, constituted by individual elements that can be easily distinguished and understood as wholly separate.[10] Human consciousness is multiple, ambiguous, contingent, roaming, and associative, and the modeless GUI helps to embed this style of thinking into the determinate, narrow, linear process of the digital.

The shift to a modeless interface corresponds to a need to make the computer more available to the user, more prepared to accommodate the contingent, arbitrary, or unpredictable nature of human needs and desires. *Personal* computing calls for modelessness, as human attention is, generally speaking, modeless, able to switch focus with little preparation or provocation. Working within the fixed linearity of a computer chip does not come easily to most of us. The modeless interface is a way of interweaving or enfolding human and computer temporalities. We might even claim that not just time but also space gets enfolded, as the linear zero-to-one-dimensional computer process gets arrayed on the flat screen to provide a convincing simulacrum of two-to-three-dimensional availability.[11]

Many of Kay's innovations arise out of a conflict in the interface with spatial and structural dimensions, and in this regard Kay acknowledges the mighty contributions of Engelbart. Engelbart's complementary developments of windows and mouse might stem from a common inspiration, the flat window of the monitor screen. The light pen, used on a regular monitor like a stylus on a touchscreen, was very handy for certain tasks but was not, in general, an ergonomic input device, especially when paired with a keyboard. Not only did it obstruct visibility of the screen on which the user was "drawing," but it also required an awkward arrangement of the user's body, to write on a monitor positioned vertically at arm's length. Confronting this awkwardness, Engelbart recognized that in the digital domain even place could be dislocated and re-placed. He virtualized the plane of the monitor screen: the mouse is the light pen moved to a more ergonomic plane, one that mirrors the monitor but is no longer coincident with it.

This relocation of the plane of input might have generated considerable anxiety, as it explicitly disconnects eye and hand. Could it have seemed intuitive to place fine input control over graphical elements onto a plane perpendicular to the plane of action, out of the central visual field, and, most of all, completely out of touch with the objects being manipulated? As argued above, however, the disconnect between eye and hand was already there, even with the light pen, as the mediation of the computer and screen already dominates this apparent direct contact.

Kay effected a similar deterritorialization on Engelbart's other major contribution to the GUI, the window. Confronted with the problem of limited monitor space, Kay recognized that windows, already understood as independent virtual spaces, could be stacked in overlapping planes, with the frontmost window remaining visible and hiding those behind it. (Codices have employed a similar principle for centuries, but the screen both technically and phenomenally acts like a single sheet and so did not readily lend itself to a virtual layering of planes.) The now-conventional GUI element of stacked windows met with resistance when first suggested, as some Xerox PARC researchers believed that users would be too confused by obstructed or partially obstructed information. This worry may have seemed more pressing because visible borders were then only just being introduced to windowing systems, so the visual clarity of frames around windows could not be taken for granted. In any case, Kay's proposal creates a false depth within the plane of the monitor, and thus opens the virtual third dimension in which windows are stacked.

This is not the virtual third dimension of Albertian perspective; the planar area of a window does not shrink as it recedes into the virtual depth of the monitor screen. There is no vanishing point, hence no simulated visual or spatial depth. Rather, the plane containing each window is infinitely thin, and they are all stacked within a single infinitely thin plane. They cover each other but they never stack up to a thickness in depth, somewhat akin to the pages of a codex (which combine to make a thick volume but do not recede to a vanishing point). The shadows and other edge effects that decorate windows in modern operating systems are thus unmotivated and even inappropriate according to the visual logic of window depth.

Modelessness does not require windows or a mouse, but it does complement them. The mouse allows for nonlinear *random* access, making it easy to choose from among many simultaneously presented alternatives. Windows visually indicate the latent condition of an inactive process, a document or object that may not be the focus of user attention but could come into focus with a simple click. Windows and mouse set the stage for an amodal operating system, but modes continued to undergird lots of individual elements of software design. Kay addresses one such nagging problem in another remarkable innovation.[12] He describes his solution to the problem of modality in a text editor (word processor).

> The most difficult area to get to be modeless was a very tiny one, that of elementary text editing. How to get rid of "insert" and "replace" modes that had plagued a decade of editors? . . . Over a weekend I built a sample paragraph editor whose main simplification was that it eliminated the distinction between insert, replace, and delete by allowing selections to extend *between* the characters. Thus, there could be a zero-width selection, and thus every operation could be a replace. "Insert" meant replace the zero-width selection. "Delete" meant replace the selection with a zero-width string of characters. (Kay 2001, p. 130)

Prior to this zero-width selection technique, text editing required that a user first switch the computer into a mode suitable for her next operation: inserting, replacing, or deleting. Kay's trick is to make each of these operations digitally equivalent by programming the editor so that when the user has no text selected, the computer, nevertheless, "has" a selection consisting of the nonspace, the boundary between characters where the cursor is currently positioned. Instead of a selection of a few contiguous characters or a single character, such as a space or a letter, the selection has a width of zero. As Kay explains, this allows for each of the three operations to work the same way: whatever is next typed replaces the selection (and if a backspace or delete is typed, this replaces the current selection with a zero-width selection).

The zero-width selection provides an archetype of virtualization. In order to connect the digital and human domains, the interface posits a strange nonentity, a purely digital or virtual object, a selection that consists of nothing. (Note that this is also the archetype of the icon, an entity that stands for something that is not exactly there.) It is the introduction of this contrivance, this digital thing that corresponds to no actual or human thing, that makes possible the most natural or human interaction with the text editor. From the perspective of the digital, a selection of zero characters is just as valid as a selection of one or twenty-one characters. The same rules apply, the same operations can be conducted, the same algorithms, the same code can manipulate this virtual object.[13]

Due to Kay, the letter is now well and truly purloined. The zero-width selection comprises a letter that is not there, a letter whose content is only the pure possibility of being filled in by text that the user has yet to enter. The text editor attains modelessness by virtue of a digital object whose only reference is to itself, an absent letter, not missing from its place for it is an abstraction that defies the sticky demands of the material letter that must always be somewhere. It is not a letter missing from its place but a place that has only a missing letter. (The digital is often compared to spoken or written language or to the alphabet, and though they all share a crucial quality of abstraction, the digital intensifies this quality much further to divorce itself altogether from the particularity of the material.) Not (yet) filled in, this zero-degree selection could (but does not) have any of a number of predetermined values; its value is to not be any of those values, but to be ready to become any of them. This noncommittal readiness is the heart of modelessness.

The zero-width selection may seem like an odd contortion, a *kludge*, as programmers would say, but this virtual shadow in the real typifies the workings of the digital. The simplest difference between 0 and 1 determines the ontological modality of the digital, yet this difference has no content: it is effectively missing from its place. Every bit has its determinate value, 0 or 1, but the meaning of that value is only that it might have been its other. *Might have been* is in this case substantive, not an idle counterfactual. A 0 asserts nothing more than not-1 and so also asserts could-be-1. Thus the zero-width selection, which also operates by virtue of what it might be or could be, reproduces the fundamental dynamics of the binary at a higher level of interactivity: the ontological mode of the digital is precisely the might be, pure possibility rendered materially effective in the technology.

The might be, the defining character of the bit, casts the digital as a technology of material abstraction. That is, by reducing all difference to the difference between 0 and 1, the digital captures a manifold world including the processes that manipulate it. But only because 0 and 1 carry with them the subjunctive modality of the binary, the abstraction of the digital always includes its pure possibility. This is not a merely metaphysical claim about the digital, an undetectable fact operating behind the scenes; rather, the might be thoroughly infuses the culture of the digital. From its origins, the dominant mood of digital technology has been futural; the digital promises more to come, a world of endless possibility. (Recall the cursive *hello* on the Mac's screen in 1984. It was clearly inadequate, all too digital, but it conveyed a promise about the future of the digital. The digitally rendered humanity of the *hello* and the smiley face icon were the shape of things to come. Moreover, *hello* is usually a promise of more to come, not an end in itself.)

At the intersection of input and output, serving as a primary mediating element, we discover the icon. The icon defines an area of geometric equipotential, an area within which a click anywhere will mean the same thing. This is its unity or coherence, its object-orientation. Presenting the general availability of a digital object, the icon occupies a continuous planar field, an enclosed shape whose geometric integrity corresponds to the purported coherence of the object it stands for. Frequently, a click anywhere within an icon has a uniform effect. But icons can also be internally differentiated, where a particular part is highlighted, or a click on one part of the icon produces a different result from a click elsewhere within the icon. In general, the meaning of an icon derives in part from these internal differentiations and from the possible visual differences that distinguish an icon from others like it or from the same icon in a different state. (An icon selected looks different from the same icon unselected. An icon representing an alias to a file looks marginally different from an icon representing the original file. An unavailable process or menu item appears dimmed or grayed out, a possibility repealed, deferred, or aborted.) The icon must be read against a field of its possibilities, what it is not. The computer is a machine of possibilities, and the icon tracks those possibilities, relating them to a set of objects and conditions or states of those objects.

The icon reports back the results of alterations to the object, showing both current and possible states. It exists as a collection of similarities and differences, with families of icons potentially common to multiple objects. The icon relates by similarity to a group of other icons that it resembles, which tells the user that it represents a particular kind of document or is associated with a particular application or can perform some particular kind of function. Icons for mathematical operations might have a different visual style than do icons for alphabetic manipulations, for example. An icon is related by difference to every other icon, including even itself. That is, its differences not only distinguish it as the particular icon it is (for one application vs. a different application, or a cut operation vs. a copy operation), but also distinguish its current status.

Its confinement to a vertical plane coincident with the monitor screen gives the icon two sides. On one side, the icon presents information and accepts instructions. On the other (virtual) side, the icon invokes a digital process, to open a file, or change a font, or start a calculation. Thus, the flatness of the icon is no technological limitation, as though the monitor imposed a final constraint on it. The interface may be graphical or visual, but the objects to be manipulated in the computer and the manipulations themselves are digital, formal rather than spatial, abstract rather than material. Some data lend themselves to three-dimensional representation, but there is no inherent connection between data and visuality, so presentation is generally a question of chosen design.

Convention has dealt with icons and other interface abstractions largely in two dimensions, or rather, in planes. Fantasies about a digitized spatiality, a three-dimensional, digitally simulated world, are overstated. The flat icon is actually the easiest way to get to the computer. There may be a number of things that we do with computers that benefit from a representation in three dimensions, but not most things. Simulated three-dimensionality could become wildly popular as a medium on the computer, but the primary computer interface will remain stubbornly two-dimensional—icons, windows, documents, layers, desktops. Some scientists and engineers can work effectively in three dimensions, as can plenty of artists, educators, and businesspeople. Gamers have a field day in a simulated three-dimensional space, and recent technological developments may popularize stereoscopic interfaces that can present to vision three realized dimensions rather than a projection into two dimensions. But as long as information is primarily abstract, textual or structural, its presentation will be best suited to two-dimensional planes. For Kay, two-dimensional representation has the added advantage of a leveling effect, the flattening of hierarchy: "What seemed to be required were states in which there was a transition arrow to every other state. . . . In other words, a much 'flatter' interface seemed called for" (1993, p. 72).

As discussed above, the visual interface follows the logic of the icon throughout. Not just the small images that stand for files and folders, not just the pictograms that populate palettes and toolbars, but every element of the visual interface, from menu items to scroll bars to characters of text, all adhere to an iconic logic. Each object in the interface stands as representative of some nonpresentable version of itself, a binary encoding whose visual presentation is only one face, one aspect. What one sees on the screen is, in principle, generic, iconic, representing a digital artifact that is both more and less than its material analog. It exceeds its material analog in that it includes possibility as part of its way of being, a set of possibilities for how it might otherwise be. But it falls short of its material analog in that it lacks the generative specificity of the material, the creative renewal that is the unique ontological mode of the material world.

> For example, let us look at the concept of icons as interface devices. Icons are designed to be precise and accurate and discrete—on or off. They are designed to present a closed set of possibilities. They are not capable of subtlety, ambiguity or question. An interface of choice and control makes sense for a word processor, an information retrieval system or a game, but not as a metaphor for interactivity or dialogue. (Campbell 2000, p. 133)

From modality to modelessness, from corporate to personal, from expert to novice user, the GUI coalesces at the convergence of many strands of computing progress. Kay's dream was to bring computing to the masses, but at the same time to transform the computer from a rapid calculating machine to a locus of creative expression. The means were to be windows, menus, icons, and a pointing device. Windows and mouse answer to the most general conundrum of interface design: the human and digital domains are at odds, and the interface must negotiate the awkward or uncomfortable juncture of their meeting.

Kay offers a clue to his fantasy of the interface in his insistence on *late-binding*, which is a principle of interface design in which one attempts to maintain a separation between the digital and the interface so that the elements of the interface are allowed to "float" for as a long as possible before being fixed or tied down to a digital code. Kay offers a theory of the history of hardware development, wherein many hardware standards came about as an attempt to incorporate late-binding mechanisms into the operation of the machine. For Kay, late-binding tends over time to incorporate its principle progressively, first as software and eventually in the design of the hardware.

> One way to think about progress in software is that a lot of it has been about finding ways to *late-bind*, then waging campaigns to convince manufacturers

> to build the ideas into hardware. Early hardware had wired programs and parameters; random access memory was a scheme to late-bind them. Looping and indexing used to be done by address modification in storage; index registers were a way to late-bind. Over the years software designers have found ways to late-bind the locations of computations—this led to base/bounds registers, segment relocation, paging MMUs, migratory processes, and so forth. Time-sharing was held back for years because it was "inefficient" but the manufacturers would not put MMUs on the machines, universities had to do it themselves! Recursion late-binds parameters to procedures, but it took years to get even rudimentary stack mechanisms into CPUs. Most machines still have no support for dynamic allocation and garbage collection, and so forth. In short, most hardware designs today are just re-optimizations of moribund architectures.
>
> From the late-binding perspective, OOP can be viewed as a comprehensive technique for late-binding as many things as possible: the *mix* of state and process in a set of behaviors, *where* they are located, *what* they are called, *when* and *why* they are invoked, *which* HW is used, etc., and more subtle, the *strategies* used in the OOP scheme itself. The art of the wrap is the art of the trap. (1993, pp. 87–8)

Each of these technical advances, driven by late-binding, pushes the line dividing actual from digital deeper into the machine, so that human desire pends its conversion to a binary code. Consider the last line: the notion that to get something digital in hand, to wrap it, is to submit it to a late-binding scheme via the *trap*. A trap is a virtual redirection scheme, a process whose instruction to the computer is to look up in a specified memory address another (as yet unspecified) memory address and then begin execution of the code at that new memory address. The code that ultimately gets executed by the trap can thus be easily changed at run-time, since another program (or another part of the same program) can rewrite the trap table, the set of addresses to look up, so that a new and different set of subroutines is invoked by the same code that was previously used to call on the old routines. This double indirection, like the RTTI techniques discussed in Chapter 2, is thus a way of deferring until run-time what might otherwise be decided at compile-time, yielding more control to the user. But as the next chapter suggests, such techniques of indirection and deferral also open the machine to a kind of pure formality, in which the code awaits a content that may never arrive. This perspective paints the interface as a problem, a problem of converting between ontologies that do not always find ready points of contact.

It would be folly to question the need for a user interface. Human beings are not calculators; they do not think or act in the 0s and 1s that constitute the digital domain. But this chapter has argued that the problem of the interface is more intractable than a matter of translation. It is not just about finding a way to make the interface more convenient or appealing or efficient. The gap between digital and human stems from an ontological incommensurability for which there is no natural or correct resolution. Every interface involves its share of compromises, every interface encourages certain choices over others and presents the digital to the human in a particular light. The history of the interface is the story of the ongoing negotiation between digital and human, and the two domains do not invariably approach each other. Individual elements of the interface represent this negotiation in progress, a dynamic compromise that avails the user of some aspects of the computer while hiding or burying other aspects. How to represent abstraction using colors and shapes; how to make available something of the pure possibility of the digital in an icon; how to offer an invitation and a provocation, a learning environment and a productive one; how to stimulate creativity in a context of prescribed choice—these are the challenges whose response is the developing design of the user interface.

4

From the Interface to the Web

Though computers, and microcomputers in particular, had by 1990 already engendered widespread changes in habits of work and leisure, it was the subsequent popular explosion of the internet that cemented computing's ubiquitous influence on culture. The search for "killer apps" continues, propelled by both need and greed, but the easy networking of digital devices may already have been the killer-est app of all, reshaping media, knowledge production, textuality, and altering not only the means of communication but also its pace, its purposes, and its participants.

David Jay Bolter and Richard Grusin identify two tendencies that have a share in all media but achieve a degree of intensity in new media, driving the advance of computing and fueling the internet revolution. Writing a sort of primer for students of new media, Bolter and Grusin in *Remediation* (1999) trace two simultaneous and loosely opposed characteristics of new media. On one hand, new media answer to the fantasy of immediacy, wherein one wishes to get the interface out of the way and to remove all reminders that one is interacting with a machine. This would be an immediate experience, one unmediated by screens, keyboards, and mice, or, at least, it would be an experience in which these trappings of technology become so peripheral as to disappear from consciousness. On the other hand, new media introduce an extraordinary range of new possible manipulations of digital information and objects, and provide such a ready and constant stream of possibilities that one wishes to have everything available all at once, leading to a layered and aggregated presentation of possible action, in which diverse streams of data and other representations coexist alongside icons and widgets and menus and more, offering in its plenitude the very idea of the simultaneous availability of (nearly) everything: hypermediacy. As Bolter and Grusin discuss, there is a tension between these two tendencies, as the drive to immediacy attempts to diminish or remove the interface while hypermediacy adds buttons, windows, and layers that offer powerful choice but also serve as reminders that one is using a machine and a designed interface that stands between user and machine.

> Binary coded machine instruction once gave way to the mnemonic letter-codes of assembly languages; assembly languages were in turn translated into high-level languages with a syntax resembling that of natural languages. Then arbitrary words were supplanted by the motivated signs of icons on the screen. When machines are enabled to respond to spoken commands, the keyboard will become superfluous. Next to go will be the screen and the sight of the machine: visual displays should occupy the entire field of the user's vision, rather than forming a world-within-the-world, separated from reality by the frame of the monitor. Last but not least, language itself must disappear, at least in those areas where it can be more efficiently replaced by physical actions. (Ryan 1994, §8)

In this quotation, Marie-Laure Ryan peers down one path of computing's future, toward the highly popular and universally recognized fantasy of computer teleology, *virtual reality* (VR). The primary aim of VR is to provide a world for the user to experience, a reality in the virtual, filling her sensorium with rich stimulation to engender a sense of her own presence within the digital. As Coelho et al. put it in their discussion of virtual reality, "The definition of presence [is] the *perceptual illusion of non-mediation* produced by means of the disappearance of the medium from the conscious attention of the subject" (2006, p. 28), which Ryan calls the "virtual reality effect." The development of VR progresses by *removing the interface* piece by piece, leaving nothing to mediate between user and computer, thus affording the user an *immediate* experience of the virtual world. Manovich confirms the desire to eliminate the interface: "When we use computers as a general-purpose medium for simulation, we want this medium to be completely 'transparent'" (2013, p. 70). This immediacy of VR renders the user present to/in the machine. Ryan notes that the user's sense of presence depends on the credible response of the virtual world to her actions. If the virtual world did not respond, at least somewhat predictably, to the user's pokes and prods (or clicks and keystrokes), she would lose a sense of the virtual world's reality and fail to feel suitably enmeshed in it. Ryan concludes that VR must strike a balance between contingency and predictability; virtual worlds have to be surprising enough to captivate the user's interest but not so surprising as to stop making sense.

The very immediacy that makes (the fantasy of) VR such an immersive and, thus, extraordinary experience also carries a hint of the ominous. Once the computer is capable of providing a plenary reality, human beings will be confronted full force with worries about the authenticity of their experiences and with the metaphysical issues that accompany such worries.[1] When the computer can fully simulate the real, how will we know for sure of any given experience that it is real or authentic? Films like *The Matrix* and *eXistenZ* most explicitly depict this fantastical threat of VR, but examples abound, and one can scarcely find a VR fiction that does not engage at some level with this question. "Meanwhile, computer graphics experts, computer users, and the vast audiences for popular film and television continue to assume that unmediated presentation is the ultimate goal of visual representation and to believe that technological progress toward that goal is being made" (Bolter and Grusin 1999, p. 30). They thus acknowledge the cultural currency of virtual reality, which they describe as "the paradigm for the computer as a graphics engine," and "a label for the digital revolution" (p. 161).

Despite its inherent immediacy, and despite the importance of some measure of interactivity for effective simulation, virtual reality nevertheless prolongs the traditional medial schema: a designer/programmer fashions a virtual world that is then experienced by a user, whose role is relatively passive and not fundamentally creative or constitutive. Though the desire for increasing immersion and verisimilitude surely drives the development and adoption of digital technologies, VR's emphasis on the passivity of the user should signal its inadequacy as an authoritative account of the future history of computing. For the digital, though masterful at simulation, is first and foremost a workshop, *a set of tools for the realization of its users' desires*. The telos of the fantasy of VR—the perfection of immersive simulation—elides the digital's more significant function as canvas or workshop. Ryan, like other media theorists, understates the import of interactivity for computing, subjugating it to the computer's power of simulation rather than recognizing interactivity as the computer's defining characteristic. A *fantasy of intuition*—that emphasizes not only the elimination of the interface but also the increasingly intuitive accommodation of the user's desires—would better reflect the essential dream of the digital's future. Immersive environments are great for showing off the technical potency of the digital, but hardly are they ideally suited to the main work of computers, which is to save labor and aid in creative endeavors. Only with an eye to this less celebrated fantasy of computing's future can we understand the force of hypermediacy, which is propped up by the desire for digital ability and not digital immersion.

Thus, immediacy as a concept must be more carefully analyzed to yield the most salient predictions about the future of the computer. Part of this future involves a progressive erosion of the interface to produce the most natural or intuitive user experience; a sufficiently *intuitive interface* would encourage an immersive experience such that the user might forget that she is working in an artificial medium. But a more important dimension of the progress of immediacy is an ever-closer meld with the desires of the user; an *intuition machine* would anticipate or articulate the user's desires. Of course, this is itself quite complex, since the desires the user wishes to express/fulfill may well be influenced or even defined by the software and hardware. One does not approach the computer with a predigital desire but with a desire already preformed by one's sense of the possibilities and projects suitable to computers. In this sense, the computer is like a musical instrument: one sits at the cello with a nonspecific desire to do the sorts of things that cellos can do, although there is also always a leading edge; that is, part of the desire is always about extending the reach of the cello, making it do something, possibly something very subtle, that has not been done before. The greatest artists work at this liminal surface, pushing the instrument beyond its established possibilities. *Technique* is the name given to the ability to utilize existing possibilities, but it is primarily on the basis of technique that one exceeds technique, performs not so much the impossible but the parapossible. According to the fantasy of intuition, the ideal computer would expose the parapossible, negotiate a contact with the leading edge of what the computer might do.

The analogy with musical instruments highlights some of the current deficits of digital machines. To engage with an instrument is to draw on forces that are not fully within one's conscious control, to make a new body out of the encounter between human and instrument bodies. One coaxes sound out of the instrument according to an immediacy that leaves no room for articulated desire; the musician in tandem with her instrument must *discover* what comes next, her fingers, her ears, her affective condition propelling the music forward faster or finer than consciousness can keep pace. But this fine edge can rarely be found in digital machines, whose discrete logic requires an articulated input, one which could, in principle, be made conscious. Technique on a computer never exceeds its positive description as keystrokes and mouse movements, such that the actions of even the fastest-twitch gamer are amenable to a full accounting. (Indeed, such actions are necessarily accounted in the sense that every action of significance to the digital system is at some point rendered as a particular numerical value moving through the machine at a specifiable moment of digital clock time.) If intuition is precisely the body and the unconscious running ahead of consciousness, computing machines thus far seem like poor catalysts for its cultivation.

The two dimensions of the fantasy of intuition are somewhat at odds with each other. We would expect an intuitive interface to be so straightforward that one could use it perfectly in a first encounter. It would respond in just the way one expects it to without requiring any experience or knowledge on the part of the user. But an interface that supplements the user's intuition, such as a musical instrument, tends to demand from that user a significant training, as the tools for the realization of desire can be quite complex. (Think of the vast expertise required for the proficient use of Photoshop, for instance.) With extensive experience, mastery of these tools leads to a sense of immersion in which hypermediacy is no longer characteristic of the user's experience of the technology, even if someone watching over her shoulder might find the various keystrokes and menu options counterintuitive and baffling. In other words, hypermediacy comes to be experienced as immersive and immediate when the tools become sufficiently familiar. As Bolter and Grusin hint, hypermediacy and immediacy are superficial features of the interface and their distinction begins to blur when the focus shifts to the experience of the user rather than the appearance of the screen.

In virtual reality, the user is invited to experience the simulated world as present, become "as if" present to the user. The user's body is made to feel as though it is absorbed by the machine, which, in its holism, substitutes for the world or becomes the world of the body. The converse characterizes the fantasy of intuition: the most intuitive interface allows the user to extend her presence into the machine. Or, rather, she comes to experience her desire as immediately present (in the machine) and its realization as proximal, a minimal gap (the single click?) between desire and its fulfillment. The machinic system is integrated into a system of desire that is primarily mental and relatively disembodied; the features of the interface come to constitute not a shell for a pseudo-embodied subjectivity but elements of a libidinous world whose center is in the autonomous subject. (Or rather, its center is in the knot of desire around that user.) While VR typifies the traditional medial schema and places the user in a world not of her own making, intuition calls forth the user's creativity, inviting her to make her own experience, to exploit the computer as a creative tool rather than a preformed expression of someone else's creativity.

If in the cultural imaginary VR remains the promise at the end of the digital rainbow, this no doubt serves the interests of existing corporate institutions. VR places users in the role of (relatively) passive receivers of content that would be provided by, presumably, Hollywood studios (or a suitable successor). These same institutions allied with the high-tech industry work hard to hide the continuity of this structure, insisting, instead, that VR is a radical break from previous media modes. Images of VR are presented as liberatory, since one can choose to be anywhere at all, live any life whatsoever. The emphasis on a plenary sensory stimulation masks the concomitant restriction on creativity; with your senses full, you will not feel any need to express yourself! And that is a good thing, since in VR one's range of possible responses is determined by the authors of the software and the limitations of the engine, not by one's own reservoir of creativity. Passive wonderment substitutes for creative desire. This also explains the rhetorical emphasis on forgetting in VR, where a successful implementation is one that encourages the user to forget that she works at a machine. (As many theorists have remarked, in most implementations of VR, the restrictive nature of the experience is legible in the many wires hemming in the user's motion, the allowed rate of movement, the disconnect between proprioception and virtual motion, etc.) In the fantasy of intuition, by contrast, the user is burdened with responsibility, forced to learn the ways of the machine, and this feels restrictive and laborious but the reward is a genuine opportunity of expression. No wonder that most people opt for the former relationship to the machine since it claims in part to represent the latter.

Consider the word processor. This software/hardware system is only loosely based on the simulation of a typewriter; its interface is driven not by the dream of an immersive virtual typewriting experience but by the need to manipulate text. Undoubtedly, there are plenty of assumptions built into word processing software about how it will be used, such as the general bias in favor of prose over poetry, the typographical and lexicographical preferences that reflect mainstream printing practices in book and magazine publishing, etc. And while some of these assumptions are holdovers from the simulation project whose end point is a fully virtual reality, for the most part they are driven by function and not by the arbitrary desire to mimic a predigital writing experience.

Authors do not so much need an immersive environment to help them compose and edit texts. Rather, what helps an author is software that abets the writing process. Today, software flags and corrects misspellings, cites violations of rules of grammar, allows the recall of previous versions of a document, evaluates style through a statistical analysis of the sophistication of vocabulary, and even summarizes documents by attempting to elucidate their key points.[2] Following the fantasy of intuition, future word processors will assume even more of the labor of writing, modifying or generating style for a specified audience, expanding ideas, linking terms to definitions and other reference materials, strictly enforcing rules of grammar, typography, and even semantics according to criteria chosen by the author, and more. As a writing instrument, the computer should not simulate an idealized writing environment but should partner in the writing process, the computer as intuitive ghostwriter assistant.

Subsuming the fantasy of virtual reality under the fantasy of intuition, we must recast Bolter and Grusin's description of immediacy as a tendency of computer development. They describe a progressive elimination of the interface that eventually places the user in "the presence of the thing represented" (2000, p. 6), which is indeed the aim of VR, an unadulterated simulation of presence. However, given the more central role of the computer as a tool for the realization of the user's desires, it would be more accurate to aim not for virtual reality but for a *real virtuality*: not the presence of the thing represented but the presence of the user to the thing, "extensions of the user's will and purposes, shaped from and embedded in the stuff of the computer" (Kay 1999, p. 134). We do not need computer-based documents to appear more real, and we certainly do not want to go through the simulated motions of threading sheets of paper into a virtual typewriter; what we want from the computer is the most powerful means of manipulating documents, a far-reaching extension of the user's will into the machine, so that her very intuition guides the creative processes that take place on the computer while the interface anticipates and fulfills her desires.

Though virtual reality has largely captured the popular imagination as a story of the history and future history of computing, the broader fantasy of intuition does not lack for prophets. Vannevar Bush's memex—often cited as a remarkably foresighted conceptualization of the World Wide Web—is not a prescient fantasy about immersion in a virtual reality. Rather, it is a fantasy of ready access to a vast store of information, wherein the computing device takes over the roles of memory and association that must otherwise be performed by the user. "The process of tying two items together is the important thing" (Bush 1945, §7). Indeed, Bush proposes quite explicitly that we allow the computer to do more of the thinking for us.[3] This proposal—that the computer take over the labor of thought—signals that the anxieties that attend virtual reality in the popular imagination should not disappear when the focus shifts to an intuitive interface. In modifying the fantasy of VR to give interactivity its proper and more prominent place, we have not forestalled the threat that lurks at the extremes of this dream of computing's future. Sandy Baldwin's incisive critique of Microsoft Word (2002) notes with dismay that Bush's wish has in part come true, with potentially deleterious effects on what is called thinking. For as Word software does more of the thinking, the space for creative human thought becomes more narrowly circumscribed, and there arises a troubling question about whether there is room to think at all.

Correcting the fantasy to reflect accurately the nature of the computer as a tool for the realization of desire changes the threat but does not eliminate it. Even without simulating reality, a computer that anticipates the desires of its user threatens the subjectivity or integrity of that user. If Amazon can decide what your next music purchase should be, or if Netflix tells you which films you are likely to enjoy, where is the room for the accident that is crucial to the creative development of aesthetic sensibility? If the computer ghostwrites one's essay or novel, what has happened to authorship? If the computer responds to intuition without an intermediate corporeal effort by the user, does this leave room for one to have an original intuition, or has the determinacy of a binary logic replaced the contingency of human thought and action? A user absorbed in a VR simulation still maintains her individuality even if the response of the world to her actions has been determined in advance by digital algorithms; a user who cedes her decision making to a computer is harder to locate as an individual, as she has effectively melded her identity with those algorithms. The threat of absorption into the machine informs fictional accounts of the computer's future, but these accounts are necessarily more subtle and confused than those surrounding the shared fantasy of VR where the relative passivity of the user makes the nightmare scenario an easy target for fictional depiction. If immediacy brings with it its own threat of absorption, we should look again at the World Wide Web to examine whether its insistence on mediacy shelters it from the loss of creativity and freedom wrought by the immediate. Can mediacy temper the threat of the immediate, to negotiate the right measure of intuitive responsiveness without denying the user her own creative input?

Befitting its claim to mediacy, Web 1.0 eschews the headlong rush toward a transparent interface so characteristic of other digital phenomena; rather than attempting to eliminate the interface as in virtual reality, the Web embraces its interface, the browser. Browsers have changed quite a bit over time, to accommodate alterations in standards for content encoding on the Web, to allow greater customization of the appearance and experience of browsing, and to render more efficient the most common browsing maneuvers; but the basic interface of the browser, including, especially, the strictly windowed display of information, shows little sign of erosion.[4]

Despite the persistence of the browser, the Web—even 1.0—is not immune to the fantasy of immediacy that propels so much of digital culture and technology. Immediacy seizes the Web not via a frontal attack that would simply eliminate the interface (the browser), but via an end-run that recapitulates the interface in a diversity of devices and channels. The Web's particular brand of immediacy is most manifest in the increasing availability of access. No longer restricted to the personal computer, the Web is now available on smart phones, PDAs, handheld gaming systems, electronic readers, and other *personal* devices. Further, even while the browser remains dominant, its functions have been cannibalized and regurgitated piecemeal, to render key information available more immediately and effortlessly: specialized software constantly displays certain time-sensitive data from the Web, such as stock quotes, weather reports, or sports scores, while other software selectively browses and packages specific material like film reviews and search results, or sends a text message when your plane is late or your auction has ended. The dream underlying this diffusion of the Web is a dream of unmediated and fully intuitive access: anytime, anyplace one should be able to retrieve any information. "The compulsion of the virtual is the compulsion to exist *in potentia* on all screens, to be embedded in all programs, and it acquires a magical force: the Siren call of the black box" (Baudrillard 1993, n.p.). In fact, ideally, desire should be adequate to its own fulfillment, so that one should as soon have the information as seek it. (Vannevar Bush might have forecast even this development, though to his credit he restricted his description of an associative universal database of information, the memex, to technologies that were practically realizable even in his pretransistor era.) Wearable computing, universal wireless coverage, a world encrusted with ID chips, ubiquitous computing, all aim toward the goal of immersion, not in a simulated sensorium (VR) but in a sea of data.

Thus, at least one popular account of the topology of the World Wide Web must be amended. The Web has been heralded as a flat space; lacking a center, growing rhizomatically and without imposed architecture, the Web refuses hierarchy, so that each site is equally central, each page can lay claim to a perspective as valid as any other. The Web has no starting point and no inherent order, though there are plenty of local organizations and *ad hoc* impositions of structure. The lack of hierarchy has, it is claimed, significant economic and political consequence. For example, the availability of news from the broadest variety of sources with no official sanction given to one or another source means that audiences can choose whom to trust and can consider perspectives that would never show up in mainstream media. Because the flat organization of the Web implies a sort of populist economics of information, commercial interests that lack the resources to compete against the largest corporations can still find a healthy number of buyers. Moreover, the viral model of marketing, bolstered by the antihierarchical topology of the internet, means that the little guy might even come out on top: may the best product win! The flat Web, it is said, implies a level playing field. Hubert Dreyfus offers a sober account of this hope.

> When information is organized by hyperlinks, however, as it is on the Web, instead of the relation between a class and its members, the organizing principle is simply the interconnectedness of all elements. There are no hierarchies, everything is linked to everything else on a single level. Thus, hyperlinks allow the user to move directly from one data entry to any other, as long as they are related in at least some tenuous fashion. The whole of the Web lies only a few links away from any page. With a hyperlinked database, the user is encouraged to traverse a vast network of information, all of which is equally accessible and none of which is privileged. (Dreyfus 2009, pp. 10–11)

Though these claims about the social and political implications of Web topology may have real merit, it is mistaken to describe the organization of the Web as an "infinite flat surface" (Manovich 2001, p. 76).[5] Lacking an architectonic structure, the Web's particular fantasy of immediacy implies a topology best described not as flat, but as a *black hole*: each point next to each other point, any page on the Web but a single click away, the maximum density of information. The image of a flat surface encourages the imposition of a metric on the space, a measure of distance that describes some points as closer and others as farther away. By contrast, the black hole distorts space and defies an overarching metric, allowing local and provisional measures of distance but ultimately insisting that any point might be proximal to any other. "The sudden generalization of communication into a single diagrammatic media produces a concomitant effect of the immediacy of every point of the world to every other point" (Baldwin 1996, n.p.).[6]

With most points equally distant, the problem is not how to get to a given page but how to find the right ones. At its extreme, the dream of the intuitive interface implies an immediate access to information, such that the desire to know something would without effort call to mind its desideratum. Though this dream is driven by immediacy, it is not the typical fantasy of the virtual, for the black hole collapses the simulated space of VR. Rather, on the Web we dream of incorporating the machine into ourselves, making it part of consciousness. To swallow the machine not only keeps it always close but also eliminates the interface. (As we will see below, the dream of integrating the machine such that it becomes equal to one's will is the driving force behind Web 2.0.) The transition from the fantasy of the virtual to that of intuition alters the corollary threat: taken to its fantastic limit in fiction, VR usually threatens to overwhelm its users. By contrast, at the limit of the fantasy of intuition on the Web, desire equals its fulfillment, so that the user herself becomes part of the flow of information: information as knowledge, information as memory. The black hole crushes into indistinction anyone caught in its orbit, flattening the division between user and data. The interface is thus replaced by intellection, at least according to this dream of internet immediacy. (Ryan [1994, §8] too calls forth this equivocation of desire and its fulfillment, describing the future [absence of] interface as a "language of the angels," in which it is enough to think something that it become real.) In this fantasy we see the result of the collapse of the medial chain, where a total interactivity dissolves the distinction not only between author and audience but even between audience and content. Floating in a sea of data, the user has simply become those data, their availability part of her consciousness or memory.[7]

This end point should seem farfetched, even improbable, but the Web beckons to this fantasy of intuition.[8] The unification of all information, the elimination of division among dataspaces, the database of databases, the desire to index everything, the increasing inclusion and proposed standardization of metadata, the heads-up display of contextually appropriate information, even the banality of the push delivery of sports scores through cell phones—these are the policies and products of the age of universal availability. "The dream is an old one: to have in one place all knowledge, past and present. All books, all documents, all conceptual works, in all languages" (Kelly 2006, n.p.). If the dream of the digital is to eliminate the interface, to make the user's desire equivalent to its realization, then on the Web, this dream amounts to the elimination of the subject, who simply *has* the data, without having to wrestle an interface in order to get it. One must sacrifice only one's self to become all-seeing and all-knowing. (Absorbing data into oneself also means becoming data to some extent, and indignation over being "targeted" by marketers and surveilled by governments or other security organizations constitutes the loudest protest against the growing pervasion of the World Wide Web. Caviglione and Coccoli affirm that

> The aggressive integration of user-generated content and canonical webpages allows Web 2.0 to be pervasive and inescapable. As a result, users can be tracked web-wide, and their interests acquired via *ad hoc* plugins, such as the Facebook Like button, and Google +1. Under the facade of a constant collective experience, the risk of meticulous and non-stop user profiling is more than real. (2011, p. 17)

The diminutive *single click* turns out once again to be crucial, for it sustains the user as (unique) subject and so also the Web as medium. Choosing not to click, the subject staves off the collapse of the Web into itself and the collapse of the subject into the Web. A minimal resistance, the quantum unit (one bit) of information, the single click (or rather, the option to withhold that click) holds at bay the entirety of the World Wide Web, placing just this page before the user and not the others. Absent the click, the Web would effectively collapse into itself, the user would no longer be separate from the data and would drown in those data, user and data dissolving into the *formless* digital that makes no distinction without a subject.[9] Choosing not to click, or choosing to click here and not here, the user defines her unique perspective on the World Wide Web, establishes her own experience as limited and tied to a place and time.

The single click, therefore, defines the subject as a subject; it represents her sole power not only to choose which page appears before her, but also to separate herself from the mass of data that is the black hole of the World Wide Web. Maintaining her subjectivity—as the one who stands above and apart from the Web and also as the one who chooses which particular page will be viewed—the single click renders the Web a medium, for only as what stands *between* the subject and the data is the Web medial. The browser, even as it breaks apart and reconstitutes itself within Web 2.0, remains the symptom of the Web's mediacy, the software that accepts and directs the single click. (While push delivery of information to computers and personal devices circumvents the single click, users must be very choosy about which feeds to display. Push delivery only works for a few choice bits of information before it becomes overwhelming; relinquishing the power of the click, we teeter on the brink of the black hole.)

The space of information has previously been compared to a black hole, though with a very different resonance. Martin Rosenberg (1994) describes hyperlinks as black holes, passages from one page to another. Even while employing the figure of the black hole, Rosenberg cautions against the uncritical appropriation of new physics as a revolutionary discourse, noting that such borrowings from science fail to recognize the ways in which science, even when tied to nonlinear or discontinuous functions, still imposes a stable geometry on its objects of study, denying them the truly dynamic character that a revolutionary theory would seem to require. In this regard, he privileges the moment of passage through the hyperlink (what I have called the single click) as the sole possibility of a disorientation severe enough to count as a revolutionary destabilization, but he warns that this moment is too fleeting, and that the reader soon reorients herself in the new space.[10] Readers are momentarily uprooted from normal consciousness when they click on a link, but soon reestablish a stable perspective in relation to the new page that comes up. Though provocative, this view of the Web is dated, reflecting the excited sense of potential that surrounded the notion of hyperlinks at the end of the last century. Linking, which was only a marginally revolutionary possibility even in Rosenberg's account, has now become simply a normal experience and no longer destabilizes the reader. Moreover, one effect of the rise of digital textuality has been to reveal the traditional linear model of text (and reading) as a cultural norm rather than a natural attitude. Clicking a link could only be destabilizing for a reader who expects each word to follow the previous one without interruption, a model that page-turning in a traditional codex already undermines. The black hole does not represent the possibility of escape from the banality of linear text but only the promise of a total availability of information, which is also the threat of a total absorption into the machine.

Though the hyperlink may not destabilize the reading process on the World Wide Web, it does both promote and defer the fantasy of the Web as black hole. As the clickable passage from page to page, the hyperlink represents the immediate proximity of every linked page, the tie that binds. In this spirit, Manovich (2001, p. 172) cites Paul Virilio: "At least in principle, every point on earth is now instantly accessible from any other point on earth." But inasmuch as each page contains only certain links and not others, the reality of the hyperlink (as opposed to its fantasy) is to render only a tiny subset of the Web immediately available. The logical space of the World Wide Web consists of numerous organizations or perspectives, wherein each page brings near some part of the Web and places more distant the rest.[11] Just as the resistance of the single click makes the user a subject and the Web a medium, so each page constitutes a unique perspective on the Web, an organizational overview of the information space, (literally) underlining some pages and leaving most of the space of the Web to hover implicitly in the background.[12]

This role of the hyperlink as structuring element gives meaning to the claim that the Web is a metamedium. Certainly the Web mediates other media, and certainly the Web has brought about the creation of new genres and even new media. But its most essential function, its most consistent purpose across its many genres is to organize information, to present other media and other Web pages as more or less distant from the subject. To construct a page on the Web is to create a perspective, to privilege selected content and encourage ready access to particular information, to thrust forth and even forge certain relationships.

This suggests a new reason for applying Kay's neologism *metamedium* to the World Wide Web[13]: the Web is a metamedium in the sense that it is *a medium for the organization or structuring of information*, a medium for providing diverse perspectives on a vast and unwieldy mass of information. "This may imply that new digital rhetoric may have less to do with arranging information in a particular order and more to do simply with selecting what is included and what is not included in the total corpus presented" (Manovich 2001, p. 78, fn. 13). *Meta-* here indicates the shift from an emphasis on content proper to an emphasis on its structure or organization. Inasmuch as each page offers a perspective on the entire Web, the Web pushes content into the background, privileging instead the presentation of structure or form. A Web page organizes information into a hierarchy of near and distant, and its metamedial function is precisely the presentation of this hierarchy. Each page is effectively an index to the entirety of the Web, but it is a critical index whose meaning derives from the choices of what to frontload and what to leave in the background.

This metamedial charge of the World Wide Web prompts its past and current development. To promote the role of the Web as organizer of information, technical standards increasingly mandate the separation of form from content, effectively allowing the independent analysis and manipulation of the perspective itself, regardless of what content it provides a perspective on. Cascading style sheets (CSS) explicitly divorce the appearance of information from its content, and more fundamentally treat appearance in terms of structural characteristics. That is, a given object on a Web page (paragraph, image, sound, etc.) is labeled in terms of its structural properties, placed within a hierarchy that records its functional relationships independently of its actual content. By analyzing CSS, one can read something about the structure of a Web page without attending to the specific content of the text or other elements on the page. Alan Liu puts it in terms of *data pours*, which hide the data on a given page from the coder but present it to the user as level with other data on the page; such organizational techniques of deferral of content "open the prospect of a new model of authoring predicated on technologies enforcing ever more immaculate separation of content from presentation" (2004, p. 62).

CSS, which has been widely adopted across the Web and incorporated into all recent Web design software, is only one prominent example of the push toward foregrounding structure as the Web's *modus operandi*. More broadly, HTML is slowly being superseded by XHTML, which latter standard is based on the greater flexibility and syntactical rigidity of XML, and this also means increasing facility in treating structure without regard to content. (One could gloss XML as a system for formalizing content so that it becomes encodable as structure.) The incorporation of metadata into the underlying code for Web pages similarly provides information that describes the structural relations of that page to its outside. Metadata are keywords and other information that do not appear when a page is viewed normally (as in a browser), but that are incorporated into the page code to help identify the nature of its content. The Semantic Web project is one extreme example of this practice, where metadata provide information, for example, about the relationships among terms on the page and not just the appearance of those terms. Even the Document Object Model (DOM) instituted early in the life of HTML (and manipulable using JavaScript) furthers this goal, encapsulating each element on a Web page (as well as the page itself) under a single name, so that its relationships to other elements come into sharper focus.

Liu (2004) identifies this push to separate form from content as the driving force behind the progress of networking technologies. Though he acknowledges the extraordinary power of this approach—which allows a reader (or, as Liu underlines, a machine) to gain a perspective on information independently of the information itself—he also notes a sinister dimension to this trend. Given the Web's power to manipulate perspective, content is increasingly deemphasized to the point "where an author in effect *surrenders the act of writing* to that of parameterization" (p. 59, my emphasis); content comes to fall "outside the normal play or (as we now say) networking of discourse" (p. 60). The desire to rein in an unruly overload of information (the World Wide Web) through technical measures that organize that information according to structural categories leads to the abdication of authorship. The Web as metamedium is a tool for creating perspectives on information, but this tends to hypostatize the very idea of a perspective to the detriment of meaningful information itself. The user, focused on establishing perspectives, no longer engages critically with content, entrusting the generation of content to the vastness of hyperspace. "The World Wide Web . . . encourages the creation of texts that consist entirely of pointers to other texts that are already on the Web. One does not have to add any original writing; it is enough to select from what already exists" (Manovich 2001, p. 127). Once again, the fantasy of intuition—already intruding upon reality in this case—cuts both ways, providing a more efficient access to just those data the user desires while in the same stroke eliminating the singularity of authorship by yielding authorial responsibility to the network. To cast the Web as a metamedium is to void the medium in favor of the *meta-*; for all its massive gravity, the black hole, at its limit, turns out to contain nothing.

Two brief examples, search spaces and blogs. Search engines use algorithms to filter information. While some of this filtering is based on content, what usually distinguishes one engine from another is how it evaluates structure. That is, a search engine chooses to filter and order its results largely on the basis of noncontentual aspects of the pages being searched, such as how many other pages link to it or how frequently it has been accessed. This privileging of structural features was the great innovation of Google and the primary mechanism of Google's PageRank algorithm. Search engines thus provide perspectives on information by analyzing perspectives on information, doubly earning the prefix *meta-*.

Blogs are as often as not about the act of blogging, a reflexivity that demonstrates explicitly the way in which content disappears in favor of the analysis of form. "It is noteworthy that many of the A-list bloggers are particularly known for their interest in blogging as a topic of inquiry and comment" (O'Baoill 2004). This may be less true a decade after O'Baoill's remark, but blogging remains a prime example of a certain self-conscious disclosure, a way of performing and so creating culture. Moreover, the genre of the blog nearly mandates that each blog must refer to other blogs, so that the dynamics of the blogosphere are based largely on the interlinking or cross-referencing of various blogs. Bakardjieva and Gaden (2012, p. 406) refer to the "widespread practice of bloggers to post links to and excerpts from media texts," establishing the skeletal schema of a blog entry as just a link to another blog entry. Offering a still more extreme diagnosis, Anna Munster reiterates Geert Lovink's description of "a nihilistic impulse in contemporary online culture, where 'meaning' is erased from media via incessant blogging about 'nothing' (Lovink 2008: 1–38)" (Munster 2011, p. 69).

Web 2.0 coincides authors and readers, producers and users. The collapse of the medial schema makes for a particularly strange form of mediacy, as the equation of author and audience generates a kind of immediacy by default. Self-expression and, thus, also self-recognition become the defining experiences of Web 2.0, such that the Web is both mediate and immediate at the same time. How far does this paradox extend?

Galloway might credit standards, or *protocol* in his terms, for deemphasizing content and promoting, instead, the Web page as placeholder, a canvas on which the user can paint what she will. Standards like TCP, XML, and CSS are neutral with respect to content. By formally separating content from the package that surrounds it, our computers can work with those packages regardless of their content, a protocological agnosticism. Since protocols remain "indifferent to the content of information contained within" them (2004, p. 52), one can *author* a Web page without actually creating any content, just by leveraging available standards. Web 2.0 then appears to be a natural consequence of the ubiquity of standards; mature standards help to vacate content on the Web, so that Web pages start blank and their contents appear eventually to spring up as if from culture at large. "Instead of people being treated as the sources of their own creativity, commercial aggregation and abstraction sites presented anonymized fragments of creativity as products that might have fallen from the sky or been dug up from the ground, obscuring the true sources" (Lanier 2011, loc. 284–6).

The mathematical theory of communication supports this development. The more universal and specific the standards that regulate the passage of information are, the less information any given message contains. Mathematically, information is a measure of how surprising or unanticipated the data that arrive are, while a standard makes the possible data more anticipated. A rigorous standard allows the receiver to predict much about the message to be received. It is as though more and more of the information is itself built into the infrastructure of computing, so that we no longer pass information but just conduct ourselves according to the standard. Inasmuch as Web 2.0 establishes standards on top of standards, templates awaiting completion by users who fill in the blanks, the range of information narrows. To contribute to Web 2.0 is not so much to originate an idea as to adopt an available position.

No wonder that the fantasy of Web 2.0 recasts the nature of authorship. First, the mantle of authorship moves from authorized content-creators to users. Those who formerly provided content now generate forms awaiting contributions, portals that fill with data from other sites, blank slates on which users may inscribe their desires. But even those users mostly defer full-fledged authority, choosing instead to circulate or affirm existing information. Bloggers link compulsively to other blogs, reproducing content or just redirecting readers with any number of gestures that boil down to "Check this out!" YouTube videos bury the author and assert his insignificance as an individual; his role in creating the video is relatively minor compared to that of the many who comment on it ("Sick!" or "Adorable!" or, of course, "LOL"), and who, simply by viewing, promote the video to the point of broad recognition, voting with their clicks. These masses supply Web 2.0 with its content, not only by uploading but by transmitting, by referring, by linking, and by starring in all their banality as the subjects of the videos. The content of the video only confirms its collective authorship, as most YouTube clips are remarkable for their mundanity. YouTube documents ordinary lives, the silly things that anyone might do, the footage that could have been shot in your backyard. A significant portion of the meaning of a YouTube video derives from its claim to everydayness, its status as generic cultural expression. The subjects of these videos are us, just as the directors and the viewers are also us. Collectively, we must be the authors of these videos, for they claim to represent and define us. Jaron Lanier again:

> If the books in the cloud are accessed via user interfaces that encourage mashups of fragments that obscure the context and authorship of each fragment, there will be only one book. This is what happens today with a lot of content; often you don't know where a quoted fragment from a news story came from, who wrote a comment, or who shot a video. (2011, loc. 849–51)

Social networking sites provide a particularly indicative case, as such sites are explicitly intended as vehicles for constructing and disseminating self-identity. Bakardjieva and Gaden (2012, p. 404) draw quotations from Anthony Giddens to express the immediate result:

> The reflexive project of the self "consists in the sustaining of coherent, yet continuously revised, biographical narratives" and "takes place in the context of multiple choice as filtered through abstract systems" (p. 5). The more daily life involves a dialectical exchange between the local and the global, the more individuals are "forced to negotiate lifestyle choices among a diversity of options."

They conclude that selfhood becomes not a creative pursuit, but a matter of choice among discrete possibilities:

> The user is invited to perceive and create his or her world of friendships through that technical interface. From this moment on, the technical carrier is going to select and structure the kinds of interactions that constitute friendship. The drop-down menu is going to be the mode through which the self is presented to his or her group of friends; these friends will be counted and quantified in precise ways and the interactions between and among individuals will unfold on a highly visible public stage. Like it or not, the self of the profile holder will be constituted by these different data streams. He or she will be easily compared to others, ranked and placed into categories for different purposes including marketing. In short, the self will continuously expose its thoughts and deeds to the scrutiny and judgment of its network in the hope to achieve not moral guidance, pardon or salvation, but the major reward that this environment offers, the main currency which animates its moral economy: popularity. . . . (p. 410)

YouTube videos seem to become popular by already being popular, an information-age version of the adage about the rich getting richer. There is a strange kind of circularity or bootstrapping underlying Web 2.0, visible in countless examples but best seen in that hallmark of Web culture, the meme. (YouTube is home to many memes.) Memes come from nowhere in particular. They succeed not because they are exceptional but because they are quotidian. We view and enjoy them with a wink, marveling as much at their clumsiness or amateurishness as at their humor or pathos. What we most enjoy in a meme is the bizarre realization that "this is culture," that the meme represents ourselves. Their provenance rarely matters, for they thrive, regardless of where they come from, by virtue of being passed around or referenced. Transmission eclipses content in a meme; a meme is what it is because it gets passed around, affirmed by a collective viewership. Neither the content nor the medium, but participation itself, is the message. Deprecating its banal content, a meme foregrounds its status as meme, inviting viewers to click as the formal acknowledgment of participation. To view a meme is not to appraise its content but to assert its status as representative of culture and to assert one's own status as purveyor of that culture. We pass along a meme because that is what it means to belong to this new Web culture: Web 2.0 is undoubtedly a fetish.

The fantasy is that, with enough participation, content arises from out of culture at large, reflecting our collective beliefs, opinions, and ideas. Each user gets to assent to those expressions that suit her, authorship having disappeared in favor of selection, a menu-driven collective creativity. Individuals are represented just to the extent that they subjugate their individuality to the *zeitgeist*, proclaiming in many voices nothing more than their willing complicity, a common message whose content *is* its commonality. ("I love Big Brother"?) Each contributes to Web 2.0 but only as a generic representative, not an individual but a subject position that rightly claims authorship of the collective expression that is Web 2.0. Caroline Bassett asserts that Web 2.0 "explores participation itself as the motive force that may enable the real and/or final fulfilment of these networks" (2008, n.p.).

From online shoe stores and book stores to recipe sites and film review databases, users chime in with perspectives that are their own, but at the same time, enunciations of culture. That is, Web users feel obliged to speak for themselves precisely because their ideas and opinions are representative, how others will also likely feel. (This is partly why so much discourse on Web 2.0 is me-too-ism. One writes not in order to say something but in order to have one's say.) Writing under generic pseudonyms that express roles more than individuals ("frequentbookbuyer1001" or "iluvvideocameras"), users shoulder the burden they have welcomed, to generate the future by weaving the Web. Each capsule review, each editorial response, each partisan contribution is an assertion of belonging to a collective that owns the products of its self-fulfilling enterprise. The opinion aggregator, from tag clouds to last.fm to Netflix to StumbleUpon, captures the essence of Web 2.0, masking its users' identities behind the collective weight of their approval. One freely offers one's valuable opinions, knowing that they inevitably become the views of the collective. This is not altruistic as much as it is a means of constructing culture and simultaneously constructing oneself as its representative. The Digg is the minimal representative gesture of Web 2.0, the simple thumbs-up that, combined with everyone else's thumbs, constitutes content. If the single click as described above maintains the Web as a medium, the Digg, expressed in a single click, dissolves the individual into the participating collective, the owners of culture. "You won't find editors at Digg—we're here to provide a place where people can collectively determine the value of content and we're changing the way people consume information online" (Digg.com 2008).

The pretzel logic of Web 2.0 finally realizes the immediacy that has been the dream of the digital since its inception, driving its relentless progress. Abdicating content and recasting authorship, Web 2.0 presents itself as a blank page on which each user selects what to foreground, representing her individuality as a matter not of creativity or desire but of perspective. The Web becomes a reflexive nest of perspectives on itself, a simulacrum that severs its ties to the ground of authorship and declares itself equal to culture, from which it arises autochthonously. No gap exists between culture and its expression, no individual can fail to recognize herself in this new Web of perspective since she is, after all, invited to generate there her own perspective, representing her *unique* relationship of collective belonging. Alienation on Web 2.0 is impossible, for there is no individual who could be alienated. The fantasy of intuition returns full force: of course Web 2.0 knows what you want, for Web 2.0 is you. Emptied of content, Web 2.0 expresses only the fact of belonging to culture, the formal declaration of participation that is the collective auto-constitution of culture. When users are producers, when audiences become actors, all the world's a stage and performance equals reality. Web 2.0 achieves immediacy by default, not a reflection of culture but the total of culture, the *zeitgeist* materialized as medium. A strange paradox it is then that this immediacy of Web 2.0 should be so highly mediated. The new Web expresses you just to the extent that you affirm your belonging by embracing a mediated existence. The immediacy of Web 2.0, its claim to be culture, operates only as long as culture itself contains the structure of technological mediation. You are not a member of our culture unless you express yourself and discover yourself on the Web, which is to say, via the computer. The persistence of the browser evinces a residual mediacy, but this mediacy is now a mere formality, an element subsumed under the immediacy of Web 2.0. Finally, the computer knows what you want.

5

Abstraction and its Consequences

From the elemental logical units of computing to the social networks that tie together digital culture, abstraction anchors the operation of the digital. Chapter 1 showed that bits are defined by abstraction and that it is their power of abstraction that allows them to serve as a universal code for the data and instructions that underpin and define digital technologies. In Chapter 2, examination of the basics of programming revealed the abstractions that structure code in order to subject digital objects to digital actions. Chapter 3 studied the interface as a site of abstraction, where three dimensions of motion flatten into Cartesian coordinates, desire flows through the buttons of a keyboard and mouse, and every object becomes iconic. Chapter 4 tracked the priorities of Web 2.0, which favors form over content, choice over indeterminacy, and network over node, each binary selection a promotion of abstraction. The bit's ontology repercusses throughout the digital domain to determine the character of computing from its technical arcana to its cultural concomitants. Lev Manovich calls this mirroring of digital ontology across scales *transcoding* and nominates it as a basic principle of new media, "the projection of the ontology of a computer onto culture itself" (2001, p. 223). Elsewhere Manovich acknowledges the bit-like character of that ontology: "In short, the ontology of computer dataspace as a whole and the individual objects in this space is atomistic on every possible level" (2002, n.p.). And Jaron Lanier decries the implications of this universal atomism for the computer user: "Computers have an unfortunate tendency to present us with binary choices at every level, not just at the lowest one, where the bits are switching" (2011, loc. 1154–6).[1]

If the ontology of the bit suffuses the whole of the digital, this accounts both for the digital's far-reaching power and for its blunt limitations and brittle requirements. As discussed in the first chapter, the bit pushes so far toward abstraction that it largely separates its significance as an operative element of a digital system from its instantiation in a material substrate, driving a wedge between its ideal, logical meaning and its material basis. Thus can bits work (almost) flawlessly at unimaginable speeds over inconceivable numbers of iterations, for they are but little hindered by the inertial resistance of material actuality. But this same detachment from a materiality that would drag the bit back into the world removes the bit to a domain of ideal, formal reality, rendering it perfect but generic, productive but static and without any character of its own. By stripping away resistance, the resistance of difference, abstraction pushes the digital toward a universalism, the treatment of all difference as bits. Can every object and every action accommodate a description as discrete abstraction? This final chapter examines the implications of discrete abstraction more closely. What do the foregoing chapters reveal about the digital and its multiscalar abstraction? More than previous technologies, beyond even the abstraction of language, which remains bound to a concrete form in sound or figure, the digital takes abstraction far enough to realize another ontology, a way of being that follows different rules and confronts different problems from those of the actual.

If the digital and the actual differ ontologically, their encounter necessitates a negotiation of sorts, a working out of the problem of their difference. There are plenty of well-known symptoms of this problematic transport as the digital troubles large social categories; property, money, authorship, media, place, aliveness, knowledge production, and more, all demand reconfiguration and redefinition in the wake of the new digital hegemony. At a more personal scale, the human-computer interface offers plenty of further examples of the necessity of renegotiation across an unfamiliar gap, as one never quite touches what one reaches for on the computer, digital objects lack their own integrity, rich sensation must confine itself to fewer dimensions and pregiven vehicles of expression, and modality is squeezed from the contingency of potential into the mechanism of the possible. Dominating the visual interface, the icon both presents and stands in place of a digital object and its possibilities, shrouding the ontological status of the digital in ambiguity. Digital-to-analog (and analog-to-digital) conversion never quite connects the two sides of the gap that separates what is to be converted, trading space for time or leveraging a mechanism of *induction* between one field and another. Making the world abstract requires a considerable cooperation from the actual, the material, which must offer itself as discretized and generalized in order to be ready for the digital. If something passes from one side to the other, it must cross an *edge*, a digital divide that separates the digital from the actual world, setting it into its own slippery domain of great efficiency by reducing all difference to the single, simple difference of the binary code. The edge is a knot that both disrupts and conjoins digital and actual, a passage between that breaks but at the same time connects our world to the digital, crossing "the profound divide between its materiality and our own" (Hansen 2004, p. 143).

At its core, the ontological split between digital and actual begins with the break between the materiality of the bit and its value. This structure, known familiarly as the *black box*, establishes an opaque housing or container that does not know its contents, separating its inside from its outside.

> That is, the details of how the procedure was implemented could be suppressed, and the particular procedure itself could be replaced by any other procedure with the same overall behavior. In other words, we could make an abstraction that would separate the way the procedure would be used from the details of how the procedure would be implemented in terms of more primitive procedures. (Abelson and Sussman 1996, p. 83)

The black box, which can contain procedures or algorithms just as well as objects or data, casts its shadow over the entire domain of the digital, characterizing the bit and also, the programmer's objects and the icons of the interface. In the digital, things present a public, accessible face, an interface by which they can be queried or instructed, but their interiority remains obscure, reinforcing the vague otherworldliness that sets apart the domain of the digital. An icon is a black box, offering at most a hint of what it captures in its "insides," and that hint is itself only a convention or convenience with no necessary relationship to its actual contents. Portals on the World Wide Web may be drawn in as literal black boxes, rectangular areas of the screen cordoned off by a border that indicates the indirect information housed therein.

In coding contexts, black boxing is often called *encapsulation*. Encapsulation is the name given by programmers to the possibility of referring to a whole structure by a single name or a whole set of actions using a single command. The name or label then stands for the data structure it names, and other algorithms can manipulate that structure (or instruct it to manipulate itself) without knowing anything about its contents. To enclose an object, a set of algorithms, or a group of digital parts within a named container makes it possible to treat that object or group as a simple entity. Other algorithms can make use of that name to *point to* or *reference* the encapsulated object, simply by invoking the name assigned to its capsule. Placing data inside a structured container and then labeling that container (with a name or an index) makes it possible to manipulate data as structure without knowing any particular values. On the plane of the digital, a pointer allows a sender to pass a package to a receiver without seeing what is inside. Internet communications are based on *packetized* data, wherein a sequence of bits is packaged and addressed according to a protocol that delivers the addressed package without regard for what data the package contains. This serves in some ways as the current standard for cultural production, where digital artifacts are constructed from borrowed or referenced or *crawled* information gathered from elsewhere, the *hyperlink* as the model of action, propping up the value of citation, recontextualization, mashups, and remixing. At a technical level, indirect reference makes possible all sorts of computing techniques, from trap tables to sophisticated variable typing. Reference-by-address recapitulates the most rudimentary structure of software, to treat an object by its name or place. The black box undergirds software, encapsulating each program behind its opacity, but at the same time encapsulating the smallest moves on the digital plane behind higher-level program commands.

The very idea of software manifests the principle of encapsulation, each piece of software serving as its own tightly sealed black box. Commercial software often includes licenses that insist on the opacity of this box, denying users the right to decode the machine language instructions that produce the running program in the interface. Kittler marvels cynically at the possibility of typing a single word, even just two characters, to invoke a massive system for coordinating input and output, also known as a piece of software (1997, p. 149). A single word, an executable file, a command—these simples encapsulate the complexity of industrial software, which is often referred to as a software *package*. Like Kittler, Chun notes (with some suspicion) the historical trend toward increasing encapsulation: "In the name of security, structured programming, which emphasizes programming as a question of flow, is itself giving way to data abstraction, which views programming as a question of interrelated objects and hides far more than the machine. Data abstraction depends on information hiding, on the nonreflection of changeable facts in software" (2004, p. 37).

Reiterating the original encapsulation of the bit to separate its value from its material, the encapsulation of software as a package, abstracted from the hardware on which it operates, opens the path to the world now called *virtual*, a cyberspace distinct from real space. The abstraction of software deterritorializes the hardware, hinging the computer at the divide between them. Software, become abstract, is freed to operate on other hardware, but at the same time freed from the matter of its processes. Writing thus takes over from engineering as the verb applicable to software production, but it is a stunted writing, constrained by inflexible rules of syntax and an isomorphic relationship to its "meaning."

Many hardware and software systems interpose additional layers of abstraction between names and their referents in physical memory, such as virtual memory systems or handle-based indexing systems. A named variable that holds the memory address of an object is called a *pointer*. The term *handle* in programming contexts refers to the practice of storing not the memory location of an object, but the memory location of a pointer to the object (which is the memory location of a number that serves as an index to the memory location of the object). Double-indirect referencing intensifies the abstraction of the code, allowing it to operate in more general or less specified contexts. Handles require more overhead, but their excessive abstraction also offers advantages, in that the referenced object can be moved around in memory or otherwise altered without the handle needing to know anything about it. The handle points consistently to the same pointer, which latter must be changed when the object is moved, else the object would be effectively lost in memory, unreachable by its handles.[2] Code using handles is more abstract, more general, less attached to its particular machinic instance.[3]

As Chapter 3 analyzed, the central gesture of the human-computer interface is pointing, designating without touching. The digital, both in the user's intention and in the structure of representation that underlies the interface (input and output), behaves indexically. Users point to something they intend by way of the interface; they *select* from available options laid out flat in two dimensions in order to generate an anticipated outcome. The mouse presents its on-screen visual correspondent as a pointer, sometimes an arrow, sometimes an iconic fist with index finger raised. A simple keystroke or click triggers a multistaged process across various layers of the digital domain, eventually producing a glyph on the screen and a value in one or more memory locations and data stores. The user's reach with a digital tool intends not only the production of that glyph but all of the consequent effects and their associated possibilities. Even a single keystroke thus encapsulates an extended sequence of digital actions.

Corresponding to the pointing (and clicking) action of the user, the interface presents icons to be pointed at and clicked on. The mouse click as a deictic gesture is vital to the useful operation of computers, partly because computers do not do very well with the deictic on their own. Computers operate without context, they do not distinguish between central and peripheral, between the center of attention and its horizon. The computer does not *have* a sense of past or future; it occupies an immediate present, which consists of a perfectly defined (but possibly very large) set of data, the values stored in its memory at that instant.[4] For the computer, attention as such is only a list of numbers, the current values of memory and registers. To move the mouse is only to proceed from one pixel to the next, a value measured by Cartesian coordinates referring to a matrix of screen memory. If the single click, the deictic gesture, is to mean anything, the computer must offer something clickable, something more than a pixel or bit to point to. Corresponding to the single click, supporting the world in which one can indicate by clicking, is the icon. The deictic gesture thus comes from without, and just as the user must constrain her expression to what can be made discrete and abstract, so the interface prepares for the user's commands by offering clearly marked visual indicators of what can be pointed to. The icon thus mirrors the mouse pointer, itself a discrete abstraction that allows the user to indicate *this* rather than that.

Encapsulation gathers a complex into a simple bundle, but this black boxing only provides its great advantage to the digital if the box can be named, referred to, or pointed at. Unsurprisingly, these tools, encapsulation and pointing, are already manifest at the level of the bit. The bit gathers its value inside of itself, always a 0 or a 1, but this value derives its meaning as an element in a sequence of bits, referenced when needed using some form of an index. This is a structure of double articulation, one distinction of value within and one distinction of place without. That these two distinctions are themselves distinct, such that neither reduces to the other, attests to the edge at work even in the simple bit. The asymmetry of the double articulation that constitutes and designates the bit provides a texture, a rough surface that allows the bit to reach beyond itself and ultimately to connect with its outside. Even the intrinsic distinction, 0 or 1, overflows the bit's interiority, in that these binary values must remain consistent not only within a bit but also from one bit to its neighbors; a 0 or 1 must be recognizably the same value when bits are actualized in different substrates or at different times or at different indexes in a sequence. Paired with the relativity of an index, which locates a bit not in absolute memory but relative to some chosen starting point, this identity (and disidentity) of values is mobile, in the sense that groups of bits can be moved, preserving the values of individual bits by preserving their places in the overall sequence. A digital object, made of bits, is therefore neither self-identical nor ever-changing; rather, it has a *mobile* identity, a sameness defined by its parts and their values, such that it can be equal to a copy of itself.

The double articulation that defines the bit also defined the *dividual* in Chapter 2. The bit serves as a prototypical dividual, a bottom line that cannot be further subdivided. Built out of bits, the whole territory of the digital carries forth this dividual structure. Digital abstraction engenders a kind of enframing, a general gathering together of both a category (extrinsic) and its values (intrinsic) to form a dividual. A dividual typically comprises other dividuals, objects defined both extrinsically according to a division and intrinsically according to a character or value. But ontologically, there is no category difference between an object and its parts; neither is more complete, more stable, more finished. Which is to say, the ontology of the digital does not distinguish except as binarity: this is its only tool. The difference between part and whole does not matter anymore than any other difference in the digital code. All of the mattering has to come from without. It is the user who finally affirms the formal coherence of a digital object, whose dividuality is never enough to guarantee that coherence. The dividual thus represents the digital's most concerted attempt to rise above its own formality, to make a difference by multiplying and interlocking its only difference, the simple difference of the bit. Inasmuch as the dividual defines the nature of digital objects as a doubled distinction of inside and outside or quality and value, it helps to spread the ontology of the bit throughout the digital domain.

The designation of internal and external depends on the chosen level of analysis; the inside of a part becomes the outsides of its subparts, as when the color of a part of an object is made of three subparts (*color channels*), each of which encloses bits in a sequence that determines the value for that channel, some magnitude each of red, green, or blue, for instance. But even these bit values that (in sequence) represent the magnitude of each color channel are ultimately given from outside the computer, whether by the programmer as she chooses the background color for an alert window or writes an algorithm to determine it or by the user as he chooses a color for the bow on the *evite* he is sending to his friends. The structure remains intact at the level of the individual bit: it does not spontaneously become one or another value but is assigned a value according to a flow of logic-electricity that can be referred back to an origin in a person outside of the machine. To determine a bit as 0 or 1 is to make a decision about the actual within a given structure; prior to its instantiation, a bit is first a possibility, the possibility of 0-or-1. We will examine further the notion of possibility as the modality of bits and so also of the digital domain.

One further clarification is that both articulations, that of parts and that of values, come in two flavors. Each articulation may be with respect to the particularity of the object being encoded or with respect to a medium or substrate in which that object appears. In the case of the articulation of parts, the parts could be generic elements of a medium, such as the pixels that divide any two-dimensional (visual) space into regular elements and are not, as such, specific to an image. Or the parts could be distinguished and determined (though still conventionally) by the nature of the object, as a database of insects might represent a given species by storing distinguishing characteristics for each of its three body segments, head, thorax, and abdomen. Likewise, the articulation of quality can refer to a quality independent of the object, such as color, or a quality specific to the object, such as a code to record the nature of a relationship between two people, where possibilities include *married*, *friends*, *family members*, *strangers*, *classmates*, etc. This is not a general quality that applies to many kinds of objects but is particular to the kind of data being encoded in this case. (Even in the case of a temporal division, the division may slice time as a background medium, as when sound samples are taken every forty-four thousandth of a second, or it may take its slices from the nature of the object, as when a task is modeled as *assignment*, *acceptance*, *in-progress*, and *complete* phases.)

With the structure of the dividual as the stamp of the digital, difference in the digital comes to have a particular shape. Because the dividual, as the digital's attempt to assert a difference that makes a difference, distinguishes interior from exterior, it tends to build its objects and actions in layers or tiers. The lowest layer is made of individual bits, but these are treated as parts by placing them in a sequence, and then sequences of bits themselves become parts of a more complex data structure. Each aggregation of parts into a larger whole establishes a higher layer, but the whole structure remains a house of cards, held up by the conventions that affirm the structure even as it threatens to fall back into the individuated bits from which it is constructed. Between user and CPU, in the windows and desktops of the interface, in Photoshop, in the digital object, there are stacked layers governed by deterministic interrelationships. Source code becomes executable code through a series of temporal layers, as it is written, tokenized, compiled, assembled, linked, and run, each a discrete step or phase of its transformation.

Many commentators on the digital take note of the layers that it accrues and sometimes hides behind. Chun quotes historian Paul Ceruzzi describing the computer as onion-like, "with many distinct layers of software over a hardware core" (2004, p. 28). Hayles (1993) discusses the layers of signifiance that lie between human action at the computer and the machinic result of that action. Kittler (1997) makes passing mention of two different sets of layers, the layers that interpose between source code and executing software and the layers that settle over hardware to build up an opaque software surface structured as an interface. Kim Cascone carries the layering into digital production, finding "a clear indication that contemporary computer music has become fragmented, it is composed of stratified layers that intermingle and defer meaning until the listener takes an active role in the production of meaning" (2000, p. 17).

Given her unusual degree of access to the machine, the programmer has a perspicuous view of the layered ontology. If something passes from programmer to user, it does not travel from one to the other without numerous interruptions, stages of re-representation, encoding, and decoding. Each such stage is a layer, a degree of abstraction, that bears more or less rigid relations to the layers on either side of it, producing isomorphisms and other topological effects between layers. Not surprisingly, the idealization of the digital object carries all the way through to the interface. Lionel Kearns figures this layering that collapses into the immanent plane of 0s and 1s in his digital sculpture, "Birth of God/uniVerse," which ironically asserts that God, or everything, turns on the reflective interdependence of 0 and 1 iterated at multiple scales. There is no better illustration of the principle of digital layering.[5]

As Kearns demonstrates, the layers in the digital are only formally distinguished; they threaten constantly to collapse into each other and finally into the bottom layer, the flow of 0s and 1s. The leveling effect follows from the combination of hermetic confinement to a plane of internal deixis and dematerialization or idealization. Cut off from the irreducible resistance of the actual and without tools of strong distinction of its own, the plane of the digital foregoes absolute hierarchy and turns itself over to the universalism of code. Kittler puts it most succinctly in "Protected Mode": "The entire hierarchical standard of self-similar program levels—from the highest programming language down to elementary machine code—rests completely flat on the material" (1997, p. 163). Kittler conceptualizes the collapse of the stacked layers onto the hardware, but this collapse occurs more generally in relation to the whole domain of the digital, which treats everything using the same binary tools, making no distinction that is not already equal to every other distinction in its domain. As Manovich describes "new media objects," "They are collections of individual items, with every item possessing the same significance as any other" (2001, p. 218). This same confinement and idealization give rise to multiple layers, however, inasmuch as the plane of the digital, divorced from the actual, is reconnected to the actual through a series of idealized, symbolic transformations. Each successive transformation produces another layer, but each remains flat inasmuch as each retains the fundamental abstraction of discrete distinction. A sequence of symbolic transformations leads from molecular abstractions to molar ones and, finally, to phenomenal, iconic representations.

In his recent work, Manovich argues that the ontology of computing encourages layers, and that layers define our access to digital objects. He reasons that raw data are meaningless to human sensation such that access to them must be always mediated by software: "Actual data as it is represented and stored in a computer is no longer directly accessible to our senses" (2013, p. 155). Each piece of software offers its own modes of access, which appear to be properties of the underlying object, but are better understood as aspects of the software being used to access those data. "The 'properties' of digital media are defined by particular software as opposed to solely being contained in the actual content (i.e., inside digital files)" (p. 152). We encounter digital objects only through mediating layers, like a Photoshop mask. This is also the reason that Manovich believes that digital media are in a state of permanent innovation: objects derive a mutability from the necessarily indirect or mediated mode of encounter with them because there will always be newly invented techniques for looking at (the same) data; an object is always new when it is presented through a new interface.

The ambiguity of layers that collapse into each other supports a basic property of code, the lack of formal distinction between data and program. Since both operations or instructions and the objects to be operated on are made of the same stuff, each can be treated the same way; program code can be manipulated as data and data can be interpreted (in some contexts) as instructions. "The Von Neumann architecture recognizes no difference between commands and data" leading to "an incurable *confusion between use and mention*" (Kittler 1997, pp. 157 and 147). The strength of this conflation of use and mention is the possibility of reflexivity. When program code is treated as data, the computer becomes capable of operating on itself, of changing its own instructions, of analyzing and automatically altering its behavior. (This is not to grant the machine an original autonomy, but only to indicate the reflexive structure built into its operation, such that it effectively always operates on itself.) The digital takes the distinction between data and program into itself, constructing a soft boundary, maintained by conventions expressed in the formal protocols of hardware and software. The power of abstraction thus leaves the machine metaphysically vulnerable, since its structure of command and control issues from a position of imaginary authority. There is no difference in principle between the commands and the objects to be commanded, such that command is potentially subject to the same control as what it commands. Only a subject outside the machine stands in a firm hierarchical relation to the code, though the question of *access* problematizes this hierarchy.

Software, too, relies on the conflation of program and data; an executable program on a computer is a set of instructions captured as a list of 0s and 1s, program as data. Inasmuch as the data produced from storage, derived from analytic processing, or introduced by the user, also instruct the computer to behave in one way or another depending on their particular values, data also function as coded instructions. To separate instructions from hardware, to *write* programs independent of any particular machine, in the same ideal language used to express the data, these gestures pry open a new dimension, suspended between the ideal digital plane and the interface that presents the digital to the actual. The binary encodes data and program indifferently, such that each is equally available, reservoirs of possibility. Whereas in practice the indistinction of code and data rarely concerns the programmer explicitly, it remains basic to some critical possibilities of programming and computing generally.[6] "The classic distinction between functions and arguments, operators and numerical values has become permeable. However it is precisely this breakdown of the alphabet which also permits operations to be applied to operations, and ramifications to be automated. Which is why computers in principle comprehend all other media and can subject their data to the mathematical procedures of signal processing" (Kittler 1996, n.p.).

Even beyond the interface, the weak distinction between use and mention in the digital bears on the culture of computation. It is this same indistinction that means that each act on the computer is reproducible and, hence, becomes an object that can circulate. To make something in the digital is to propose a legacy, to demonstrate a possibility, to create an object or action that can then be repurposed, reappropriated, reproduced, plugged in. Most media admit some distinction between content and medium, whereas the digital makes every content also a tool while every tool and technique gets objectified in code. Whatever one makes or does in the digital can be packaged and reproduced in principle: the digital as automatic archive.[7] This potential invites a culture of quotation, reuse, versioning, borrowing, joining, but so challenges provenance, authority, authenticity, originality, and other attempts to pin an object to its origin. Defying singularity by its universal and self-identical binary code, the digital object shakes off its origin to rise as the gift of culture to itself.

Leveling or flattening also establishes another significant power-limit of the digital, the capture of semantics by syntax. Restricted to formal evaluation (rather than more invested discernments), the digital lends itself well to the capture of syntax, which is more formal, but less well to the capture of semantics, which is less formal, at least in the details. Using 0s and 1s it is considerably easier to represent formal rules, for example, categories like parts of speech, or measurable relationships among parts, than it is to represent the vagaries of meaning. (Hence the slower-than-anticipated progress toward computer speech and comprehension.) But semantics cannot be strictly divorced from syntax, and digital contexts increasingly include tools to capture (something like) semantic value as syntax, to identify and encode meaningful information in formalized, intercomparable structures. The simple technique of associating keywords with a digital object provides a ready example: keywords augment the power of search and offer other benefits by codifying meaning in an isolated term, a formalized abstraction of semantic content.

With a finer resolution than keywords, mark-up languages can be used to encode or index properties and parts of a digital object, including properties that might be aesthetically or ethically contentious or otherwise significant. The Semantic Web project proposes to store along with each web-accessible object a set of properties of that object describing various categories and values of semantic information applicable to it. Galloway paraphrases web-founder Tim Berners-Lee to describe this supplement to Web 1.0: "The Semantic Web is simply the process of adding extra meta-layers on top of information so that it can be parsed according to its semantic value" (2005, p. 194). This allows web pages, for example, to provide search engines with more human-relevant data about each page's content, including not just subject matters but relationships among words and concepts.

Perhaps the reduction of semantics to syntax is inevitable in the digital. The plane of the digital, given its simple but effective tool of discrete distinction, cannot distinguish semantic content but operates piecemeal on every bit using a complicated but deterministic logical syntax. Even, or especially, at this proximity to the plane of the binary, the leveling tendency asserts its ontological influence. In a vocabulary made only of bits, there is no resistant difference between use and mention, or between data and program, or between process and object. This was Kurt Gödel's trick, to make numbers refer to themselves by building a code that uses numbers to represent claims about (other) numbers. The digital has this capacity at its core, as the same code represents processes and objects, such that processes can be analyzed as data, while data serves as instruction, directing the flows of electricity one way or another when those data pass through the processor.

The indifference of bits, or rather the simple difference of bits is reflected even in the social dimension of the digital. A prominent consequence of the rise of digital communications is a similar lack of distinction on the socius. The spread of digital technologies has not realized the fantasy of direct democracy, and the promised populism of the internet is thoroughly sullied by corporatism and other oligarchies. Such visible centralizations notwithstanding, the erosion of regulable borders does institute a general reversal of long-established hierarchies to allow a more distributed mechanism of evaluation in the marketplace of ideas. Media production and distribution are changing rapidly to catch up with Web 2.0 and its many-to-many medial schema. Traditional news outlets experiment with new structures of reporting and new services for their audiences, desperate not to be left behind by a technology that makes any witness a reporter and any commenter an editorial author, leveling hierarchies of authority. Political campaigning adopts untested strategies to collect, respond to, and manipulate opinion, which now gets expressed in commonly accessible forums, whether it comes from the grassroots or the political action committees. The leveling of distinction rewrites the rules of privacy, as strict boundaries are hard to maintain in the digital. Code can be strongly encrypted, which for the most part limits access to those who have the right password, but the dematerialization of hardware means that the physical (geographical) locations of the storage devices often fail to separate entirely a data store from the general flow of information.[8] As the mechanisms for maintaining privacy lose their potency in the face of dematerialized data, the weakness of boundaries also unravels the conception of property, which has historically been tied to materiality and a privative notion of possession, while intellectual property hovers on the blurry edge of capital accumulation, taking its place alongside other postmodern commodities like timeshares, bundled debt instruments, and pocket change auctioned on eBay. Manovich identifies the leveling of the distinction between public and private as the primary motivation behind social media: "In fact, the whole reason behind the existence of *social media and social networking services and hosting websites* is to erase this boundary [between personal and public] as much as possible" (2013, p. 28).

The theme of digital leveling seems to be commonly intuited, expressed in different ways by many theorists thinking about digitality. Anne Friedberg, for example, focuses on the question of the digital medium, concluding that "digital technology inherently implies a convergence of all media forms" (2002, p. 32). Matthew Fuller looks instead at the interface and the underlying representations of data, but also arrives at a certain indistinction in the digital: "Boolean logic ties any interface action into a yes or no, where any mark into data is as fixed as any other elements. Equally, every object or element of data in a file, once it has been saved from the buffer, has the same status" (2003, p. 113). The question then is how the digital, in its apparent indifference, serves, nevertheless, as a locus for so much creative activity. For the leveling effects of digital technologies are not accidental but stem from the ontology of the bit. According to the mathematical theory of communication, a code requires a prior agreement between sender and receiver regarding what messages can be sent, and there can be no meaningful exchange of information without such an agreement. In practice, this means that at some level all of the messages in the digital domain have already been determined, the language of possible expression has been delimited, and this squelches the potential for original claims in the very structure of the technology. The digital does not admit contingency or accident, except as catastrophic possibilities that negate altogether the effective use of the technology.

As this book has argued, the topology of the digital combines a flat space, or stacked layers of flat planes, with a random access that implies the proximity of every point to every other. This paradoxical spatiality results from the availability in the digital of only one kind of difference, the double articulation of the bit. Though this single and absolute difference limits the expressive powers of the digital, its abstraction also offers the digital a significant freedom in that this single difference is removed from the inertial grip of materiality. *Dematerialization* functions in two different orders of the digital. Not only does it drive the history of computing hardware, which has become smaller, faster, more energy efficient, and less wired, but dematerialization also names one of the great powers of digital content, the submission of time and space to an arbitrary manipulation in the digital domain. Rendered digital, space and the objects within it can be divided and manipulated, subjected to deformations of any complexity, and constrained by (simulated) natural laws of physics or entirely imaginary laws or no laws at all. A given process can be executed once or many times, slowed down or sped up, reversed, repeated, reordered, and, of course, observed and analyzed in every dimension with arbitrarily fine precision. Given the construction of its world from a single, uniform difference, the digital makes only minimal demands on the spatiality or temporality of its representations; a computer can simulate a galaxy as easily as a molecule, can compress eons into milliseconds, and can abut incompatible geometries, places that violate the familiar spatial logic of embodiment. Even writing, already on the way to dematerialization, gains dramatic powers under the sway of digitality: "The immateriality of the text derives from a translation of mechanical leverage into informational patterns that can undergo transformations unthinkable if matter or energy were the primary basis for the systemic exchanges" (Hayles 1993a, p. 165).

Some commentators push the notion of dematerialization to extremes, claiming, for example, that programs are not tangible or "physical, material entities which occupy specific regions of time and space" (Eden and Turner 2007, p. 22). Mary Ann Doane discovers in this dematerialization a dream of the disappearance of media:

> The digital seems to move beyond previous media by incorporating them all . . . and by proffering the vision (or nightmare) of a medium without materiality, of pure abstraction incarnated as a series of 0s and 1s, sheer presence and absence, the code. Even light, that most diaphanous of materialities, is transformed into numerical form in the digital camera. . . . Digital media emerge as the apparent endpoint of an accelerating dematerialization, so much so that it is difficult not to see the very term "digital media" as an oxymoron. Is the digital really a medium, or even a collection of media? Isn't its specificity, rather, the annihilation of the concept of a medium? Its information or representations appear to exist nowhere and the cultural dream of the digital is a dream of immateriality, without degradation or loss. (2007, pp. 142–3)

Dematerialization, here emphasizing the progressive amelioration of material *resistance*, thus underlies the notorious power of *simulation* that stands for some theorists as the headline ability of computing. Control over time and space enables scientific simulation, wherein processes normally beyond human perceptual thresholds can be closely examined as they (virtually) occur at any level of detail. The possibility of *authoring* dynamic space and time opens up new forms of expression, notably the medium of video gaming, which bases many of its ergodic pleasures, including its narrative elements, on the manipulation of time and space. (Many games replace a linear narrative with a variable sequence of events that unfolds geographically, as the player explores a map and discovers new locations. The typical mechanism of saving and replaying scenes in a game gives a hint of the unique temporal possibilities of video gaming.) And the computer clock, whose successive ticks coordinate the various subsystems of the machine and regulate the flow of commands through the CPU, establishes a time that runs independently of human time (though not outside of human time), pushing the operation of the machine along at a pace determined by its internal timing. The machine thus carries its own temporality with it, another remove from the times and spaces that we inhabit.[9]

The user interface, usually painted with a desktop metaphor, submits time and space to the control of the user, allowing the instantaneous summoning of files from long ago and far away, such that they appear without fanfare next to the most recent and most familiar icons. The internet, so the story goes, was designed to operate from nowhere in particular, to defy localizability, privileging the most convenient pathways rather than choosing a central trunk, and diverting flow according to a local directionality rather than an overarching control over a fixed map. In example after example, the vaporization of hardware complements the malleability of digital time, space, and matter to create a new set of relationships to forms of materiality, while communications, research, and life in general move at a pace and along paths inconceivable prior to the massive rise of the digital.

If the digital carries with it its own spaces and times, this facet of digitality rests once again on the ontology of the bit. Divorcing its meaning from its materiality, the bit removes itself to a realm where space and time gain a share of flexibility, as the bit does not behave quite like a material object, which would accrue a singular history by tracing a unique path through time and space. Rather, the bit asserts not so much an actuality as a possibility, and it retains this possibilistic character to determine the unusual and challenging modality of the digital. Generically or ideally, the bit hesitates between 0 and 1, or occupies both positions at once. (The ontology of the bit thus already points toward the ambiguity of the qubit, the quantum bit, an element of a quantum computer, that can physically obtain a superposition of two values at the same time.) When actualized, the bit must occupy only one of those values, but the other remains as a nonactualized possibility, the might-have-been that gives the bit its unique significance. A bit is, thus, first of all a simplification or apotheosis of possibility, a mark whose meaning is precisely that it is one of two values *and* that it might have been the other value. This hesitation, this actualization of one value that simultaneously possibilizes the other, carries into the character of the multibit digital object. Not only is its structure, constituted of part-qualities, amenable to a similar calculus of possibility oriented around individual parts that have a finite number of possible values, but each of its bits also expresses this same might-have-been, which then describes the object as a whole. As Galloway puts it, emphasizing the ontological gap wrought by the bit's ideality, "Code does not reach its apotheosis for people, but exists within its own dimension of perfection" (2008, n.p.). The digital presents itself according to a combinatorics, a set of possibilities that is virtually fully realized, but actually realized only one way.

This Saussurean reading of the bit and the digital object discovers their meanings in the fact that they did not end up having the "other" values that they might have had. But it differs dramatically from the Saussurean model of linguistic meaning in that Saussure understood language as occupying a field without a prior differentiation, or a number of such fields, such that the divisions within the field (of words and concepts) are themselves selections and are *a posteriori*. Whereas in the digital, the divisions are foundational and *a priori*, the discrete difference between one value and the other, or between one bit and its neighbors in sequence. Thus, language remains in touch with potential as the basis of signifiance, while the digital has always already been flattened into a list of possibilities.

Responding to this modality of the digital, the user does not approach digital objects with the same attitude or objective relationship as she does actual, material objects. The potential of actual objects already lies in their ontology, which includes their ways of relating to the subjects who encounter them. As Heidegger emphasizes in *Being and Time*, we do not first find a world filled with independent and autonomous objects but can only encounter that world and those objects as already related to us, to our desires, our needs, our embodied space, our being in time. This relatedness is a precondition of experience of the world and the things in it.

But if digital objects must retain at least some of this ontology of the object, they also recast this prior relationality by presenting themselves according to a set of possibilities. To encounter an object in the world is to move within an open-ended potential whose horizon is indefinite. Whereas to encounter a digital object is to confront a finite list of possible manipulations determined by the structure of the object and software that surrounds and sustains it. Even a user who does not know all of the specific possibilities for manipulating a given digital object knows that those possibilities are part of the object and are clearly delineated in its structure. Rather than the open-ended horizon of a world, the digital object offers itself as a set of possibilities. The objects thus defined present an algebra of the possible as opposed to a calculus of probability, and every digital object is accompanied by a penumbra of possible alterations. "Therefore, in practical terms today you cannot simply 'access' media without automatically being offered some ways to 'modify' it" (Manovich 2013, p. 153).

The extreme abstraction of the bit produces a logic unfamiliar to empirical sensibility. If the bit is made of pure possibility, then any set of data might be the next discrete state of the machine. Any configuration of bits is, in principle, possible. Hansen makes a similar observation in the context of digital images: "The image becomes a merely contingent configuration of numerical values that can be subjected to 'molecular' modification, that lacks any motivated relation to any image-to-follow, and indeed that always already contains all potential images-to-follow as permutations of the set of its 'elementary' numerical points" (2004, p. 9). Hansen contorts the modality of the actual to locate the digital image's future in its present; the images that might arise through algorithmic manipulation (and given the appropriate algorithm, any image could be thus generated) are "always already" there. Including its possibilities as explicit in its discrete, numeric code, the digital suggests that any next state is possible.

Galloway offers further corroboration in relation to the protocols that center his inquiry: "To follow a protocol means that everything possible within that protocol is already at one's fingertips" (2004, p. 53). Both of these theorists couple the notion of pure possibility with a sense of the mechanized or algorithmic limitation on possibility. A bit might take on any next value, but the next value it takes on (and the subsequent ones) are not all indifferently or equally possible but are restricted by the digital context, whose logical rules determine available transformations. All the possible transformations are already given, not just because in principle every possibility is already pending in the set of bits taken as an aggregate of abstraction but because the transformation rules are already materially inscribed. The actual possibilities (not just abstract possibilities) can be circumscribed, the actual sets the most possible outcomes in relief on the plane of possibility.

Elsewhere Galloway makes the case even more directly, equating possibility in the digital with reality:

> And in the logical world of computers, if it is possible then is the real [sic]. Can you break into a computer?—not "should you" or "is it right to." When poured in a vessel, water will fill the vessel completely; when poured into a computer network, the hacker will enter any space available to him/her. In fact, possibility often erases the unethical in the mind of the hacker. (2008, n.p.)

The hacker takes the ontological suggestion of the digital object, that all of its possibilities are in some sense already realized within the virtuality of the digital, and attempts to fulfill this plenitude of possibility, to exercise an ethics that would satisfy the intrinsic destiny of the digital.

Both Galloway and Hansen temper the sense of arbitrary possibility by locating their general claims within an instance or realization. They imagine a particular image or a particular protocol and can therefore also include the constraint of this (general) particular, the way in which an instance includes particular logical possibilities. All such possibilities are available, not only because every possibility is available but also because the particular available possibilities are explicitly spelled out by the logical context. We would feel no need to note the strange role of possibility were it not for this particular kind of constraint. For instance, one might say of an unexposed sheet of photosensitive paper that it already contains all the possibilities of any image that might be printed on it, inasmuch as the individual particles of light-sensitive chemicals coating the paper contain, virtually, every color and intensity that they might eventually fix. But the discrete specificity of the digital situation exaggerates and foregrounds a sense of prescribed possibility. Because we can specify and enumerate every possible transformation of the digital image (using available hardware and software), there is a stronger or clearer sense of these possibilities being already contained in the situation, already given in the image.

The digital demonstrates its affinity with possibility even in its everydayness. Users interact with digital devices in a manner that anticipates possibilities. Choices (menu items or keypresses) are made with respect to the possibilities that they represent, possibilities of a particular outcome. As Chapter 3 details, the human-computer interface lays out possibilities before the user, a graphical array of icons and menus, each of which crystallizes, materializes one or more possible objects or operations. Manovich insists on this as a principle of digital media, noting the inclusion of techniques for modification as part of the object, on the same plane as the digital object itself: "The building blocks used to make up the computer metamedium are *different types of media data* and the *techniques for generating, modifying, and viewing this data*" (2013, p. 110). A program is a set of possible outputs already mapped to possible inputs. In general, a digital object includes its possibilities; it is what it is, largely because of the ways in which it can be altered, edited, manipulated, which is to say, because of its possibilities.

Espen Aarseth describes the logic of cybertext as essentially including an awareness of the paths not taken. He reinforces the notion of possibility as the rule of cyberexperience, partly because one can make explicit all the possible options, the choices one could make: "When you read from a cybertext, you are constantly reminded of inaccessible strategies and paths not taken, voices not heard. Each decision will make some parts of the text more, and others less, accessible, and you may never know the exact results of your choices; that is, exactly what you missed" (1997, p. 3). This field of choice defines the experience of digital objects, providing the object with a sense of the many might-have-beens or could-becomes.

Software-based composition, offering a menu of possibilities, pushes writing in the direction of selection as the digital mode of composition. Fuller's cynical reading of Microsoft Word speculates on the future of document production based on software's presentation of combinatoric possibilities: "The end point of this [sensing and matching patterns of text in MS Word], of course, is that every possible document will be ready for production by the choice of the correct template and the ticking of the necessary thousands of variable boxes" (2003, p. 148). Baldwin draws a similar conclusion, noting that the act of writing is increasingly a matter not of composition but of coding, such that "documents dissolve into the flexibility of possible document models and formats" (2002, p. 7).

To act at the computer is to choose among possibilities. As Brian Massumi bluntly puts it, "The medium of the digital is possibility, not virtuality, and not even potential. Digital coding is possibilistic to the limit" (1998, p. 309). Each choice refines the field of available possibilities. This is the nature of digital action: to act is to select. But in selecting, one both closes and opens possibilities.[10] This structure corresponds to the inside-outside or dividuated character of the digital more broadly, a machine of absolute determination. From the outside, determination is suspended, a form to be filled in. From the inside, determination is complete but indifferent, data awaiting their meaning.

Programming, too, deals principally with the manipulation of possibilities: the programmer's job is to constrain possibility in some useful or interesting way. As is often the case, digital games present a typical example: if many digital games tend to be played only once, it may be because their interest wanes once their possibilities have been exhausted or fully revealed. The emphasis on possibility as the building block of the game also contributes to the ludic dynamic of exploration as a substitute for fixed narrative; games are about discovering and exploiting possibilities, which may include mutual interdependencies, but which otherwise offer themselves equally and indifferently to the user (rather than in some necessary or motivated order). The user chooses a direction to explore and then pursues whatever possibilities lie in the chosen direction. The computer offers a broad field of possibilities, one whose borders may be unknowable in practice. The programmer creates an environment that makes some set of these possibilities most immediately available, arraying other possibilities at a greater remove from the user, and leaving many others untouched in a presumptive default state. To program is to determine the values of some bits so as to form a structure made of bits in hesitation, bits with determinate relationships to each other but without determinate values (other than possibilistic insistence on binarity, 0-or-1). These structured but suspended bits await the user, who chooses further determinations, qualities, within the structures supplied by the programmer via the program. The programmer therefore sculpts an indeterminacy, which describes her task in general: to make available some constrained set of possibilities as an aid to creative pursuits. The determination of this structure is the meaning of the program, the contribution of the programmer. The determination of the not-yet-determined qualities is the making of meaning for the user. Though these distinctions are not strict, this could be an *ad hoc* means of distinguishing the orientation of *programming* from the orientation of *using* a computer: the programmer makes determinations that produce a structured indeterminacy, whereas the user makes determinations that produce fixed values. Every action at a computer is a matter of fixing a hesitation, there is only actualization of possibilities. At the level of the bit, even an instantiated and determined one, there remains the ghost of its opposite value and so also a hint of its hesitation, a possibility unrealized but still there.

A digital object is a conventional aggregation of part-qualities, the convention itself being specified and enforced through encoded structures that determine how the sequence of bits assigned to a given object or part is to be divided into smaller parts or qualities represented by values. The possibilities of a digital object are the possible alterations to those part-qualities, changes of value that represent a given quality for a given part. A record in a database is divided into fields, each of which contains some information that is taken as pertinent to or descriptive of the whole record. To alter a record is to alter one of these fields, which equivalence already defines a limited set of possibilities. In some cases, it is possible to add another field, just as it is sometimes possible to add another part-quality onto an object. The code determines whether or not this augmentation is an available possibility, which keeps the whole operation in the realm of possibility and limits the intrusion of potential on a digital object or record.

Without an internal sense, vivisected into layers by a strange ontology, verging on its own combinatoric possibilities, easily and exactly replicable and mutable, constituted in part by its ideality, lacking a strongly unified identity, the digital object resists even a simple count. If the object fails to cohere as a unit and implies its capacity for production, how many of "it" are there? We can enumerate identical files in a file system, deciding, for instance, that there are "five copies" of a given file stored on hard discs and data back-up tapes. Five copies of a file represent an insurance policy in the case of certain kinds of damage to one copy, but closer to the rule-bound plane of the digital, at a remove from the contingencies of the actual, one copy, or five, or five thousand, these are logically so close that their differences almost disappear. To make a copy in the digital is trivial, to reproduce millions only slightly less so. Characterized by pattern rather than presence, as Hayles (1993) argues, the digital perplexes counting. "For within the digital realm, there is no difference between original and copy, and information outlasts its material support" (Doane 2007, p. 143).

A pattern is a capacity for production, a capacity implicit in the being of the pattern, that it might be continued, and while one can distinguish instances of a given pattern from each other using familiar conventions like contiguity, orientation, scale, structural aberrations, and other variables that leave the essential pattern intact, it makes sense neither to say that these instances are one pattern nor to say that they are many. *Pattern* is more verb than noun, such that a count of instances misses the essential, the *patterning*. In the digital object, this ontological defiance of the simple act of counting—unlike most of the material world where things can generally be enumerated—produces some of the most recognized consequences of digital culture, such as the restructuring of legal and social institutions based around property and its scarcity, which cannot apply their usual measures and controls to digital objects. Hardware and software contrivances attempt to restore a scarcity and countability to digital artifacts, to make them behave like worldly objects whose unique paths through time and space stamp them with a singular distinction; digital signature systems, copy-protection schemes, bulky hardware media, and the honor system all try to assimilate digital objects to the old economic order, but these techniques push against the ontology of the objects they are designed to govern. Objects can be easily reproduced because they are equal to themselves as code, specifiable as a group of bits, and thus subject to reproduction and to alteration, dissolution, etc. The possibilities of a digital object accompany it, but as extrinsic, as self-actions that still appeal to an externality that chooses or triggers them.

This combinatoric character of digital objects and actions may be particularly evident in the case of gaming, though gaming here serves as an archetype of computing more generally. "The experiential basis of the computer-as-medium is prediction and control of a limited set of variables. The fascination with all computer technology—gamesware or straightware—is figuring out all the permutations of a limited set of variables" (Bernstein 1991, §35). Wark extrapolates this combinatorics into a digital ethos:

> The algorithm can produce every possible combination of the resources mapped in the database—and a few impossible ones as well. The possible and the actual reverse positions. It is the possible that is real. If the algorithm can produce it as an outcome from the database, it exists. The mystery is why the recalcitrant debris that litters the actual sometimes refuses to get out of the way. This insistence on the reality of the possible, on what resides within resources, is the American dream. (2009, card 073)

Manovich traces the same phenomenon into the interface:

> Digital culture tends to modularize content, i.e., enabling users to create, distribute, and re-use discrete content elements—looping animations to be used as backgrounds for videos, 3D objects to be used in creating complex 3D animations, pieces of code to be used in websites and blogs, etc. (This modularity parallels the fundamental principle of modern software engineering to design computer programs from small reusable parts called functions or procedures.) All such parts also qualify as "content." (2013, p. 25)

John Simon's 1997 digital artwork, "Every Icon," concretizes and thereby parodies the combinatoric character of the digital. This work consists of a 32 × 32 grid of boxes, each of which can be either blank (white) or filled (black). A simple algorithm, basically a counter, iterates through every possible combination of filled and blank boxes in the grid, thus—eventually—reproducing every possible icon. Given the grid of 32 × 32, there are on the order of 10^{308} possible combinations of filled and blank boxes, such that even at 100 iterations per second, it would take (by the artist's reckoning) "several hundred trillion years" to cycle through all the possibilities, which is considerably longer than the universe is likely to exist. Simon expresses succinctly the ontological ambiguity of the digital that sustains his digital sculpture: "Every Icon presents all possibilities. . . . The grid contains all possible images" (1997, n.p.).[11]

Perhaps we are living increasingly in an age of possibility. The digital substitution of the modality of possibility for the openness of potential aligns with the creeping positivism that has burgeoned for half of a millennium in Western culture. The rationalism, positivism, and logicism of the digital machine do not of themselves produce the exclusive valuation of facts and statistical truth that now dominate the epistemologies of our moment, nor does the computer on its own bring about the eclipse of potential by the distributed determinism of possibility. Rather, the machine contributes to and reinforces these broad trends of culture, trends already dominant in Descartes' attempt to found a reliable and certain understanding of the world on the basis of rational (hence self-evident) argument. Digital technology does not, therefore, originate this epistemological hegemony, but provides the ideal occasion and means to promote it; digital tools lend themselves most willingly to a cognition of discrete facts and desire defined according to category.

If the strict determinism of digital logic[12] operates in accord with this positivist epistemology—a way of relating to the world that emphasizes discrete facts in logical relations—it may be less clear how the use of digital technologies imposes that epistemological outlook on its users and the members of the cultures in which those technologies are prevalent. As was detailed in Chapters 2 and 3, the user also makes a contribution to the digital in order to cross the gap between digital and actual and so participates in its logic. To make sense of a digital machine, to engage in a digital operation, is to contribute a coherence that would otherwise be lacking. But we have also seen that this contribution cannot take any form whatever, but must be presented in a form that has been anticipated by the software and hardware of the digital technology. Only an expected input can be effectively entered into the machine; all other expressions, desires, attitudes are excluded from the digital by the design of the system. The rage of swinging a bat or the gentleness of stroking with a feather will encounter the plastic surfaces of the machine with violence or passion but cannot penetrate the abstraction of the digital domain of 0s and 1s. As Kay puts it, "We have the *object* first and the *desire* second. This unifies the concrete with the abstract in a highly satisfying way" (2001, p. 130). Consequently, to use a digital machine effectively is to bend one's cognition toward the digital, to mirror its world of discrete objects made in part of possibilities by making one's own desires discrete and casting them in terms of specific outcomes that are part of the preordained possibilities of the machine. Computers demand not only abstract thinking, but a particular kind of abstract thinking that absorbs the rules given by the logical possibilities of software and hardware and shapes one's input according to those rules.

> The computer's role is only to ask how our engagements might be facilitated, but it does so with a staggering range of provisos and conditions. Upon opening a programming manual, one discovers that all data must be expressed as strings or numbers; that ontologies may only take the form of lists, trees, or matrices; that everything is an object of a certain class. And over and above these, the computer demands abstraction and encapsulation of its components. (Ramsay 2011, p. 67)

> In effect, the conventional PC is a filter which filters out all aspects of our complex embodied intelligence except that small part which can be encoded as strings of alphanumeric characters. Rhetorics of computing, both marketing rhetorics and the more complex and subtle characterisations of the computational in literature and film, commonly contain extropian and anti-corporeal sentiments which imply that human experiences which are not amenable to serial Boolean logical expression are somehow irrelevant. (Penny 2008, n.p.)

Though processes of abstraction take place throughout the space between the actual and digital, abstraction reaches an ultimatum on the plane of the binary, and its hold weakens as one moves farther from that domain of logical purity. The rigid idealization of the digital code bubbles up into the interface, producing an icon, which is not just an output but also a site of input. What this icon makes available retains from the idealized plane of the digital an immateriality: the object can be seen and sort of touched, but these and any additional material factors exhibited by the object are simulated, readily mutable numerical abstractions lacking the heft of real materiality. A digital object, ambiguously represented by the icon, straddles the divide between digital and actual, channeling characteristics of the digital plane into the image-objects that appear in the interface. To interact with a digital interface is thus to interact with an ideal, an idea, but this formula points in two directions: the digital plane presents its ideality in the icon, but at the same time, the user confronts the interface *as an ideal*, a set of discrete, provisionally unified objects made of qualified parts that can, in principle, be manipulated stepwise.

These two directions of analysis mirror the curious phenomenology of the interface: the bidirectional travel of data—input going from the human through the interface and into the digital depths of the machine and output reversing this path—corresponds not only to a digital articulation of data and processes but also to separate hardware components assigned to separate functions and to separate sensations devoted to different functions as well. In other words, the division between input and output, separated by the entire complexity of the operation of the computer as the data go all the way in and come all the way back out, also divides monitor from mouse and vision from touch. The computer includes components to deal individually with input and output and the human body respects this articulation, separating touch from vision.

The message is that, if the interface has one foot in the human world and one in the digital, this is a problematic negotiation. It means that the digital retains something of the human all the way to its core, while the human user must also give herself in part to the digital in order to use the computer. As part of her self-digitalization, she becomes corporeally articulated, not only aligning her body at orthogonal angles for efficient operation but splitting vision and touch into independent systems (output and input) that are connected by the mediating mechanism of the digital. Correspondingly, the computer divides its systems into output devices and input devices, each with its own separate hardware, with separate electrical pathways and separate (but coordinated) software. Engineers at Apple Computer recognized the need for an intimate connection between touch and vision on the computer, responding to the split of those functions by the design of the machine. One of the subtle but important user interface design characteristics of the Macintosh is the low-level integration of mouse and screen: the subroutines to track mouse movement and represent it in terms of screen coordinates were originally inscribed in specialized hardware to ensure reliable operation even when application software malfunctions.

To point to the user's requisite capitulation to the machine is not to claim that creative use of digital technologies relies exclusively on a choice among pregiven possibles. Perhaps this is the digital's contribution to creativity, an inducement to positivism, but to use a digital device is to reach across the gap between the abstract plane of the digital and the actual world, requiring ontological compromise and contortion on either side. The user submits to the rigidity, the formal demands of the interface in order to purchase the extraordinary array of benefits of abstraction. Though these benefits are limited by the same abstraction that produces them, they enable another purpose, sometimes called *content*. The user can work with words, images, structures, sounds, and more, applying principles *that are not themselves abstract* to objects that are, principles that transcend the digital and lie entirely beyond it. Composing a good sentence, painting a striking image, deploying a subtle irony, all of these can happen in a digital medium but without submitting to its order, as though they hover above the plane of the digital on which they are invisible, buried in an indifferent logic, to appear only in higher layers where flat code has given way to expansive icon.

Nevertheless, the creativity of content cannot be strictly divorced from its digital environs, for its objects remain digital. To write in a word processor is to engage with dividual glyphs, words, sentences, and paragraphs, which submerges textual continuity in favor of combination. Cut-and-paste (and the dividuality it demonstrates) reorganizes the concrete task of writing, as the *structure* of words and ideas becomes a primary object of direct manipulation, reducing the need for a prearticulated progression of argument or narrative. The way the writer approaches her task, the cognitive habit of seeing linguistic and ideational structures as combinatoric, engenders a writing process comprising possibilities different from those of typewriters and pens. (The reorientation of text by the hyperlink suggests even more dramatic changes to writing and its practice.) Even crafting an elegant sentence now follows a different path, no matter if the results frequently converge on the older aesthetic. The digital both influences and constrains what happens within it, as digital writing—at least some forms of writing—foregrounds formal structure to make an afterthought of content. "The functionality of Word is a mirroring and repetition of the hierarchical document structure its interface implies. . . . Microsoft Word is a black box. Where once we fed in keystrokes to produce printouts, we now feed in codes and get multiple views. The new Word no longer mimes a document, but transcodes text into algorithms and programs" (Baldwin 2002, pp. 6–7).

To use an interface effectively demonstrates a tacit understanding of digital ontology, an awareness of the lightness of digital being and its invitation to mutation. No doubt, the user rarely thinks in such terms, and may never come face-to-face with a buried code behind the interface. (When a computer crashes, it sometimes reveals a hint of underlying code by *dropping into* a text-based interface closer to the plane of the binary code; but this was more common in an earlier age of the personal computer, as even the process of crashing is more polished than it once was, shielding users from the disorienting innards of the machine.) Though she may not, in general, explicitly formulate the logic governing the objects in the interface, the competent user behaves under the assumption that there is such a logic: she executes particular commands in the expectation of producing a specific alteration to an object or some of its parts. One enters a command (using keyboard, mouse, finger-tap, or other input mechanism) with a result in mind; even in cases where the particular result cannot be or has not been anticipated, one expects the result to be particular, the precise result of the entered command, reproducible as such. Commands—examples include typing a key in order to produce a glyph on the screen (and in the document), double-clicking a volume icon in order to make visible its contents, and steering one's avatar suddenly to the right using the joystick in order to avoid oncoming obstacles—generally aim at objects and their parts, intending to alter or query properties/values. To engage with the interface is to aim for properties that can be altered piecemeal, according to predictable rules.

Which is to say, the user approaches the interface as though it were filled with ideal objects, things made of divisible parts that are qualified precisely and specifiably and that react predictably to a range of possible manipulations. Thus, users know, for example, that the same command executed in the same circumstance will produce the same result, and they know this because users internalize the digital's mechanism, its ideality. Gamers train their bodies to twitch in mechanistic response to a particular repetitive output from the monitor and speakers, eventually shooting the bad guys before they have a chance to think about it, once their bodies internalize the pattern. Graphic artists develop techniques represented as sequences of steps for processing images in specific, reproducible ways to achieve a desired (and fairly predictable) effect.[13] Suburban teenagers let their lightning-fast thumbs do the talking, sending messages without even needing to take their phones out of their pockets. Just as programmers break down their goals into smaller goals (and so on), so do users achieve their ends at the machine by making each task into a set of smaller tasks. Bodies were always machines, but the standardization of input and output, the simple discrete distinction at the core of digital technology, the reliable predictability built into the code, the static ideality of the digital, these make the body-machine more mechanical, more rigid, more narrowly expressive.

This boundedness and determinacy of the digital experience once again finds its origin in the bit. Bits function according to strict logical rules, such that every bit's value can be predicted from its previous value and the state of the other bits in the digital system. There is no break from this rigid process, no moment when a bit might depart from its expected destiny. Indeed, this is the great strength of digital machines, that they are so wholly reliable, without accident, utterly predictable in their simulated ideality. Absolute predictability makes the bit a powerful building block, for even when there are billions of them recalculating their values millions of times per second, they still do precisely what they are supposed to, just what they have been designed to do. Drained of all character of their own, submissive to any command expressed in the appropriate language, the bit gives itself to instrumentalization: as long as one can specify a digital end, that end can be achieved with bits. And instrumentalization thus becomes a rule of the digital domain, which can accomplish any simulated task, but only if it is instructed to do so. To use a computer, one must have something in mind, must at some level already know the possible outcomes of one's efforts.

This description of the user underlines her accommodations to the digital, but that is not the whole picture. Typically, the user does not bring an algorithm before her consciousness in order to interact with a digital object but, instead, musters *affect* in relation to the machine, a desire intended toward a roughly specified end or no particular end (e.g., write a letter or play a game or learn Spanish or check up on a friend or relieve boredom). Flows of logic tied to their shadows on the plane of the digital meet flows of affect expressed by the user, the material, and the actual. These two sets of flows entangle and adjust to each other so that the code bends in a dimension that was not prior to this entanglement (ontologically) available and the affect breaks down, disrupted into various yes-or-no possibilities of expression, partial sensations, and nonreciprocal interactive modalities. "The constant interactivity in a simulation game—the perpetual feedback between a player's choice, the computer's almost-instantaneous response, the player's response to that response, and so on—is a cybernetic loop, in which the line demarcating the end of the player's consciousness and the beginning of the computer's world blurs" (Friedman 1999, p. 137). A primary role of the interface is to ease a transfer of what is, first of all, affective and hence, by definition, concrete into an abstraction that can be hosted on the plane of the digital.

The interface invites this transfer of affect by its aforementioned structure of split-mediation. Its iconic objects are affectively resonant; the letters, images, menus, motions, and more on the screen generate affect in excess of any logical implications. And they respond to affect provided that it is expressed in the language and through the channels that the digital device accepts. However, given its necessary confinement to an encodable stream of information in the digital, communicated affect rarely dominates human-computer interaction. For at the same time as the interface presents digital objects that are affectively resonant, those same objects stand for or re-present an underlying code, and the user intends her actions at some imagined version of this code, parts with numerically definable qualities that can be predictably altered by the application of a calculable sequence of steps. To engage with the interface is to know that one's object is a strange façade, a mask that stands for and is connected to the object behind it, which gives it its form, a dancing marionette whose strings were designed by many but held now, it would seem, by an automaton offstage. Perhaps this makes a tripartite schema of the digital object: its presentation in the interface, its representation of an underlying code (or encoded object), and the user's intended nonspecific idealization.

Two ontologies reaching across a gap—the edge at the juncture of the digital and the virtual must be crossed to connect the plane of the digital to the material, actual, and human worlds. The edge textures the plane of the digital and the layers above it, breaking up flat contours to invite a creative friction, to point in a new direction. By reducing its reach to only the forms of things, the digital all but abandons material reality, foregoing at one stroke both material singularity and material resistance. The abstracted plane that results from this technical obstinacy, an insistence on only 0 and 1, yields the wondrous possibilities of digital technologies but operates on the other side of an ontological chasm. The digital constantly recovers the edge, coding it as just another formal, discrete distinction, pulling the edge back into its plane. The question is how to provoke the encounter of ontologies, to transgress the edge of the flat surface of the digital whose lack of texture eludes the grip of the human. Only an always-new edge will ensure that the digital remains creative instead of falling into the homogeneity that results from the ascendance of abstraction.

The problem of crossing the gap between actual and digital, solved again every instant that someone types a keystroke while using a word processor or flicks her thumb across the screen of a smartphone, this problem and its renewable solution find an archetype in *the interrupt*. An interrupt is a common technical feature of many hardware/software systems. It exists to address a problem of computer engineering that arises out of the relentless linearity of the CPU: computers pay no attention. Hermetic, confined to its stream of bits, the digital has no context, no permeable border surrounding the logic that constitutes its processes.[14] The CPU processes instructions in sequence, one after another. It has only these commands in sequence, its entirety is the execution of these commands.[15] The computer is thus effectively single-minded (or null-minded). It is wholly occupied with the task at hand, entirely consumed by the operation being executed. Centered in its CPU, the computer is equivalent to the execution of a given command, followed by the execution of the next command, and so on. Binary-encoded commands are the basic units of a computer's process, the lowest layer of abstraction where the digital plane and the hardware cease their distinction.

At this low level, an individual command is a number, an ordered sequence of bits that enters the chip as electrical impulses on small wires specifically devoted to that purpose. Different chips are distinguished by different sets of commands that they can accept, a given set of commands constituting a particular *machine language*. Each machine language designates a model of computer chip, and the name of the language is generally also the name of the chip that it runs on: 8088, 6502, G5, Xeon, etc. (There are also families of chips wherein each branch of the family works with a similar, but not identical, language.) Generally, when programmers write in machine language (which is increasingly rare), they use alphanumeric mnemonic codes (*assembly language*) that stand for the strictly numeric codes of the machine language, just to make the code easier to write and read. (For example, if the number 01100100 is the numeric code for a multiplication operation, the programmer might type into the computer the more easily remembered alphanumeric code `mult`, which prior to execution gets translated into the binary number 01100100 by a piece of software called an *assembler*.)

When a given command is fed into the CPU, it enters the CPU as a binary number, a sequence of 0s and 1s that are the binary representation of the numeric machine code.[16] These 0s and 1s are flows of electricity that trigger the opening and closing of junctions on the circuitry of the chip, thus allowing other flows of electricity to flow (or not). The binary number (command) flows through the logic inscribed on the chip, a series of gateways that, admitting or blocking the flow of electricity, eventually produces another binary number at the other "end" of the chip, the output. This process of reading in a number that controls the flow or stoppage of electrical impulses is the entirety of the CPU's process. There is no place in this scheme for something like attention. Utterly occupied by the execution of the current command, the computer does not attend to its surroundings.

It is largely by not paying attention that the computer gains the speed and consistency that constitute much of its fantastic utility. The commands that the computer executes are not themselves complicated; they are things like "multiply two small numbers together" or "shift a row of 0s and 1s one place to the right" or "copy the integer in one memory location into another memory location." These commands, the basic operations of the CPU, offer no intellectual challenge, no problem in themselves. On the contrary, the commands executed by the CPU are conceptually extremely simple. But no person could focus on such tasks efficiently for long, as a human horizon of attention extends well beyond the task at hand. Just having a body ensures that one is already distracted by one's immediate surroundings; in fact, one is already distracted by one's body, with its various needs and its autonomous and autonomic desires and habits. Lacking a body, lacking a world, the computer's strength is its ability to perform simple tasks with astonishing rapidity and perfect accuracy. Millions of times per second the CPU can multiply two integers together or copy a number from one location in memory to another. And it (practically) never makes a mistake; instead, the computer does *exactly* what it is programmed to do, for years at a time, billions and trillions of operations in a row without error.

As Chapter 2 describes, the commands that the computer executes are organized in sequence and packaged into discrete functional units or *algorithms*. Algorithms usually take the form of loops, sequences of commands that are executed in order, to begin again when the end of the sequence arrives. The loop does not cease to run until its termination condition is reached, which might be the achievement of the desired result (e.g., an algorithm to find the prime factors of a given number would not terminate until it had discovered all of these factors), or it might be some fixed number of iterations (e.g., an algorithm that processes calendar data might execute twelve times, once for each month), or it might be some other condition (e.g., a loop might continue to execute until a given time or until an error occurs).

Locked into its loop, the computer has no mechanism by which to recognize that the user wants its attention. Looping indifferently and incessantly, how would the CPU undertake a new project, head in a different direction? The CPU just executes one command after another. What happens when one needs the computer to perform a task other than the one currently being executed? There are a number of solutions to this dilemma.

First, one could simply allow the computer to finish the task at hand, reach the termination condition of its currently executing loop, only then directing it toward the next task to be performed. Computers are very fast, so it probably would not be too long of a wait. This effective strategy is frequently employed in software design. But it leaves something to be desired. For instance, what if the algorithm currently being executed tends to repeat many times before reaching its termination condition? While some loops terminate in milliseconds, others may continue for seconds, hours, or even days. In fact, there is no guarantee that an algorithm should ever terminate.[17]

A second solution compensates for the inadequacy of the first: write the code so that each pass through the loop checks whether the user is pressing a key or holding down the mouse button. If so, read in and act on the user's new command, suspending indefinitely the operation of the currently executing loop. When the user presses a key on the computer keyboard, this closes an electronic circuit, allowing electricity to flow. This flow of current passes through the USB chip inside the keyboard,[18] which reacts by sending a digital message (usually in the form of electricity) through the wire that connects the keyboard to the computer. The USB subsystem on the computer's motherboard receives this message and appropriately interprets the message as a keypress. The USB subsystem on the motherboard then adds this key (or, rather, the numeric code that represents this keypress) to a buffer, a digital queue of keystrokes held in memory, waiting for the CPU to access these data. In addition, the USB subsystem sets a flag, that is, it changes a value stored in some prearranged memory location (from 0 to 1, for example), to indicate that there are data waiting in the queue, much like the flag on a mailbox used to indicate the presence of outgoing mail.

If the loop executing in the CPU includes code to check whether the user is pressing a key, this is tantamount to code that checks whether the flag has been set. A set flag triggers a branch to some other algorithm that reads in the data from the queue and acts accordingly. This is what happens in the principal mode of operation of a word processing program, for instance, where the default loop checks whether a key has been pressed and, if so, reads in the data and updates the display to reflect this new input (by making the appropriate character appear at the insertion point on the screen, for instance).

But this method too, though frequently employed, has a significant drawback: while many loops execute only a few times before reaching their termination conditions, others terminate only after millions of executions. And some algorithms perform operations so basic that they are triggered all the time, thousands of times per second. If each algorithm included code to check whether the user-input flag has been set, the computer would waste a lot of processor cycles checking for input that, for the most part, is not there.[19] The result would be a computer that feels slower, possibly a lot slower, since the computer would waste processing resources checking for nonexistent user input instead of using those resources to work on the task at hand.

The interrupt offers another way that answers to these problems of inefficiency and inconvenience. It works most reliably when engineered into the system at a low level, inscribed in the hardware of the machine. It acts as a direct line of transmission, a *hotline* to the CPU of the computer. When the user triggers an interrupt (say, by pressing a key combination or even a special key specifically designed to trigger an interrupt), the CPU, no matter what operation is currently executing, abruptly ceases its linear progress through some sequence of code, and begins executing a new algorithm as directed by the interrupt. The CPU need maintain no awareness and can go blithely on its way, as the interrupt works like a tap on the shoulder, or perhaps a carjacking would be a more apt simile, given the metaphoric violence of the interrupt.

Most computers have a number of interrupt mechanisms. Pressing Ctrl-Alt-Del on a Windows machine or Opt-Cmd-Esc on a Macintosh triggers an interrupt, which is why these key combinations tend to function even when the running program has become unresponsive. (Built into the hardware, the interrupt does not rely on the proper operation of the currently executing software.) Widely employed in the design of modern computers, the interrupt is not technically remarkable. But this blunt technique, a jolt to the CPU, epitomizes the encounter of human and digital, worlds with divergent rhythms, values, and ontologies; there is always some violence in this meeting, some upheaval, some interruption, as the edge cuts across a digital layer that would otherwise proceed unperturbed.

The interrupt illustrates *the ontological markers of the edge*, the structure of creative intervention in the digital. That is, there are recognizable tropes that come into play along an edge, and the interrupt as example renders them neatly schematic. As the role or meaning of an edge is to effect the meeting of actual and digital, the edge cuts through the flat plane of a layer, introducing *a new dimension*, typically a passage to another layer. Topologically, the interrupt demonstrates this added dimension in the heart of its structure. Whereas the algorithm operating within the CPU is effectively a line or a closed loop, the interrupt implies a perpendicular or transverse direction that cuts into this loop, redirecting the computer onto a different path unrelated and indifferent to the one the CPU had been treading.

The additional dimension is not immediately assimilable on the plane of the CPU's traverse. The violence of the interrupt presents a difference in kind, a momentary dominance, an aggression that curtails the operation executing in software and redirects the CPU based on a message sent through hardware. Carving out another dimension, the interrupt instates a *hierarchical distinction*, asserting the priority of the new dimension over the old one, as hardware takes priority over software, at least for the moment of the interrupt. No matter what process was executing at the CPU, no matter what algorithm is running, the interrupt trumps it, altering the course of operation of the machine.[20] As we have seen, such hierarchical absolutes are not easily maintainable within the digital, which flattens all distinction; the edge perturbs the digital's ontology.

The difference between a process taking place in software and a redirection command sent through hardware implies a specific topology, the *topology of inside and outside* or interior and exterior. The interrupt itself comes from an outside of the process, a human world beyond the self-contained hermetic world of the CPU. A process operating within the material-ideal inside of the machine gets terminated by a message sent from without. As long as the CPU plods from one command to the next, there may as well be no outside, no world beyond the plane of the digital. But the interrupt implies an outside, a realm of contingency that disrupts the hermetic indifference of the linear process of the CPU.[21]

These three closely related ontological features of the edge, increase in dimensions, hierarchical distinction, and inside/outside topology, often serve a fourth characteristic: *the edge enfolds logically, temporally, and spatially heterogeneous domains*, so that they overlap or interpenetrate each other. The encounter of alien logics in the interrupt becomes apparent in a comparison between the interrupted flow of the CPU and the normal, noninterrupted termination of an algorithm. When an algorithm terminates normally, it generally "cleans up" after itself, zeroing out certain registers, deallocating used memory, setting flags to indicate successful termination, saving files that have been altered, and returning a value to the subroutine that called it. But when an algorithm gets interrupted, these housekeeping measures are preempted; the interrupt is comparatively brutal, wresting control of the CPU from the process underway and not even giving it time to grab its stuff on the way out. This has the effect of destabilizing the entire system to some degree, since the bookkeeping chores ordinarily performed when an algorithm terminates maintain the computer in a predictable and normal state, the condition anticipated by the various subsystems and subroutines that operate within the machine. If memory is not deallocated and no value returned to the triggering subroutine, the overarching system may be more likely to crash in the wake of an interrupt.[22]

Divergent temporalities also come together in the interrupt, the human time of the user and the machine time of the computer. For the computer, time is effectively indifferent, undifferentiated. The computer operates according to a clock that does not so much keep time as mark off successive clicks. A calculation process might take twenty milliseconds or two centuries; the computer addresses it exactly the same way in either case and does not distinguish between a short time and a long time, between morning and evening, between summer and winter. Human beings have a textured experience of time. For us, it often matters whether a given event happens now or now. Important, even life-altering events may depend on whether a task is accomplished in two seconds or two minutes. (Thirty seconds late for a bus may change the course of a career. A fiftieth of a second may decide the outcome of a sporting event. On eBay, the action happens in the last five seconds of the auction.) The interrupt represents the imposition of human time on the undifferentiated time of the machine. An interrupt coaxes the computer into respecting, at least somewhat, the lived time of human being, a temporality of vicissitudes and accidents, without altogether negating the homogeneous temporality of the machine.

The new dimension and enfolded heterogeneities of the interrupt do not typically make a lasting alteration to the operation of the machine and are not intended to. Like other edges in the digital, the interrupt happens in a moment and then fades into normalcy. Edges admit the virtual not through a constant or abiding event but by establishing a dynamic threshold, a boundary between two other states. Soon after the interrupt occurs, the computer returns to its "normal" operation, the CPU begins to execute a new algorithm (as determined by the interrupt), and the system continues as though nothing has happened. The interrupt does not persist, does not usually produce an evolution, but only a hiccup, an aberration, a flash in which the system makes a contact with its outside. (Compare Massumi's reference to "the fleeting of the virtual" [1998, p. 306].)

This illustrative example of an interrupt may not be the most typical. Interrupts are frequently used internally, within the machine itself, as when a particular subsystem needs to alert the CPU to an emergent condition. For example, when an input/output or *I/O* subsystem (a disk driver, for instance) has a buffer full of data, it lets the CPU know about this condition using an interrupt, so that the CPU can deal with the full buffer before going on to process further data (and before the buffer overflows when more data are added). Systems with multiple CPUs (or multiple CPU cores) may employ interrupts as a mechanism of queuing: when one CPU wants access to a shared resource, it triggers an interrupt so that the other CPU knows to relinquish this resource, making sure that the resource is in a safe condition to be handed over. (This sort of interrupt is not so brusque as the kind described above, since the interrupted CPU gets a chance to tidy up before passing control of the resource over to the interrupting CPU.) In another application, interrupts maintain security by mediating among different levels of access. Access to certain data may be restricted to subroutines that operate at a given level of security; while a higher (less secure) level may not be able to access these data directly, this higher level can trigger an interrupt that executes a lower-level algorithm to process the data without anything passing back and forth across the level security boundary.[23] The interrupt signal does not so much cross this boundary as circumvent it; it adds a dimension, an outside of the security system that escapes its regulation, and could grant access to any level of security. Note that such interrupts, internal to the computer, do not directly involve a human user, but still manifest the associated characteristics. At bottom, security interrupts also constitute a crease in the topology of the digital, an edge that borders all the flat levels of security access, reaching beyond the digital to afford a contact with the actual.

Increasing dimensions or jumping of layers, hierarchical distinction, an inside structured from within and an outside open to the virtual, and an adjunction of disjoint times, places, and logics—these are the symptoms of rupture in the digital plane, the ontologically subtle and potent tools that allow the digital to jump its closed borders and touch the actual. These are the features of the digital edge. A concluding claim of this book is that the edge is *the* mechanism by which the digital connects to the human and actual; only by virtue of the edge does the digital become creative. Absent this ontological imposition, the digital collapses into a closed determinism, an electronic idiocy,[24] the impotent ontogenesis of the possible, a flick of a switch that offers no account and no understanding of the genesis of creativity in the digital. Instead, we must discover how even in the midst of its rigid determinism, its seizure by possibility, its material of indifferent bits and discrete states, the digital opens itself to a real virtuality, ambiguates or blurs at its borders to engender a friction with the actual that serves virtual creativity. The identification of an edge as an element of digital ontology also thus imposes an imperative: to make the digital creative, one must seek out and ramify its edges.

* * *

This analysis could perhaps be summed up in a simple formula: the digital has no virtual. This usage of *virtual* is not at all how that word now resounds in our culture, its contemporary meaning, instead, labeling whatever comes from or inhabits a digital environment. What both meanings share is a reference to something that is effective but not quite *there*, something productive but not fully present. Again, this superficial similarity masks a more profound distinction. Deleuze's *Difference and Repetition*, especially in Chapter 4, describes a virtuality that is connected to or inherent in the actual and produces it: "When the virtual content of an Idea is actualised, the varieties of relation are incarnated in distinct species while the singular points which correspond to the values of one variety are incarnated in the distinct parts characteristic of this or that species" (1994, p. 206). This could be a description of the double articulation of digital objects, the dividual, were it not for the crucial reference to "singular points." The *Idea* whose virtual content is actualized is not an image or intention in the mind of a subject but is the event of encounter among singular points—encounters among objects, thoughts, desires, actions, nature, history, all the forces of contingency—as they work out their tensions in things and relations, producing sense and sensation in those things and relations as a consequence. The iconoclasm in Deleuze's ontology is to place the virtual Idea ontologically prior to the actual.[25] Plato had done this a few years earlier, but Deleuze's Ideas are dynamic encounters of singular points, not perfections that are eternally equal to their definitions. Deleuze understands Ideas as the constellations that coalesce and diffuse when black holes (the material *ne plus ultra* of singular points) and their tortured gravities meet each other in a field of stars.[26]

The virtual thus produces the actual, not as something from nothing, nor as a succession of states each proceeding from the one before, but as the solution-in-progress to a problem of the encounter of forces determined as ideal structure, "the reality of the virtual" (1994, p. 209). This must be understood in contrast to the structural abstraction at the core of the digital. Whereas digital structure meets its limit in a discrete distinction, namely, the bit as a principle of finite resolution, distinguishing objects as *wholes* by imposing boundaries from above to divide the homogeneity of a field of bits, the structuring of the virtual admits no whole but opens each Idea onto a complex of other objects, parts, and Ideas, placing pieces in relation. The Idea lacks nothing, it is fully determinate as to structure, not whole but *complete*: "What is complete is only the ideal part of the object, which participates with other parts of objects in the Idea (other relations, other singular points), but never constitutes an integral whole as such. What the complex determination lacks is the whole set of relations belonging to actual existence" (Deleuze 1994, p. 209). Deleuze distinguishes in ontology between a fully articulated structure, mathesis, and the qualities that accrue to its actualization, graphesis. This structure, the Idea, is actualized not by an external imposition according to a prescribed possibility in the Idea, but by a differenciation, a development of the Idea *into* a complex of objects and parts. The key point is that determination in the Idea, *actualization*, is an organic and dynamic process, one that restructures its parts and their relations, leaving nothing unchanged. By contrast, determination in the digital is of disintegrated parts, conventionally regarded in the aggregate, which produces no inherent sense, no resistance, only a representation.

In *Difference and Repetition*, representation occupies the negative, noncreative pole of the ontology, the impotent façade that hides the roiling virtuality inherent within it. Representation is the remnant of the Idea severed from its virtual dynamism. Deleuze locates the beginning of the negative in the proposition (of language), which corresponds to a state of affairs and can be measured according to truth and falsity. As the possible truth of a proposition invokes also its possible falsehood, the proposition points the way toward a combinatorics like that of the digital, a world made of possible states of affairs. This shadow world of states of things elides the dynamism of its genesis in the virtual, instead advancing a "negative" logic of rules and forms.

> Forms of the negative do indeed appear in actual terms and real relations, but only in so far as these are cut off from the virtuality which they actualise, and from the movement of their actualisation. Then and only then, do the finite affirmations appear limited in themselves, opposed to one another, and suffering from lack or privation. In short, the negative is always derived and represented, never original or present: the process of difference and of differenciation is primary in relation to that of the negative and opposition. (1994, p. 207)

At so many points, the ontology of the digital and the ontology given in *Difference and Repetition* are in parallel: a mathesis no less real than its graphesis, the ideality of the generative domain, determination by a double articulation, object parts that are structured and qualified in separate processes, negation as a totalizing logic, representation as stasis and product. But if Deleuze's account of the negative stands, it would seem to condemn the digital to negation, for the digital is always derivative and always representational. Negation arises precisely when positivism fills the field of meaning, when the world corresponds to a set of true-or-false propositions, and the future is made of conceptual possibilities.[27] The digital described in this book approaches such a world, a world where every object and every event is made of simple responses to yes-or-no questions, a world structured as to detach the teeming activity in the depths of the digital from the placid interface seen by the user. The virtual, as generator for the actual, finds scant purchase in this world of the digital, for the rigidity of the digital plane admits naught but posits, that is, values that submit to a logic of only true and false. How there can be any edge, how a rapprochement between actual and digital becomes at all possible, that is the pressing question of a digital politics.

Notes

Chapter 1

1 Though today's computer components have fairly standardized material construction, computing history includes mercury and cathode ray tubes, punch cards and floppy discs, and plenty of other materials used to store and process bits. See the timeline at the website of the Computer History Museum for examples: http://www.computerhistory.org/timeline/.

2 Though the size in bits of a byte depends on the hardware in question, it has been conventionally defined as eight bits in the international standard IEC 80000-13:2008, which includes other definitions such as the standard prefixes for naming powers of two, kilo-, mega-, giga-, etc.

3 See the official definition document scanned at http://worldpowersystems.com/J/codes/X3.4-1963/ (accessed December 4, 2014).

4 For example, consider the casual cynicism of Kittler's early conclusion in "There Is No Software," "As one knows without saying, we do not write anymore" (1997, p. 147).

5 It might not be very efficient, but a property such as temperature could also be used as the basis of binary encoding. It would require an apparatus that could control, read, and maintain over time stable temperatures at distinguishable points in some space.

6 This is not to discount the importance of digital materiality as it relates to questions of access and distribution of digital technologies, issues around exploitation and ecology in the acquisition of those materials, or the material conditions of production in the construction of digital technologies. If the demands of its materiality have been mostly sidestepped in the ontology of the bit, those demands resurface as issues of access, disposal, resource use, and more.

7 Aliasing is a particular kind of distortion, or deviation from the original signal, that occurs in sampling systems: if a component of the original signal to be sampled has a frequency greater than half of the sampling frequency, then the sampling process yields an extra element in the sampled signal, an *alias* of the uncapturable portion of the original signal. In image sampling applications (such as digital photography), aliasing shows up as *jaggies*, triangular shapes (half of a rectangle or square) filled in with the wrong color.

8 Jim Campbell's work frequently explores the boundaries between digital and analog. More examples and information are available at the Daniel Langlois Foundation, http://www.fondation-langlois.org/e-art/e/jim-campbell.html. Or consult the collection of essays on Campbell's work edited by Steve Dietz, *Jim Campbell: Material Light*. As regards *Portrait of a Portrait of Harry Nyquist*, note that the scrim acts as an antialiasing filter by distributing a range of brightnesses over a continuous two-dimensional space and eliminating hard edges of both light intensity and image geometry.

9 The hardware and software built around a system that includes more than two values might present some novel problems and possibilities—the transistor demonstrates a natural binarity—but these systems remain logically equivalent to binary ones, and, in fact, binary systems can simulate n-ary systems and *vice versa*.

10 There is no reason in principle that digital processes must be carried out using electrical circuitry. Digital machines could use flowing water, moving people, or symbols drawn on paper to perform their operations, though these methods would likely be clumsier and less reliable (and marginally slower) than the electricity that flows through most digital machinery today.

11 Wikipedia underlines the role of abstraction in the Philips head screw, noting that the invention and popularization of this screw head design were motivated by the need to automate screwdriving on assembly lines. Philips head screws allowed the machine-controlled screwdriver to "cam out" when the applied torque exceeded a certain amount, thus preventing damage to the screw or driver.

12 Moore's law (due to Intel co-founder Gordon Moore, 1965) as formally stated predicts a regular geometric increase over time in the planar density of transistors on computer chips, where the measurement at any given time applies to chips manufactured with minimal production costs. (Thus the law does not claim to apply to costly chips at the leading edge of research.) But in practice, increasing transistor density is tantamount to increasing the speed and decreasing the size of computing technologies.

13 Compare Figure 7 at http://queue.acm.org/detail.cfm?id=2181798 as generated by the online resource, *CPU DB* at http://cpudb.stanford.edu/. Figure 7 constructed by Andrew Danowitz, Kyle Kelley, James Mao, John P. Stevenson, and Mark Horowitz | April 6, 2012 in "CPU DB: Recording Microprocessor History" in *ACMQueue*, 10 (4), April 2012.

14 RGB color representation preexists the rise of digital technologies by a long stretch, having been employed not only in capture and reproduction of television and other video signals, but also in early techniques of color photography in the mid-nineteenth century.

15 While the principle of sampling and pixel-based capture remains the same throughout most techniques for digital image representation, files containing

digital images often include additional information about the image and the file itself. Further, some encoding techniques do not associate a separate group of data with every individual pixel; consider lossy image encoding techniques such as JPEG, which groups pixels into blocks and assigns a single set of values for the whole block, or vector-based image representation, which describes an image as a set of line segments connecting one point to another.

16 A vector-graphics digital system treats an image not as a flat field of individual pixels but as a collection of lines, polygons, and other shapes. But it remains a collection of discrete parts, called *primitives* in vector graphics.

17 The sampling process as a basis for encoding sound digitally is not the same as the notion of sampling as it is employed in music production, where it refers to the use of (usually) short segments of sound from preexisting sources (such as other recordings). Though distinct, these two notions of sampling are connected, each appealing to a standardization or homogenizing process that is typical of the digital and to the possibility of an ideal or perfect reproduction of these standardized data.

18 In this context, a token is a character or sequence of characters that is given a logical meaning, setting it semantically above the raw character data in which it is embedded and which it may describe or effect. "Raw" text can also be tokenized, which would be necessary in order to perform an operation as simple as spell-checking: a sequence of characters has to be tokenized at least as separate words in order to properly check the spelling of each word. To a digital machine, a space (as generated by pressing the space bar on a keyboard) is just another character, and such a machine has to be instructed to interpret a space as a special marker that divides one word from the next.

19 There are not really rules but rather common models. Some computer languages can perform an analog of compilation in real time, an operation called *interpreting* the code, such that the code can be executed as soon as it is written, without having first to conduct a compile process. Interpreted code tends to run less efficiently and more slowly than compiled code, in part because the translation process happens while the program is running, using up resources such as time. LISP is a classic example of an interpreted language, but while languages are usually either interpreted (Java) or compiled (C++), the question of how the language is to be executed is really independent of the language itself, such that a compiler could be created for a language that is typically interpreted and *vice versa*.

20 In "There Is No Software," Friedrich Kittler (1997) marvels at the magic of this invocation, wherein to type a name, or click a mouse, is to set in motion a myriad of essential processes.

21 A *constant* contrasts more naturally with a *variable*. I emphasize the particular kind of constant called a *literal* to stick with text-oriented examples.

22 Abelson and Sussman (1996, p. 83). Though the very notion of a variable is already an abstraction, the quotation refers to *data abstraction* as a way of hiding not just the value behind the name of the variable, but also the internal structure of the variable itself.

23 Though particular implementations will vary, in general there is a trade-off between speed and memory when comparing literals and variables. A variable takes slightly longer for the running program to access, as it has to execute instructions to read the appropriate memory location. A literal, written directly into the machine code, is more immediately accessible, saving a few microseconds of look-up time, but at the same time possibly making the executable file size larger. Depending on how they are implemented, literals can also make program code harder to debug or reuse, since literal values are fixed and have to be changed one at a time in the program code.

24 The difference is not entire. Modularity frequently shows up in the temporal and spatial structure of the interface, while coding must engage and to a degree emulate the linearity of the executing machine code to come.

25 The standard for C++, for example, allows the programmer to use or ignore the object-oriented features of the language.

26 To trigger a procedure from another procedure is typically a matter of writing the name of the procedure to be triggered and specifying values for its parameters.

27 An opaque structure such as a procedure or a computer is often called a *black box*. Input goes in and output comes out, but what happens in between, the internals of the black box, is specified only abstractly.

28 Though modularity is typically a goal of procedural programming, the paradigm does not necessarily demand fully independent modules, but allows for global states and global data. To the extent that a module refers to data defined outside of itself, it loses a degree of modularity.

Chapter 2

1 Though OOP does build from procedural programming and represents a relative increase in organizational complexity, I do not mean to suggest a narrative of historical progress, only a conceptual order. Coding paradigms have developed in fits and starts, with advanced techniques often invented only to lie dormant for many years before their rediscovery and employ. The combination of practical and theoretical advance driving the progress of computer science ensures that no history of computing will look wholly smooth and progressive, and the cultural-theoretic resources of genealogy may reveal more about the nature of progress in computing than would a straightforward chronological account.

2 To be clear, there is nothing that can be programmed in OOP that could not be programmed in nonobject-oriented procedural language, and procedural code can be made rigorously modular with sufficient coding discipline. Rather, OOP alters the nature of the programmer's task and the way she understands the program as a set of parts. The modularity enforced by OOP also encourages the use of code libraries, self-contained mega-modules of code that offer a large set of data types and commands for their manipulation and analysis. Because they can be so cleanly separated from (and connected to) their contexts, object class libraries are relatively easy to modularize and make available.

3 In some versions of OOP, inheritance is not strictly hierarchical, and multiple parentage is possible.

4 The `this` referent is not a particularly important feature of OOP, as it sees only occasional use and could probably be dispensed with with little hardship. However, it does show most dramatically what OOP adds to the programmer's arsenal. `this` is a keyword particular to certain object-oriented languages. Java uses `self` instead.

5 There are significant technical elisions in this explanation. Clear rules allow most references to `this` to be unambiguously resolved at compile-time. Most cases of polymorphic (ambiguous) reference can be resolved from syntax and do not require run-time calculation. But the situation in which `this` is ambiguous at compile-time is not only possible but also common, and the example thus illustrates a legitimate facet of OOP. Two further caveats are to be noted: the syntax employed here is not standard in any OOP but has been invented for this explanatory context, and polymorphic ambiguity is a feature of code that can arise without using the `this` pointer, which serves here as a particularly provocative example.

6 Though he does not discuss what makes a real object whole, Cary Wolfe does underline the essential contingency of the actual, in a context that highlights this contingency as a fundamental distinction between digital and analog domains: The analog "is not wholly subsumable or predictable by programs and schemata, simply because the interplay of real magnitudes in space/time is fundamentally and even inexhaustibly contingent, creating a reservoir of complexity and contingency that is, in principle, inexhaustible. . . . The analog, in short, does not exist as a presence, a substance, an 'as such' or the 'the' of '*the* body'" (2008, pp. 89–90).

7 Galloway avers that "Deleuze more or less equates five terms: digitisation, integration, codification, homogenisation and binarisation"; taking *integration* as the composition of parts into objects, the equation of these five terms also mirrors the discussion in the previous pages of this book. That the digital is a question of binarity, of integrating parts, and of encoding has been already established.

As equivocal, these terms also capture the equivalence of part and quality, the inseparability of division into discrete elements (digitization) and grouping or partitioning (binarization as grouping into twos). Homogenization expresses the principle of abstraction, the making comparable or similar of what would be different.

8 In his essay's conclusion, Galloway takes the superfold as a structure that granularizes periodization, eliminating historical thought "by accelerating the opportunities and channels for critical thought to infinity and therefore making it impossible to think historically in the first place."

9 More correctly, everything must have been put in the code by *someone*. Whether working with code libraries not of her own invention or simply relying routinely on the operating system to take care of many common tasks to be performed during the execution of a program, a programmer leverages the investments of others in order to produce her own working code. As Marvin Minsky puts it, "There isn't any one programmer" (1967, n.p.).

10 Matthew Fuller extends the same conclusion to productivity software, such as word processors: "In Word, not only can the hand not recognise the tool, but the software also makes the generous refusal of any pretence to referral to a rational outside world or any expectation of it" (2003, p. 154).

11 In code lingo, a *handle* is a value that points to a memory location (or register) that contains another value that itself points to the memory location containing the start of the data structure that the *handle* refers to. In other words, a handle is a doubly indirect reference.

12 Hansen's second-person account of an encounter with Robert Lazzarini's sculpture works, *skulls* (2000) underlines its alien nature. After numerous attempts to find a comfortable viewing perspective, "you once again move in to focus on still another skull, until finally, having grown impatient or unable to endure the weird sensation produced by this work, you abruptly pass through the door-sized opening cut into one of the room's four walls and seek solace in some less unsettling portal to the digital world" (2004, p. 199).

Chapter 3

1 The arrow has an ancient origin, and I do not mean to claim that the arrow came into existence or prominence with the computer monitor. Consider the manicule of renaissance texts or the *yad* pointer held by ritual readers of the Torah. But the arrow of the computer interface not only is more central to its context than are these earlier examples of supplementary arrows, but it also plays an utterly crucial role, identifying a point on the screen that anchors the agreement between

user and machine, allowing them to coordinate actions across their abutting ontologies.

2 One of Merleau-Ponty's key points in his analysis of vision is to overturn the image of vision as taking place at a distance, which has been metaphysically problematic because it was hard to reconcile the sensory possession of the seen object with its being (necessarily) at a distance. Merleau-Ponty argues that this is a confusion about distance, that the spatial gap between vision and the seen is the condition of a visible world, and that it is, therefore, not so much distance as proximity as far as the logic of vision is concerned.

3 By contrast, the *appearance* of a digital object often does rely on a perpetual recreation: the image on a computer monitor, like the bits in volatile memory that store the data that describe that image, must be refreshed many times per second or it would fade from view. But this appearance, even as the end point of a production process, does not derive a coherence from the self-same underlying digital object, but remains an aggregation of independent pixels, such that the production does not produce them en masse but separately, each without relation to the others.

4 The desktop is criticized as part of a critique of the whole Macintosh interface by Cynthia and Richard Selfe. "In general, computer interfaces present reality as framed in the perspective of modern capitalism, thus, orienting technology along an existing axis of class privilege. The graphically intuitive Macintosh interface provides a good example of this orientation. That interface, and the software applications commonly represented within it, map the virtual world as a desktop constructing virtual reality, by association, in terms of corporate culture and the values of professionalism" (1994, p. 486).

5 Getting the computer to output the message "Hello, world" is a typical test run for programmers encountering a given language for the first time. Even programmers are thereby encouraged to participate in the pathetic fallacy, which makes for a strange irony: is the programmer sending a greeting to herself, or is it something else that offers its salutation in this bit of output?

6 Piaget proposes human development in four stages: sensorimotor stage, from birth to age 2; preoperational stage, from ages 2 to 7; concrete operational stage, from ages 7 to 12; and formal operational stage, from age 12 onward. Bruner borrows from Piaget throughout his career; his three stages of learning are not as chronologically anchored as Piaget's four stages and are discussed directly in *Toward a Theory of Instruction* (Harvard University Press, 1966).

7 The GUI has been criticized for hiding the inner operations of the computer behind its simplified images, for falsely presenting the computer on human rather than digital terms. This critique has real merit, but the situation is more complex: the GUI reveals certain aspects of the underlying structure of the digital data while burying other aspects.

8 "As many resources showing on the screen as possible" sounds like a user interface disaster, but it indicates the excited sense of revolutionary possibility that motivated Kay.

9 Note that the flat planes of the computer interface fall short of three dimensions not only because they are flat, but also because, aside from the top plane, the order of the planes makes little difference. The z-dimension for each plane is maintained for visual consistency and legibility, but the layering does not distinguish in any significant way between the second plane from the front and the rearmost plane. Perhaps the desktop constitutes a counterexample, as it is always the rearmost plane and so also has a kind of priority, as when a command allows the user to sweep temporarily everything off the desktop so as to access the icons that always sit on that desktop.

10 That is, one way for the digital to accommodate the GUI to its relentless linearity is by successively polling each icon, each menu item to see if it is being activated. If this polling takes place sufficiently rapidly, the user has the impression that each interface element is always at the ready. Correspondingly, the interface is available to the user as a set of distinct possibilities, a selection arranged in two-dimensions of things that might be clicked.

11 A quick note of explanation: If a point is zero-dimensional and a line is one-dimensional, then the process of the CPU in a computer is in between these two dimensionalities, as it can be thought of as the leading edge of a line being drawn, the current operation at the end of a chain of operations. The GUI is two-to-three-dimensional because it layers two-dimensional planes in a third dimension of depth. Critics sometimes call this a 2.5-dimensional or 2.5D visual perspective.

12 As is evident throughout Kay's writing and video presentations, he is truly modest and inordinately generous, deferring credit and acknowledging the contributions of his collaborators and of the many others who often inspired his ideas, labored to implement them, or developed similar ideas in parallel. I have elided from this quotation about zero-length selections Kay's acknowledgment that Larry Tesler had already developed this same idea. Kay paraphrases Goethe: "the most important thing is to enjoy the thrill of discovery rather than to make vain attempts to claim priority!" For each of the inventions attributed in this book to Kay, he acknowledges multiple authorship and a broad range of significant influences.

13 Readers who tend to think more like a computer may notice one problem with this account: if nothing is selected (the zero-width selection) and the user presses *backspace* (wishing to delete the character immediately before the current insert point often indicated by a blinking cursor), it would be ineffective to follow the usual logic of the backspace command by replacing the zero-width selection with a zero-width selection. In effect, nothing would happen. Instead, a special

code must be included for this very situation. One way of addressing the issue is to check whether this situation obtains (a *backspace* pressed when nothing is selected) and if it does, to momentarily and automatically select the character immediately to the left of the zero-width selection, and then to proceed with the replace operation. Such complications to accomplish something seemingly simple (a *backspace*) may be typical of solutions in computing, which gather together multiple cases into a common set of code but, sometimes, by leaving out certain exceptional cases.

Chapter 4

1 Such concerns are already part of the computing experience. Avid gamers in the wake of a marathon session may find themselves for a moment uncertain as to whether they are driving a real car or navigating the virtual environments of a computer-simulated driving experience. Similarly, blurry lines mean that the identity of the person at the other end of an email or chat is never guaranteed.

2 More specialized functions are also available, such as software for playwrights that automatically formats text as a script, or built-in index generation and bibliography formatting for academic writers and scientists, or brainstorming and narrative diagramming tools for fiction writers.

3 Bush is careful, however, to distinguish between the mechanical, repetitive thinking that the memex might be capable of and the creative thinking that requires a human being. But for the right application, the user of the memex would hand over part of her thinking process to the machine: the memex could be an "enlarged intimate supplement to his memory."

4 MIT Media Lab scientist Michael Bove (2000) claims that the Web will abandon its medial character to become "just a medium" when the browser's functions are divorced from the browser itself and distributed through lived space. "What has to happen before the Internet becomes just a medium is the disassociation of the services from the Web browser." Though Bove claims that eliminating the browser is the key to establishing the Web as a medium, his motive is the normalization and stabilization of the Web's function for information retrieval, which he believes is threatened by the cumbersome interface of the personal computer.

5 Though the image of the Web as flat is widely repeated, it is not commonly held among those who closely study the Web's topology. Foremost among such theorists is Galloway, whose principal argument in *Protocol* is that the lack of hierarchy is a myth and a dangerous one at that. While some of the standards that allow communication over the Web are egalitarian and decentralized, others are utterly hierarchical. This is an important and perceptive correction to the

popular image of a flat Web topology, but it applies to the structure of power on the internet and not primarily to the structure of information. Power exerts a real influence over the organization of information, so that, for example, the Web has a disproportionate number of pages written in English, but there is still no center, no index, no hierarchy of information, nor anything even approaching one.

6 Manovich describes the dynamism of new media interfaces, emphasizing not so much the inescapable attraction of the black hole but the slipperiness of a domain where everything feels proximal. "The interfaces of media access applications, such as web browsers and search engines, the hyperlinked architecture of the World Wide Web, and the interfaces of particular online media services offering massive numbers of media artifacts for playback preview and/or purchase (Amazon, Google Play, iTunes, Rhapsody, Netflix, etc.), encourage people to 'browse,' quickly moving both *horizontally* between media (from one search result to the next, from one song to another, etc.) and vertically, *through* the media artifacts (e.g., from the contents listing of a music album to a particular track)" (2013, p. 35).

7 The fantasy of intuition is not the only force driving digital development but it remains the most compelling. Witness the film *Æon Flux*, where the interface is inside the subject: computer graphics show an animated view of the character Æon's brain chemistry sparking into action, while she abandons her external milieu and finds herself, phenomenally at least, in a space of immediate communication and information. In this space, her interactions (conversations, queries) are only a matter of willing, the interface is a pure cognition. Frances Dyson spells out this consequence of ubiquitous computing in a tone of measured paranoia: "While this evolution may seem to free the user from the constraints of the stationary workstation (with all of its ergonomic problems), physical space is itself transformed to mirror the resource that the individual has become: computers become 'ubiquitous,' creating an electronic atmosphere wherein every transaction is detailed, every physical move tracked and recorded, all nodes of exchange between the individual and the world become plug-in points" (1998, p. 40).

8 The current fervor regarding search space on the Web (Google, Bing, etc.) attests to the dire need for a perspective on a set of data that is otherwise simply overwhelming. Since the beginnings of the Web's popularity, it has been said that the *killer app* is the algorithm that will find just those data one was searching for. This evinces again the ambiguity between the computer as tool and the computer as intuition: the correct algorithm will produce not only the page for which the user was searching but will also generate results that the user did not know to look for but will find eminently helpful.

9 Compare Hansen (2004, p. 11), who describes the digital as without its own form, waiting for the human perceptive body to "enframe" it and give it a form. Or

Galloway (2004, p. 52): "digital information is nothing but an undifferentiated soup of ones and zeros."

10 Rosenberg (1994, pp. 289–90): "Yet, except for the dislocations made possible by the leaps through the nodes of a hypertext, what really occurs is that the attention of an observer simply becomes shifted from one geometry to another. Differences may exist between one geometry and another, but from the perspective of avant-garde polemic, no fundamental change can occur in the framing of human awareness by regulated space and time, as exemplified by the reading process, *except* in that brief moment of nodal dislocation." Rosenberg's article focuses on debunking rhetoric that draws revolutionary conclusions in the humanities from nonlinear physics, and he spends too little time (at least given my interests) examining the exceptional situation of the hyperlink.

11 A game demonstrating the principle of distance and proximity on the Web was discussed in various forums around the turn of the century: "Web that Smut" (also called "Six Degrees of Pornography") placed each player in front of his computer, with his browser pointed at an agreed-upon "innocent" starting page on the Web. The aim was to travel to a page of pornography in the fewest clicks. The claim of this game is not only that the Web approaches an ideal of total proximity, but that this same ideal includes carnal desire, the crush of Web pages incorporating into its midst a mass of erogenous flesh.

12 The convention of underlining hyperlinks dominated browser orthography until the early 2010s, and was the default setting for most browsers and for html encoding. The fading grip of this attention-grabbing convention corresponds to the diminished excitement about links more generally, which no longer stand out as a remarkable or noteworthy feature of digital textuality.

13 Alan Kay and Adele Goldberg coin the term *metamedium*. "Although digital computers were originally designed to do arithmetic computation, the ability to simulate the details of any descriptive model means that the computer, viewed as a medium itself, can be *all other media* if the embedding and viewing methods are sufficiently well provided. Moreover, this new 'metamedium' is *active*—it can respond to queries and experiments—so that the messages may involve the learner in a two-way conversation" (2001, p. 170).

Chapter 5

1 Some pages later, Lanier offers even more concrete consequences of the multi-scalar digital ontology. "The binary character at the core of software engineering tends to reappear at higher levels. It is far easier to tell a program to run or not to run, for instance, than it is to tell it to sort-of run. In the same way, it is easier to set up a rigid representation of human relationships on digital networks: on a

typical social networking site, either you are designated to be in a couple or you are single (or you are in one of a few other predetermined states of being)—and that reduction of life is what gets broadcast between friends all the time" (loc. 1301–5).

2 Moreover, a misdirected handle would no longer point via its no-longer-valid pointer to the current version of the object but to an area of memory that might now contain meaningless 0s and 1s. Every now and then a bug or glitch allows such a monstrosity to appear in the interface, a handle that blithely points to nonsense or gibberish producing an image of orderless symbols or a block of colors, or an icon that becomes a square of random dots and blots. Perhaps the icon, the character of visual representation in the digital, participates most in the semiology of handles, code handles as well as door handles: it provides access to the object, it hides and shows parts of the object, it is itself part of the object, and it can represent the object, offering a key to its status.

3 Peter Denning proposes that the double-indirect referencing system of virtual memory, to which he contributed important elements, reflects the basic ontology of computing: "the historical record reveals . . . that the driving force behind virtual memory has always been simplifying programs (and programming) by insulating algorithms from the parameters of the memory configuration and by allowing separately constructed objects to be shared, reused, and protected. . . . Virtual memory accommodates essential patterns in the way people use computers. It will still be used when we are all gone" (1998, p. 266).

4 We might distinguish between those values at the output of the CPU, other values in the CPU cache, others in ROM, RAM, on the hard drive, and even those values that constitute the nebulous, pseudo-infinity of the internet. This might define something like a center and periphery, but note that there is still a complete lack of attention.

5 http://www.vispo.com/kearns/bog1.htm.

6 The programmer would avail herself of the lack of distinction between data and code when, for instance, she writes self-modifying code, a program that alters its own commands even while it is running, treating itself as data.

7 The auto-archive—the tendency of digital machines to leave traces of all the activity they host in the form of log files, unerased memory and data storage, back-up files, and physical imprints of overwritten data—is a central subject of analysis in Kirschenbaum's 2008 *Mechanisms*. Among his many insights in that work, Kirschenbaum restores the practices of bibliography and philology to digital media, countering the intuition that the abstraction or immateriality of the digital implies a kind of pure artifact removed from the context of its history and evidence of its production.

8 Jussi Parikka (2005) argues in "Digital Monsters, Binary Aliens—Computer Viruses, Capitalism and the Flow of Information" that digital viruses are not

so much an attack on the growing hegemony of the digital but are constitutive of it. This insight can be expanded to broader ideas around digital security: the dialectical struggle between digital security and digital hacking is essential to the growth and continuation of the digital domain, and this struggle is assured by the flatness of the digital.

9 Chris Cheshire proposes that the digital should not be understood as spatial at all, notwithstanding the well-worn notion of cyberspace. "The examples drawn from architecture, cinema, interface design, and public policy show how spatial metaphors tend to encourage a single, spatial ontology of cyberspace, and thereby restrict the multitude of potential configurations of digital domains. But cyber*space* is misleading because the digital domain is not spatial at all. Networks do not reproduce space, they eliminate it. The essence of computer technology is that it enables instant retrieval and processing of encoded signs. It allows signs to be constructed and recovered as data irrespective of their location in space or time. The vectors of the telephone and computer network compress space and effectively make it irrelevant within their domains" (1997, p. 83).

10 Gordon Calleja examines the relationship in digital gaming between the field of disjunctive possibility and the ethics of responsibility for the gamer. "Games tend to be designed in such a way as to have a specified opportunity cost to every meaningful action performed. If this is similar to everyday life, digital games emphasize the contrived nature of the contingencies players need to navigate to a more radical degree. . . . Using a game turn's gathered resources to build an army barracks excludes the possibility of building walls to protect my fledgling town or extending resource fields that yield more resources, and so on. Decisions tend to have clearly labeled costs and benefits that both facilitate and problematize the process of decision making. Knowledge of repercussions of specific actions serves to decrease uncertainty. But if uncertainty is limited enough and players realize they have the ability to plan far into the future, the situation is problematized by placing responsibility more squarely on the decision maker" (2007, pp. 339–40).

11 Patrick LeMieux's "Every Icon Editor" (2014, http://patrick-lemieux.com/Every_Icon_Editor/) allows users to draw an icon on the grid and then calculates the date and time when Simon's original version of "Every Icon" will arrive at the drawn icon. The number representing the year is typically hundreds of digits long.

12 Alan Turing makes the determinism of the digital explicit. "Even when we consider the actual physical machines instead of the idealized machines, reasonably accurate knowledge of the state at one moment yields reasonably accurate knowledge any number of steps later" (1999, p. 43).

13 This is not to say that there is no art or expertise in the digital graphic artist's work. There may be reproducible logical processes to generate consistent and predictable results in an image, but knowing which image to work with, which alterations to make, and how to do it with excellence, all rely on judgments that computers

cannot replicate or perform nearly as well as masterful artists. At the same time, in an era when the smartphone is the camera of choice, at least in terms of raw numbers, the Instagram tools (and similar *apps*) invite an increasing stylistic homogeneity, as many users employ the same filters, the same techniques, and, in a sense, the same conception of beauty. Teenagers know how to take "selfies" from particular angles to make for the most conventionally attractive "profile picture" for their Facebook pages.

14 This claim, that computers have no horizon of attention, no context, is the principal claim of Hubert Dreyfus's classic *What Computers Can't Do*. Computers are strictly tied to a predetermined set of possible inputs, they can only take in what they are expecting. The computer has no "horizon" of understanding, no milieu against which it experiences the world. Human beings make sense of their worlds hermeneutically, operating from the outside in as well as the inside out. The computer only has its inside.

15 I do not mean to elide the considerable complexity of the operation of the CPU in the real world. Though the CPU remains the central site of calculation, and continues to define the computer as a technology, a great deal of additional processing (of a similar nature) takes place in various subsystems of the computer, including, for instance, the graphics card, dedicated input/output (I/O) subsystems (such as a disk subsystem), and others. The CPU itself is not monolithic: it is increasingly common to have more than one CPU in a single computer, and the latest trend in commercial personal computing is to incorporate two or more CPUs (*cores*) on a single silicon wafer, so that they are tightly integrated. The CPU itself is subdivided into segments; it has multiple stages of operation, including a stage where it retrieves a command and another where it dispatches that command, deciding which part of the CPU should handle this particular type of command. Thus, the CPU deals with different commands differently, dedicating a particular part of its chip surface to the logic that governs, for instance, operations on floating point numbers as opposed to integer arithmetic.

16 Even when a programmer works directly in the numeric machine language, she would typically read and write the numeric codes not as binary representations (base-2) but as hexadecimal numbers (base-16), which is much easier to scan visually: 01100100 (which is a binary representation of the decimal number 100) would be represented in base-16 as 0x64, where the *zero-ex* is one of many conventions used to indicate a hexadecimal representation. (Another common convention to indicate hexadecimal notation is a dollar sign in place of the *0x*.) Hexadecimal or base-16 representation works the same as binary and decimal representation, but each place farther left represents the next power of sixteen: 1s place, 16s place, 256s place, 4096s place, etc. Also, of course, the

hexadecimal system uses sixteen digits, appending digits *A*, *B*, . . ., *F*, to our familiar 0 through 9, where the new letters-digits stand for the decimal numbers 10 through 15. Hexadecimal representation offers a good compromise between readability and the binary machine code because, 16 being a power of 2 ($16 = 2^4$), they translate back and forth very easily, with four binary bits for every one hexadecimal digit.

17 The question of whether an algorithm need necessarily reach its termination condition is at the heart of David Hilbert's famous *Entscheidungsproblem*, or decidability problem.

18 At the time of this writing, the universal serial bus (USB) is the most typical interface that connects the keyboard to the motherboard of the computer, though the wireless interface, Bluetooth, is becoming increasingly popular. Prior to USB, there were competing standards for this connection, and there will no doubt be a new standard that will overtake USB a few years from now. The principle remains the same, however.

19 Even a fast touch-typist enters data into the computer orders of magnitude more slowly than a single cycle through a loop that checks for the presence of such data. Well over 99 percent of the time there are no data waiting when the computer checks the flag.

20 Different kinds of interrupt systems work differently. Some interrupt systems include a "masking" feature that enables software to set a flag rendering it vulnerable only to certain interrupts and not to others. This masking function does not so much eliminate the hierarchy of the interrupt mechanism as complicate it, implying a kind of self-reflection and a sense of temporality, a friction with time.

21 Writing of the origins of object-oriented programming in the Simula 67 programming language, Ole-Johan Dahl underlines the importance of the inside-outside distinction. The language implements objects and distinguishes explicitly between the "inside view" and the more abstract "outside view" of the object. "This difference, as indicated by the *Car* example in Simula I, and the associated comments, underlies much of our program designs from an early time on, although not usually conscious and certainly not explicitly formulated" (2001, p. 7).

22 Some interrupt systems include means to save the state of the CPU (and the relevant data it is working on) when the interrupt occurs, so that this state can later be restored. An interrupt that saves all the relevant conditions of the operation of the computer allowing accurate and total resumption of the interrupted algorithm is called *precise*. Though perhaps still just as violent, a precise interrupt is in such a case more considerate, since it allows a return to the current algorithm after the interrupting condition has been dispatched.

23 To avoid confusion I should note that increasing security often corresponds to a *lower* layer of the system ontology; greater access often means access to more basic functions, a movement closer to the digital plane and the mechanism that is its material face. Unlike regular users of a given network, the administrator of that network may be able to override passwords of non-administrator users, or set low-level functions of hardware that regulate resource allocation within the system.

24 "Our intent is to introduce you, over the next 632 pages, to the world of computing. As we do so, we have one objective above all others: to show you very clearly that there is no magic to computing. The computer is a deterministic system—every time we hit it over the head in the same way and in the same place (provided, of course, it was in the same starting condition), we get the same response. The computer is not an electronic genius; on the contrary, if anything, it is an electronic idiot, doing exactly what we tell it to. It has no mind of its own" (Patt and Patel 2004, p. 1).

25 Deleuze never abandons the virtual as a concept, but the question of its priority in relation to the actual prompts a development of this structure, especially in the writings with Félix Guattari. If the virtual were ontologically prior to the actual, then it would be the proper domain of (political or ethical) action. But, at least in *Difference and Repetition*, the virtual appears at times transcendent, nearly out of reach, and Deleuze suggests that at best one must roll the dice, throw oneself into the "aleatory point" that ceaselessly produces difference, that one might be struck by a lightning bolt, "a *fiat* which, when we are infused by it, makes us semi-divine beings" (p. 197). Later writings destabilize the hierarchy of virtual and actual, discovering always a bidirectional relationship and a subversion of established structures, usually by the introduction of a third term.

26 To be clear, Deleuze is not here discussing the digital, but ontogenesis broadly understood, the coming to be of what comes to be. Galloway (2012) gathers Deleuze's occasional comments on the digital, focusing on the brief, late "manifesto," "Postscript on Societies of Control," and identifying the "enemy," for Deleuze, as cybernetics.

27 The negativity or paucity of the proposition gets close attention in Chapter 3 of *Difference and Repetition*, where Deleuze critiques the proposition as an "image of thought," noting that the proposition as a model of thought flattens meaning, such that thought's only misadventure could be the starkness of error.

Bibliography

Aarseth, E. (1997), *Cybertext: Perspectives on Ergodic Literature*. Baltimore, MD: Johns Hopkins University Press.

Aarseth, E. (1999), "Aporia and Epiphany in *Doom* and *The Speaking Clock*: The Temporality of Ergodic Art," in M.-L. Ryan (ed.), *Cyberspace Textuality: Computer Technology and Literary Theory*. Bloomington, IN: Indiana University Press, pp. 31–41.

Aarseth, E. (2001), "Computer Game Studies, Year One," *Game Studies: The International Journal of Computer Game Research*, 1 (1), http://www.gamestudies.org/ (accessed May 2003).

Aarseth, E. (2003), "Playing Research: Methodological Approaches to Game Studies," in *Proceedings of the Fifth International Digital Arts and Culture Conference*, http://hypertext.rmit.edu.au/dac/papers/ (accessed June 2003).

Abelson, H. and Sussman, G. (1996), *Structure and Interpretation of Computer Programs—2nd Edition*. Cambridge, MA: MIT Press.

Abowd, G. D. and Mynatt, E. D. (2000), "Charting Past, Present, and Future Research in Ubiquitous Computing," *ACM Transactions on Computer-Human Interaction (TOCHI)*, 7 (1): 29–58.

Æon Flux (2005), K. Kusama (dir), C. Theron (perf), MTV Films.

Arola, K. (2010), "The Design of Web 2.0: The Rise of the Template, The Fall of Design," *Computers and Composition*, 27: 4–14.

Bakardjieva, M. and Gaden, G. (2012), "Web 2.0 Technologies of the Self," *Philosophy of Technology*, 25: 399–413.

Baldwin, C. A. (1996), "Forgetting the Future?," *ANY* (Architecture New York), 15 (Fall): 6–7.

Baldwin, C. A. (2002), "Purple Dotted Underlines: Microsoft Word and the End of Writing," *AfterImage*, 30 (1): 6–7.

Bassett, C. (2008), "New Maps for Old?: The Cultural Stakes of '2.0,'" *The Fibreculture Journal*, 13, http://thirteen.fibreculturejournal.org/fcj-088-new-maps-for-old-the-cultural-stakes-of-2-0/ (accessed March 2015).

Baudrillard, J. (1993), "Xerox and Infinity," http://insomnia.ac/essays/xerox_and_infinity/ (accessed September 2014).

Bernstein, C. (1991), "Play It Again, Pac-Man," *Postmodern Culture*, 2 (1), http://jefferson.village.virginia.edu/pmc/ (accessed May 1, 2003).

Berry, D. (2008), "A Contribution Towards a Grammar of Code," *The Fibreculture Journal*, 13, http://thirteen.fibreculturejournal.org/fcj-086-a-contribution-towards-a-grammar-of-code/ (accessed March 2015).

Bolter, D. J. and Grusin, R. (1999), *Remediation: Understanding New Media*. Cambridge, MA: MIT Press.

Bove, V. M., Jr. (2000), "Will Anyone Really Need a Web Browser in Five Years," http://web.media.mit.edu/~vmb/papers/Bove-Montreux2000.pdf (accessed November 2014).

Briggle, A. and Mitcham, C. (2009), "From the Philosophy of Information to the Philosophy of Information Culture," *The Information Society*, 25: 169–74.

Brock, A. (2011), "'When Keeping it Real Goes Wrong': Resident Evil 5, Racial Representation, and Gamers," *Games and Culture*, 6 (5): 429–52.

Brooks, F. (1986), "No Silver Bullet: Essence and Accidents of Software Engineering," *Information Processing '86, IFIP Congress Series*, 10: 1069–76.

Bruns, A. (2008), "The Future Is User-Led: The Path towards Widespread Produsage," *The Fibreculture Journal*, 11, http://eleven.fibreculturejournal.org/fcj-066-the-future-is-user-led-the-path-towards-widespread-produsage/ (accessed December 2014).

Bush, V. (1945), "As We May Think," *The Atlantic Monthly*, 176 (1): 101–8.

Calleja, G. (2007), "Digital Game Involvement: A Conceptual Model," *Games and Culture*, 2 (3): 236–60.

Campbell, J. (2000), "Delusions of Dialogue: Control and Choice in Interactive Art," *Leonardo*, 33 (2): 133–6.

Carr, D. (2007), "The Trouble with Civilization," in B. Atkins and T. Kyrzwinska (eds), *Videogame, Player, Text*. New York: Manchester University Press, pp. 222–36.

Cascone, K. (2000), "The Aesthetics of Failure: 'Post-Digital' Tendencies in Contemporary Computer Music," *Computer Music Journal*, 244 (4): 12–18.

Caviglione, L. and Coccoli, M. (2011), "Privacy problems with Web 2.0," *Computer Fraud and Security*, 10: 16–19.

Charlton, J. and Danforth, I. (2008), British Psychological Society press release, http://www.bps.org.uk/media-centre/press-releases/releases$/annual-conference-2008/computer-game-addicts-like-people-with-aspergers.cfm?templatetheme=default (accessed December 1, 2008).

Cheshire, C. (1997), "The Ontology of Digital Domains," in D. Holmes (ed.), *Virtual Politics: Identity & Community in Cyberspace*. London: Sage Publications, pp. 79–92.

Chun, W. H. K. (2004), "On Software, or The Persistence of Visual Knowledge," *Grey Room*, 18: 26–51.

Chun, W. H. K. (2011), *Programmed Visions*. Cambridge, MA: MIT Press.

Coelho, C., Tichon, J. G., Hine, T. J., Wallis, G. M., and Riva, G. (2006), "Media Presence and Inner Presence: The Sense of Presence in Virtual Reality Technologies," in G. Riva, M. T. Anguera, B. K. Wiederhold, and F. Mantovani (eds), *From Communication to Presence*: Festschrift *in Honor of Luigi Anolli*. Amsterdam: IOS Press. http://www.emergingcommunication.com/ (accessed August 13, 2014).

Crogan, P. (2004), "The Experience of Information in Computer Games," *Scan: Journal of Media Arts Culture*, 1 (1), http://scan.net.au/scan/journal/index.php.

Dahl, O.-J. (2001), "The Birth of Object Orientation: The Simula Languages," www.olejohandahl.info/old/birth-of-oo.pdf (accessed November 8, 2008).

Danowitz, A., Kelley, K., Mao, J., Stevenson, J. P., and Horowitz, M. (2012), "CPU DB: Recording Microprocessor History," *ACMQueue*, 10 (4), http://queue.acm.org/detail.cfm?id=2181798.

Deleuze, G. (1990), *Logic of Sense*, trans. M. Hurley and C. Stivale. New York: Columbia University Press.

Deleuze, G. (1992), "Postscript on the Societies of Control," *October*, 59: 3–7.

Deleuze, G. (1994), *Difference and Repetition*, trans. P. Patton. New York: Columbia University Press.

Denning, P. (1998), "Before Memory Was Virtual," in R. Glass (ed.), *In the Beginning: Personal Recollections of Software Pioneers*. Los Alamitos, CA: IEEE Computer Society, pp. 250–71.

Dietz, S. (ed.) (2010), *Jim Campbell: Material Light*. Ostfildern, Germany: Hatje Gantz Verlag, copublished with Bruce Wolkowitz Gallery, New York.

Digg.com (2008), "Digg – Overview," http://digg.com/about/ (accessed May 2009).

Doane, M. A. (2007), "The Indexical and the Concept of Medium Specificity," *differences*, 18 (1): 128–52.

Douglas, C. (2002), "Is It Possible to Build Dramatically Compelling Interactive Digital Entertainment (in the form, e.g., of computer games)?," *Postmodern Culture*, 13 (1), http://jefferson.village.virginia.edu/pmc/ (accessed May 2003).

Dreyfus, H. (1978), *What Computers Can't Do: The Limits of Artificial Intelligence*. New York: Harpercollins.

Dreyfus, H. (2009), *On the Internet*. New York City: Routledge.

Drucker, J. (2001), "Digital Ontologies: The Ideality of Form in/and Code Storage—or—Can Graphesis Challenge Mathesis?," *Leonardo*, 34 (2): 141–5.

Drucker, J. (2009), *SpecLab: Digital Aesthetics and Projects in Speculative Computing*. Chicago: University of Chicago Press.

Dyson, F. (1998), "'Space,' 'Being,' and Other Fictions in the Domain of the Virtual," in J. Beckmann (ed.), *The Virtual Dimension: Architecture, Representation, and Crash Culture*. New York: Princeton Architectural Press, pp. 26–45.

Eden, A. and Turner, R. (2007), "Problems in the Ontology of Computer Programs," *Applied Ontology*, 2 (1): 13–36.

Eskelinen, M. (2001), "The Gaming Situation," *Game Studies: The International Journal of Computer Game Research*, 1 (1), http://www.gamestudies.org/ (accessed May 1, 2003).

Friedberg, A. (2002), "CD and DVD," in D. Harries (ed.), *The New Media Book*. London: British Film Institute Publishing, pp. 30–9.

Friedman, T. (1999), "*Civilization* and Its Discontents: Simulation, Subjectivity, and Space," in G. Smith (ed.), *On a Silver Platter: CD-ROMs and the Promises of a New Technology*. New York: New York University Press, pp. 132–50.

Fuller, M. (2003), *Behind the Blip: Essays on Software Culture*. Brooklyn: Autonomedia.

Galloway, A. (2004), *Protocol: How Control Exists After Decentralization*. Cambridge, MA: MIT Press.

Galloway, A. (2005), "Protocol vs. Institutionalization," in W. H. K. Chun and T. Keenan (eds), *New Media Old Media: A History and Theory Reader*. New York: Routledge, pp. 187–98.

Galloway, A. (2006), *Gaming: Essays on Algorithmic Culture*. Minneapolis: University of Minnesota Press.

Galloway, A. (2008), "Possibility," *subsol*, http://subsol.c3.hu/subsol_2/contributors0/gallowaytext.html (accessed August 15, 2014).

Galloway, A. (2012), "Computers and the Superfold," *Deleuze Studies*, 6 (4): 513–28.

Giddens, A. (1991), *Modernity and Self-Identity: Self and Society in the Late Modern Age*. Stanford: Stanford University Press.

Gleick, J. (2011), *The Information: A History, A Theory, A Flood*. New York: Pantheon Books.

Greaves, M. (2007), "Semantic Web 2.0," *IEEE Intelligent Systems*, 2007 (March/April): 94–6.

Hagen, W. (2005), "The Style of Sources: Remarks on the Theory and History of Programming Languages," in W. H. K. Chun and T. Keenan (eds), *New Media Old Media: A History and Theory Reader*. New York: Routledge, pp. 157–75.

Hansen, M. (2004), *New Philosophy for New Media*. Cambridge, MA: MIT Press.

Hayles, N. K. (1993a), "The Materiality of Informatics," *Configurations*, 1 (1): 147–70.

Hayles, N. K. (1993b), "Virtual Bodies and Flickering Signifiers," *October*, 66: 69–91.

Heidegger, M. (1962), *Being and Time*, trans. J. Macquarrie and E. Robinson. New York: Harper & Row.

Heidegger, M. (1977), "The Question Concerning Technology," in W. Lovitt (trans), *The Question Concerning Technology and Other Essays*. New York: Harper & Row, pp. 3–35.

Jenkins, H. (1998), "'Complete Freedom of Movement': Video Games as Gendered Play Spaces," in H. Jenkins and J. Cassell (eds), *From Barbie to Mortal Kombat: Gender and Computer Games*. Cambridge, MA: MIT Press, pp. 262–97.

Kay, A. (1986), "Doing with Images makes Symbols," QuickTime Video, from *The History of the Personal Workstation*, https://archive.org/details/AlanKeyD1987 (accessed December 2014).

Kay, A. (1993), "The Early History of Smalltalk", *ACM SIGPLAN Notices*, 28 (3): 69–95.

Kay, A. (1999), "Computer Software," in Paul Mayer (ed.), *Computer Media and Communication: A Reader*. Oxford: Oxford University Press, pp. 129–37. Originally from *Scientific American*, September 1984.

Kay, A. (2001), "User Interface: A Personal View," in R. Packer and K. Jordan (eds), *Multimedia: From Wagner to Virtual Reality*. New York: W.W. Norton & Co, pp. 121–31.

Kay, A. and Goldberg, A. (2001), "Personal Dynamic Media," in R. Packer and K. Jordan (eds), *Multimedia: From Wagner to Virtual Reality*. New York: W.W. Norton & Co, pp. 167–78.

Kelly, K. (2006), "Scan This Book!," *The New York Times* (May 13, 2006).

Kinsey, C. (2014), "Matrices of Embodiment: Rethinking Binary and the Politics of Digital Representation," *Signs*, 39 (4): 897–925.

Kirschenbaum, M. (2008), *Mechanisms: New Media and the Forensic Imagination*. Cambridge, MA: MIT Press.

Kittler, F. (1996), "The History of Communication Media," *CTheory*, July 1996, http://www.ctheory.net/articles.aspx?id=45 (accessed January 12, 2013).

Kittler, F. (1997), *Literature, Media, Information Systems: Essays*, ed. J. Johnston. Amsterdam: G+B Arts International.

Kittler, F. (2001), "Computer Graphics: A Semi-Technical Introduction," *Grey Room*, 2: 30–45.

Kohanski, D. (1998), *The Philosophical Programmer: Reflections on the Moth in the Machine*. New York: St. Martin's Press.

Kopp, J. (2008), *Easy C++*. http://easycplusplus.com/ (accessed September 17, 2013).

Kücklick, J. (2003), "Perspectives of Computer Game Philology," *Game Studies: The International Journal of Computer Game Research*, 3 (1), http://www.gamestudies.org/ (accessed May 2003).

Lammers, S. (1986), *Programmers at Work: Interviews (1st Edition)*. Redmond, WA: Microsoft Press.

Lanier, J. (2011), *You Are Not a Gadget: A Manifesto*. London: Vintage, Kindle Edition.

Liu, A. (2004), "Transcendental Data: Toward a Cultural History of Aesthetics of the New Encoded Discourse," *Critical Inquiry*, 31 (1), 49–84.

Lovink, G. (2008), *Zero Comments: Blogging and Critical Internet Culture*. New York: Routledge.

Mackenzie, A. (2002), "Losing Time at the Playstation: Real Time and the 'Whatever' Body," in *Transductions: Bodies and Machines at Speed*. New York: Continuum, pp. 145–70.

Manovich, L. (2001), *The Language of New Media*. Cambridge, MA: MIT Press.

Manovich, L. (2002), "Avant-garde as Software," http://www.uoc.edu/artnodes/espai/eng/art/manovich1002/manovich1002.html (accessed October 26, 2014).

Manovich, L. (2013), *Software Takes Command*. New York: Bloomsbury Academic.

Markoff, J. (2005), "Web Content by and for the Masses," *The New York Times*, June 29, 2005.

Massumi, B. (1998), "Line Parable for the Virtual: (On the Superiority of the Analog)," in J. Beckmann (ed.), *The Virtual Dimension: Architecture, Representation, and Crash Culture*. New York: Princeton Architectural Press, pp. 305–21.

Merleau-Ponty, M. (1964), *The Visible and the Invisible*, trans. A. Lingis. Evanston, IL: Northwestern University Press.

Merleau-Ponty, M. (1979), *Phenomenology of Perception*, trans. C. Smith. London: Routledge.

Minsky, M. (1967), "Why Programming is a Good Medium for Expressing Poorly understood and Slippily-Formulated Ideas," http://web.media.mit.edu/~minsky/papers/Why%20programming%20is--.html (accessed December 2014). Modified from a chapter in M. Krampen and P. Seitz (eds), *Design and Planning II – Computers in Design and Communication*. New York: Hastings House Publishers, pp. 120–5.

Munster, A. (2011), "From a Biopolitical 'Will to Life' to a Noopolitical Ethos of Death in the Aesthetics of Digital Code," *Theory, Culture & Society*, 28 (6): 67–90.

Nash, A. (2012), "Affect and the Medium of Digital Data," *The Fibreculture Journal*, 21: 10–30.

Newman, J. (2002), "The Myth of the Ergodic Videogame: Some thoughts on player-character relationships in videogames," *Game Studies: The International Journal of Computer Game Research*, 2 (1), http://www.gamestudies.org/ (accessed May 2003).

Nunes, M. (1999), "Virtual Topographies: Smooth and Striated Cyberspaces," in M.-L. Ryan (ed.), *Cyberspace Textuality: Computer Technology and Literary Theory*. Bloomington, IN: Indiana University Press, pp. 61–77.

O'Baoill, A. (2004), "Weblogs and the Public Sphere," in L. J. Gurak, S. Antonijevic, L. Johnson, C. Ratliff, and J. Reyman (eds), *Into the Blogosphere: Rhetoric, Community, and Culture of Weblogs*. http://blog.lib.umn.edu/blogosphere/ (accessed July 2009).

Parikka, J. (2005), "Digital Monsters, Binary Aliens – Computer Viruses, Capitalism and the Flow of Information," *The Fibreculture Journal*, 4, http://four.fibreculturejournal.org/fcj-019-digital-monsters-binary-aliens-%e2%80%93-computer-viruses-capitalism-and-the-flow-of-information/ (accessed March 2015).

Patt, Y. and Patel, S. (2003), *Introduction to Computing Systems: From Bits & Gates to C & Beyond, second edition*. Boston: McGraw Hill.

Pearce, C. (2002), "Sims, BattleBots, Cellular Automata, God and *Go*: A Conversation with Will Wright by Celia Pearce," *Game Studies: The International Journal of Computer Game Research*, 2 (1), http://www.gamestudies.org/0102/pearce/ (accessed March 2015).

Peirce, C. S. (1955), *Philosophical Writings of Peirce*, ed. J. Buchler. New York: Dover Publications.

Peirce, C. S. (1958), *Selected Writings (Values in a Universe of Chance)*, ed. P. Wiener. New York: Dover Publications.

Penny, S. (2008), "Experience and Abstraction: The Arts and the Logic of Machines," *The Fibreculture Journal*, 11, http://eleven.fibreculturejournal.org/fcj-072-experience-and-abstraction-the-arts-and-the-logic-of-machines/ (accessed March 2015).

Poster, M. (1999), "Theorizing Virtual Reality: Baudrillard and Derrida," in M.-L. Ryan (ed.), *Cyberspace Textuality: Computer Technology and Literary Theory*. Bloomington, IN: Indiana University Press, pp. 42–60.

Ramsay, S. (2011), *Reading Machines: Toward An Algorithmic Criticism*. Urbana, IL: University of Illinois Press.

Rettberg, J. W. (2008), "Quests in *World of Warcraft*: Deferral and Repetition," in H. Corneliussen and J. W. Rettberg (eds), *Digital Culture, Play, and Identity: A World of Warcraft® Reader*. Cambridge, MA: MIT Press, pp. 167–84.

Rosenberg, M. (1994), "Physics and Hypertext: Liberation and Complicity in Art and Pedagogy," in George Landow (ed.), *Hyper/Text/Theory*. Baltimore, MD: Johns Hopkins University Press, pp. 268–98.

Ryan, M.-L. (1994), "Immersion vs. Interactivity: Virtual Reality and Literary Theory," *Post-Modern Culture*, 5 (1), http://muse.jhu.edu/journals/postmodern_culture/v005/5.1ryan.html (accessed December 2014).

Selfe, C. and Selfe, R. (1994), "The Politics of the Interface: Power and Its Exercise in Electronic Contact Zones," *College Composition and Communication*, 45 (4): 480–504.

Simon, J. F., Jr. (1997), "Every Icon," http://www.numeral.com/appletsoftware/eicon.html (accessed December 8, 2014).

Stern, J. (2007), "The Way It Woz: Steve Wozniak on All Things Apple," *Laptop: Mobile Solutions for Business & Life*, October 26, 2007, http://www.laptopmag.com/news/interviews/the-way-it-woz.aspx. Article no longer accessible (accessed February 2008).

Stone, A. R. (1991), "Will the Real Body Please Stand Up?," in M. Benedikt (ed.), *Cyberspace: First Steps*. Cambridge, MA: MIT Press, pp. 81–118.

Turing, A. (1999), "Computing Machinery and Intelligence," in P. Mayer (ed.), *Computer Media and Communication: A Reader*. Oxford: Oxford University Press, pp. 37–58. Originally in *Mind*, 59 (236), October 1950.

Wark, M. (2009), *Gamer Theory 2.0*, http://www.futureofthebook.org/gamertheory2.0/ (accessed September 24, 2013).

Weiser, M. (1993), "Some computer science issues in ubiquitous computing," *Communications of the ACM*, 36 (7): 75–84.

Wolfe, C. (2008), "The Digital, the Analog, and the Spectral: Echographies from *My Life in the Bush of Ghosts*," *Angelaki*, 13 (1): 85–94.

Index

www.ingramcontent.com/pod-product-compliance
Ingram Content Group UK Ltd.
Pitfield, Milton Keynes, MK11 3LW, UK
UKHW020144290926
15471UKWH00004B/683

9 781350 027473